The
ProDOS
Handbook

The
ProDOS®
Handbook

Timothy Rice and Karen Rice

SYBEX®

Berkeley • Paris • Düsseldorf • London

Cover art by Nicolae Razumieff
Book design by Jeffrey James Giese

Library of Congress Card Number: 85-50465
ISBN 0-89588-230-2
Printed by Haddon Craftsmen
Manufactured in the United States of America
10 9 8 7 6 5 4 3 2

To our parents

ACKNOWLEDGMENTS

We are sincerely grateful to Barbara Gordon, the editor of the manuscript, for her hard work and valuable suggestions. We would also like to thank Jeremy Elliott, for his thorough review of the technical aspects of this book, and Valerie Robbins, for a meticulous word processing job.

Timothy Rice
Karen Rice
February 1985

TABLE OF CONTENTS

CHARTS

INDEX

PREFACE

This book describes ProDOS, the new disk operating system for the Apple II family of computers. ProDOS brings new features and power to the Apple II, ensuring the continued success of the machine that some say triggered the personal computer revolution. ProDOS is more than a new version of DOS 3.3, Apple's older operating system. ProDOS is a bold step into the future that removes the constraints of DOS 3.3 from the muscles of your Apple.

ProDOS offers a number of advantages over the older DOS 3.3. It is much faster at reading and writing information to the disk than DOS 3.3 was. ProDOS volumes can contain a virtually unlimited number of files, where DOS 3.3 could handle only 105. The maximum size of a single file has been increased from 140,000 bytes to 32,000,000 bytes. The hierarchical structure allows greater control over those files. Almost all of the old DOS 3.3 commands have been retained and improved with added features, and a number of powerful new commands have been added.

This book is intended for everyone who will use ProDOS, from the novice to the veteran user of computers. The novice will find it an important guide to getting started with ProDOS. Once you are comfortable with ProDOS and want to begin programming with it, you will find this book an invaluable guide to the features ProDOS offers. The experienced programmer, seeking a rapid start and more technical data on ProDOS, will find what he wants by skimming the first few chapters before delving into the areas he considers more interesting.

The book forms naturally into two parts. The first three chapters focus on the more general aspects of ProDOS: what it is and how it compares to DOS 3.3, how to use the ProDOS utilities with an Apple IIe, and how to use the ProDOS utilities with an Apple IIc. The second part of the book discusses how to use ProDOS with programs. While some of the material covered in these chapters is necessarily quite technical, on the whole it should be easily readable by anyone who is interested in learning more about using Pro-DOS. We have tried to point out in the text the few places where the material is unimportant to a good general understanding and can be bypassed by those who are not looking for the more intimate technical details of ProDOS.

Chapter 1 begins with a discussion of the tools ProDOS uses: the Apple II computer, the Disk II drive, and disks. (Most of our discussion centers around IIe and IIc computers, although II+ computers that have been expanded to run ProDOS are also included.) Pro-DOS is compared to DOS 3.3 to show where improvements have been made and why ProDOS offers better performance. Chapter 2 describes the utilities on the ProDOS User's Disk that comes with the Apple IIe. Step-by-step instructions take you through the use of each of the available functions, allowing you to become proficient in their use in a very short time. These utilities allow you to accomplish easily the most common ProDOS functions (such as copying a disk or cataloging its contents), without having to learn any programming at all. Chapter 3 discusses the similar but slightly different utilities on the ProDOS System Utilities Disk that comes with the Apple IIc. The differences between these two versions of Pro-DOS utilities are discussed here.

Chapter 4 begins the more programming-oriented section of the book. This chapter discusses the ProDOS directory structure and how it is used to organize the files on a disk; it should be read by all ProDOS users. The casual user can skip the more technical sections (which are pointed out in the text) but should still read the chapter to get a solid feel for how ProDOS operates. The more technically minded can study the detailed descriptions of how Pro-DOS records data and organizes files.

Chapter 5 discusses the ProDOS commands that are available from BASIC. DOS 3.3 users will want to pay particular attention to the new ProDOS commands and the improvements that have been made to the older DOS 3.3 commands. The DOS 3.3 commands that no longer exist are also mentioned here. This chapter should be read by all ProDOS users—anyone who uses the machine frequently will want to take advantage of ProDOS's functions without having to go through the ProDOS utilities to access them.

Chapter 6 deals with the ways in which ProDOS uses memory. The system bit map, which ProDOS uses to record memory usage, is described here. The memory locations used by ProDOS are defined, and the ProDOS loading sequence is presented so that you will know exactly how ProDOS is loaded into memory. This chapter is recommended to both the casual reader and those interested in the inner technical details of ProDOS.

Chapters 7 and 8 treat related topics. Both cover the use of files with the ProDOS commands. Chapter 7 discusses the use of ProDOS with text files, a subject that should be dear to the heart of every BASIC programmer. Chapter 8 focuses on the use of ProDOS with binary files. Both chapters contain working examples to illustrate the use of the ProDOS commands they discuss.

Chapter 9 focuses on the use of ProDOS with graphics and sound. This chapter covers the use of binary files to load and save graphics images to and from the disk, with programming examples to show the technique in action. It also discusses the protection of the high-resolution graphics area from the growth of BASIC programs.

Chapter 10 deals with the ProDOS MLI. This is the machine-language interface that translates all your ProDOS commands from BASIC into machine-language instructions that your Apple carries out. This chapter deals with very technical material, but the casual reader should skim through its pages to obtain a better understanding of how ProDOS operates. The advanced programmer will find many details here that will aid him in mastering the use of ProDOS.

Chapter 11 concludes the book by briefly discussing ProDOS system programs and the use of the Monitor, a machine-language program that resides in your Apple and allows you to examine and manipulate the contents of memory. With it you can write machine-language programs that use the ProDOS MLI directly.

A number of appendices have been added to provide easy reference for material mentioned in the text. Appendix A lists the ProDOS file types. Appendix B lists the error messages generated by the ProDOS utility programs. Appendix C lists the error codes and messages generated by the ProDOS commands, and Appendix

D lists the Applesoft BASIC error codes that are returned in the same location.

Appendix E lists the ASCII (American Standard Code for Information Interchange) character set used by an Apple II computer. Appendix F lists the character tokens that are used to store reserved words in Applesoft BASIC files on disk.

Appendix G is a quick reference guide to the calls of the MLI and the parameters that each call uses. This is followed in Appendix H by a list of the error codes the MLI returns in the accumulator and their meanings. This information will be especially important to the machine- or assembly-language programmer.

The last three appendices all concern memory usage. Appendix I describes how Applesoft and ProDOS share the zero page of memory. Appendix J presents a memory map that charts the use of all 64K of memory in your Apple II under ProDOS. Finally, Appendix K explains how the system global page is used by ProDOS to communicate with the MLI.

Introduction to ProDOS

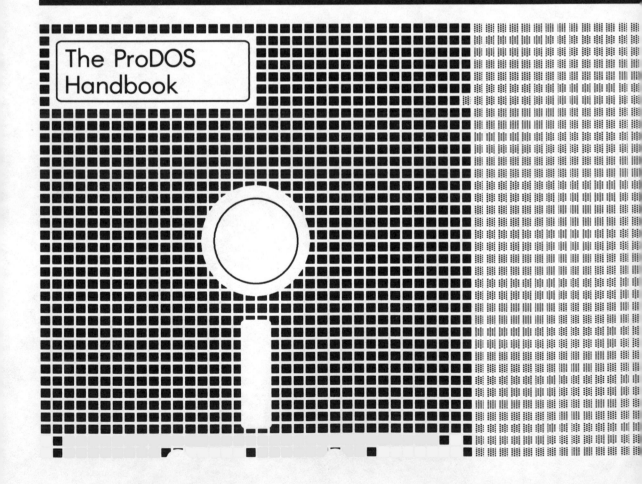

The ProDOS
Handbook

ONE

The purpose of this chapter is to make you familiar with the basic elements of your Apple II computer system and ProDOS. For those with no prior computer experience, we will take a brief look at how computers operate and the function operating systems serve. If you already have some experience with computers, you can skip the next several pages and begin with the section entitled "Overview of ProDOS." At that point we take an overall look at ProDOS and discuss how it compares to DOS, the disk operating system previously available for Apple II computers. By the end of this chapter, you will have learned all the background information you need to begin using ProDOS.

THE APPLE II

A typical Apple IIe computer system consists of an Apple IIe computer, two disk drives, a monitor, and a printer. An Apple IIc computer will look slightly different from an Apple IIe, because one disk drive is an integral part of the computer. This difference does not affect the operation of ProDOS.

The Computer

The computer is the typewriterlike instrument with a keyboard. The keyboard is your primary means of "talking" to the computer. When the computer and the monitor are turned on, every character you enter by typing on the keyboard is displayed on the monitor's screen.

If you open the top of the Apple IIe and look inside, you will see a metallic box on the left side. This is your power supply, and it is very clearly marked with warnings not to open it. There are dangerous voltages inside, and you could receive a painful shock and damage your computer if you tamper with it.

To the right of the power supply is a large green plastic board holding a number of black rectangular objects, which are the computer chips everyone is always talking about. The long chip near the center of the board with the number 6502 below it is the processor of your computer. The processor is like the engine in a car—it provides the power that makes everything else work. To the rear of the machine there are eight long slots. These are called ports or expansion slots; you can plug "cards" into these slots that will provide functions otherwise not available to your system.

If you own an Apple IIc, your machine will not look exactly like the Apple IIe described above. The Apple IIc was designed for portability and compactness. As a result, your options for expansion are limited to the plug-in ports on the rear of the machine. (By the way, you should not open your IIc computer, as that will invalidate its warranty.)

Inside your computer there are a number of chips identified on the board as RAM. This is what people are talking about when they talk about memory. There is another kind of memory in your machine that is identified as ROM. ROM is not normally considered part of working memory.

RAM stands for Random Access Memory. ROM stands for Read Only Memory. The contents of ROM are always the same, while the contents of RAM are constantly changing. ProDOS is loaded in RAM when you start up the system, and any programs you run are transferred into RAM from the disk before they can be used. Think of RAM as a blackboard that is constantly being used, erased, and used again.

Memory is measured in bytes. A byte is essentially the amount of space it takes for the computer to store one character, such as the letter a, in memory. A kilobyte is 1024 bytes. An Apple IIe comes standard with 64K (the K stands for kilobytes) of RAM memory. An Apple II+ comes standard with 48K of RAM; it can be expanded to 64K by adding a memory or language card in slot 0. An Apple IIc has a standard memory size of 128K. You need a minimum of 64K of RAM in your Apple before you can load ProDOS from your disk into memory.

Disk Drives and Disks

Essentially, a disk drive is a cross between a tape recorder and a record player. Like a record player, the disk drive uses a thin, round surface to store information. Like a tape recorder, it can both store new information and play back old information. The process of searching the disk and finding old information is called a "read" operation; a "write" operation puts new information on the disk.

A floppy disk is what is normally used to store data and programs on your Apple II. The standard Apple disk drive (called a Disk II) uses single-sided, single-density, 5¼-inch disks. Single sided means that only one side of the disk is used to store information. Single density refers to how tightly the information is packed onto the disk. The 5¼-inch figure refers to the diameter of the disk.

The disk consists of a thin layer of recording material, very similar to that used in recording tape, encased in a plastic cover. The hole in the center is used for locating and driving the disk when it is in the disk drive. The oblong slot next to the central hole exposes the surface of the disk so that the drive can read it. The disk has a write-protect notch cut into the left side. If this notch is covered with a piece of aluminized paper, you cannot write new files to the disk or make any changes to the files existing on that disk. You would have to remove the covering from the notch before you could write new information to the disk. This notch allows you to protect important information from accidental destruction.

Think of the disk as a very thin, fragile record album. If you ever touch the exposed surfaces of the disk or if you bend or damage the disk in any way, you will probably lose any information or programs you had on that disk.

When you want to use a disk with your computer, you insert it into the disk drive by opening the door of the drive and gently sliding in the disk. If the disk does not go in all the way, do not force it. Take it out and try to slide it in again. If you still have problems, check to see if there is any obstruction that should be removed. When the disk is in the drive, close the door.

Apple sells two types of disk drives for the Apple II. The most common of these is known as the Disk II and is designed to use floppy disks. The second is known as the ProFile. The ProFile is what is commonly called a hard or rigid disk. Hard disks are sealed units. You cannot remove the disk from a hard disk the way you can from a floppy disk drive. The advantage of a hard disk is that the storage capacity is considerably greater than that of a floppy disk. For example, a ProFile can store 5 million bytes of information while a floppy disk for the Apple II will store about 140 thousand bytes. (Note: As of this writing, the ProFile is not available for the Apple IIc.)

Your disk drive is connected to your Apple IIe by a flat ribbon cable. This cable enters the machine through one of the openings in the back of the case and plugs into a card in one of the expansion slots. This card is known as a disk controller card. If you have an Apple IIc, the connection between the integral drive and the hardware of your Apple will not be evident unless you open the machine (which is not advised).

If you are using Apple's Disk II interface card, the card will have two plugs very clearly marked drive 1 and drive 2. You should use the one marked drive 1 if you have only one drive. If you have two drives, both can be attached to the same card. If you add more than two drives to your system you will need another interface card to plug them into. Normally, the first interface card is placed in slot 6 and any additional drive controller cards are placed in slots 5 or 4. If you are using Apple's ProFile interface card, the card will have only one plug to connect to your ProFile.

In the course of this book, we will often refer to the disk or the disk drive. In most cases, everything we say about a floppy disk will be exactly the same in practice when applied to a hard disk. Where there is a difference, we will mention it specifically.

Monitors

The monitor is a device that looks like a television set. It acts like a window into the computer. When you type commands on the keyboard, the Apple displays them back to you on the screen of the monitor. Any messages from the program you are running also appear on the screen of the monitor. While it is possible to get an adapter kit and use a television set as your monitor, most people prefer to use a monitor designed for this purpose, as it can produce a better image.

Printers

Your computer uses a printer to put things on paper. The type of information it puts on paper or prints out can be almost anything you desire. Common examples would include letters, financial reports, and inventory lists you have created with a program; listings of programs you have written; and special graphs or charts if you have been using a graphics program.

Two types of printers are commonly used with personal computers like the Apple II. The first and by far the most popular is a dot-matrix printer. The second is a letter-quality printer.

A dot-matrix printer creates characters with tiny dots of ink. Dot-matrix printers are generally less expensive and faster than letter-quality printers. However, some people object to them for certain types of work because the characters are not as clear as those printed by letter-quality printers.

Letter-quality printers print in much the same way as a typewriter. Most of these printers have a wheel or thimble-shaped device containing all the characters you have on the keyboard. When the printer prints, this wheel is constantly spinning about to strike the proper key against the ribbon. This process is considerably slower than dot-matrix printing. Letter-quality printers usually cost much more than dot-matrix printers, and they are not able to produce the graphics and pictures that many dot-matrix printers can.

Your printer is normally connected to an interface card in slot 1 of your Apple. There are two main types of interface cards available. The first of these is a serial interface; the other is known as a parallel interface. These terms refer to the way in which information is sent from your computer to the printer. If the information is sent serially, it is sent single file, one piece of information after the other. If information is sent in a parallel mode, several pieces are sent at the same time. You can picture these methods as the difference between a single-lane road and a super highway.

(An Apple IIc computer can use only a serial printer, because it does not have a parallel port. You just plug the printer into the serial printer port on the rear of the machine.)

The important thing to know about serial and parallel interfaces is that one will not work with the other. If you have a serial printer, you must have a serial interface. If you have a parallel printer, you must have a parallel interface.

HOW COMPUTERS OPERATE

Before the computer can do anything, it has to be programmed. A program is a series of instructions that the processor will carry out in a particular order. Once they are written, programs are normally stored in a file on a disk.

Inside the computer, the processor is the boss. The processor reads every instruction and does all the things necessary to carry it out.

The disk drives can be compared to a filing room. The disks that you use in the disk drives are similar to the cabinets you would find in a filing room. Each one of them can contain many different files.

When you tell the computer to run a program that is stored on a disk, it must first load that program into memory. Memory acts as the desk top or workspace of the processor. Once the program is in memory, the processor reads all of the instructions and carries them out in the order they are arranged.

If the program needs further information that is stored on disk, such as names and addresses or the amount of money you are owed, the processor, as instructed by the program, will look on the disk for the information. The program will read the data into memory so that the processor can work on it. If the program wants to change the files, the processor will write the new information back to the disk. If there are no changes, there is no need to write it back—the original file is still on disk; only a copy was read into memory.

When the program has finished running, it remains in memory. If you run a different program, the first program will be wiped out of memory and lost if you have not stored it. The program will also be lost if you turn the machine off without first saving the program.

OPERATING SYSTEMS

An operating system is a set of rules and regulations that the computer uses in carrying out your orders. There is always a simple operating system available when you turn on your Apple. This is what interprets your commands and tells the processor what you want it to do. In addition to this, your Apple has the ability to use another operating system for instructions dealing with the disk. This operating system has to be loaded from the floppy disk into memory before your Apple can use it.

OVERVIEW OF PRODOS

ProDOS is a new disk operating system designed to maximize the power of the Apple II. ProDOS is faster, easier to use, and more powerful than DOS, the old disk operating system.

If you purchased your Apple II prior to 1984, you received DOS 3.3 as the disk operating system with your Disk II and must purchase ProDOS separately. If you purchased your Apple IIe after 1984, you were supplied with ProDOS (in the form of the ProDOS User's Disk) when you got your Disk II. ProDOS is also supplied with the Apple IIc on the System Utilities disk (which provides a rather different menu for the ProDOS utilities).

ProDOS (the letters stand for Professional Disk Operating System) manages all operations involved in storing information on a floppy disk in your drive and fetching it from the disk back into memory. The operating system acts as a traffic cop directing the flow of data according to your commands. It does nothing without receiving instructions either from the operator or from a program that is being executed.

ProDOS is an easy system to use. On most microcomputers, you have to remember all the commands if you want to use the system. With ProDOS your choices are presented to you in a menu, and you simply make your selection. If the operating system needs more information, it will ask you what it needs to know. If you hit a wrong key by accident, it will ask you again for the correct information. There is no need to remember complicated commands to use ProDOS.

When you turn on your Apple, ProDOS offers you a menu of choices. If you have any questions about what to do, a single stroke of the ? key will usually bring you the answer. (On the IIc, you have to press the Open-Apple and ? keys at the same time to get help.) This brings to the screen a feature known as the Tutor. The Tutor provides explanations of the feature you are using when you hit the ? key (or the Open-Apple *and* ? keys on the IIc). This is especially useful when you first begin using ProDOS.

ProDOS will appear to you in a slightly different fashion on an Apple IIc than it will on an Apple IIe or II+, but the operating system itself is the same. This means that all the commands that work from the BASIC prompt or from the MLI will operate in the same fashion and produce the same results. The difference in the ProDOS that comes with the IIc lies in the menu structure and the utilities that can be used from ProDOS. The next two chapters of this book will discuss ProDOS as it is used on the IIe and IIc, with the ProDOS User's Disk discussed in Chapter 2 and the System Utilities disk in Chapter 3, where we will highlight the differences in the IIc version. (Because much of the material in Chapters 2 and 3 will be the same, we suggest that you read Chapter 2 and then skip to Chapter 4 if you are using only a IIe. If you are a IIc owner, you will probably want to read Chapter 3 instead of Chapter 2.) The main menu described in the following paragraphs applies to the IIe version of ProDOS.

One of the most important features of ProDOS is what is called the Filer on the IIe version of ProDOS. The Filer allows you to copy files and disks with a minimum of fuss and bother, and it will delete files you no longer need. It also helps you organize the information you store on disk. (These same facilities are also available with the IIc version of ProDOS.)

In order to maintain continuity between DOS and ProDOS, Apple has also provided the ability to convert files from one to the other. Most Applesoft BASIC programs will perform identically under both operating systems. This upward mobility from DOS to ProDOS is a valuable and important feature of Apple's new operating system. However, programs that use direct hooks into DOS will probably not work under ProDOS, and you will probably not be able to transfer copy-protected programs from DOS to ProDOS.

ProDOS offers three more options on its main menu. If you choose Display Slot Assignments, ProDOS will tell you exactly what you have in each of the expansion slots of your Apple II. It knows the name of the disk you used to start it and how much memory it has available. If you choose Display/Set Time, you can set the date and time and have ProDOS stamp all your files when they are created or modified. If you have a clock card in your Apple, ProDOS automatically checks it for the correct time and date, making this option unnecessary unless you want to use another date for a particular purpose.

The last option on the ProDOS main menu is Applesoft BASIC. By choosing this option you can make direct use of individual ProDOS commands, bypassing the menu structures. Because once you select this option you are in Applesoft BASIC, you can also use it as a programming language to create programs of your own design.

DOS VERSUS PRODOS

DOS 3.3, Apple's previous operating system for Apple II computers, had the largest body of software available for it of any operating system in the personal computer world. It was well liked and familiar to millions. However, DOS 3.3 had some serious limitations that Apple felt had to be solved if the Apple II was to continue as a strong product.

The most serious problem of DOS 3.3 is that it limits the ways in which you can use disk space. Both DOS 3.3 and ProDOS treat the space on a disk as a volume, or an amount of space to be filled. The largest allowable volume size in DOS is that of a single floppy disk. This means that with DOS you have to divide a single 5-megabyte hard disk into roughly 40 volumes to make use of all the space. This is cumbersome, confusing, and time consuming.

ProDOS was designed to support large-capacity disk drives. Under DOS the largest possible file is 140 kilobytes. Under Pro-DOS the largest possible file is 16 megabytes—roughly 100 times the largest possible DOS file. This ability opens up a new world of opportunity for the Apple II.

Another major problem of DOS is that it is slow. According to Apple, DOS 3.3 transfers data to and from the disk drive at about one kilobyte per second. This sounds like a lot, but larger and faster disk drives can handle information much faster. ProDOS can transfer data to and from the disk drive at eight kilobytes per second, roughly eight times the speed of DOS. (Under typical conditions this theoretical advantage shrinks slightly to about five to one in favor of ProDOS.)

Under DOS you are limited to 105 files in a volume. While this number might seem very large, it quickly becomes inadequate when dealing with large-capacity disk drives such as the ProFile. As the capacity of the disk drive becomes greater, it becomes more important to organize your files in better ways. ProDOS uses a hierarchical approach to structuring the file system. This means that it uses directories and subdirectories to organize the files on a disk. Each directory may contain a number of files, some or all of which may also be directory files containing other files. For practical purposes, you will find that ProDOS allows you an unlimited number of files. The chief advantages of a hierarchical system are that it keeps the files organized and makes them easier and faster to access.

The hierarchical filing system may not be important if you are dealing with only a small number of files on each individual floppy disk. As a rough rule of thumb, you might want to consider creating subdirectories whenever the number of files on a disk exceeds the number that can be displayed on a single screen. This will allow you to split your files into categories and thus handle them in a more organized fashion.

DOS 3.3 does not support the use of interrupts, while ProDOS does. This is very important when computers are joined together in a network.

ProDOS is compatible with most DOS programs. This means that you can move programs and data files from DOS to ProDOS to enjoy the greater capabilities of the newer operating system. ProDOS is also compatible with SOS, the operating system on the Apple III.

ProDOS is easier for the first-time user to learn than DOS. This is because most of the functions you need to use are available from the menus you get when you first turn on the system. There is no need to remember commands; you simply select from the choices presented. ProDOS also has the Tutor available to give you help right on the screen.

ProDOS also allows you to make better use of the facilities of your Apple II. If you have a clock/calendar card, ProDOS will read it to obtain the proper time and date. ProDOS will also make use of the extra memory available with an 80-column text card to improve the performance of programs that make heavy use of the disk drive.

In the nature of things, Apple had to make a few trade-offs to gain all these advantages. If you have only a single disk drive in your system, DOS has certain things in its favor. ProDOS expects that certain files will always be available on disk when you change programs. This reduces the amount of storage available on any given disk. (While you can swap disks in and out of the drive when you change programs, this will soon become an annoying problem on a single-drive system.) ProDOS also uses more memory than DOS does, reducing the amount you have available for your other programs. For technical reasons that will be explained later in this book, Applesoft BASIC programs will run slightly slower under ProDOS than under DOS.

All in all, ProDOS is a major step forward for the Apple II. It vastly increases the abilities of the computer in the vital areas of storage capacity, speed, and computer networking. Compatibility with the past enables the new operating system to make immediate use of much of the software available under DOS. The effort spent by Apple to develop this new operating system promises continued support of the Apple II in the future.

Using ProDOS from
the ProDOS User's Disk

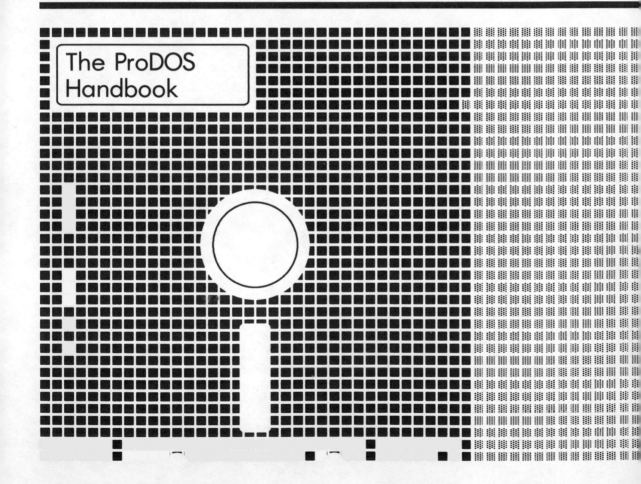

The ProDOS
Handbook

TWO

This chapter will show you how to use the standard options available to you from the ProDOS menu on the ProDOS User's Disk. These options represent utilities you can use. In computer jargon, a utility is a program that does a number of frequently required tasks for the operating system. The ProDOS User's Disk includes the following utilities:

- Tutor
- Filer
- DOS to ProDOS Conversion
- Display Slot Assignments
- Display/Set Time
- Applesoft BASIC

This chapter deals specifically with ProDOS for the IIe and not with the IIc version described in the next chapter. While the Pro-DOS operating system is the same for both, Apple has provided two distinctly different sets of utility programs for the IIc and the IIe. Although the ProDOS User's Disk is not the version of ProDOS provided with the IIc computer, it will run on the IIc almost exactly as described in this chapter. Any differences caused by the different hardware are noted at the end of Chapter 3.

TERMS AND DEFINITIONS

In order to make proper use of ProDOS, we need to define several terms. ProDOS uses these terms to locate devices and files when it needs them. If you use them improperly, one of two things will happen, the most likely of which is that ProDOS will not understand your command and will be unable to execute it. More dangerously, ProDOS may misunderstand your command but still be able to execute it. In an extreme case, this may result in deleting the wrong file.

Before proceeding to the next section, be sure that you are entirely familiar with the terms and definitions that follow—it will make the process of learning and using the system much easier.

Volumes

In the eyes of ProDOS, a volume is a disk. A volume may be either a floppy disk or a hard disk such as the ProFile. Each volume has a name that is assigned during the format process described in this chapter. ProDOS uses this name to recognize the disk you have in the drive and to try to find things when you give it a command. ProDOS searches for disks by name rather than by drive, so it is important to familiarize yourself with volume names and how they are used.

For example, suppose you have four disk drives on your system. If each one of those drives contains a disk, you have four volumes for ProDOS to choose from. If each one of them has a distinctly different volume name (PRODOS1, PRODOS2, PRODOS3, and PRODOS4), ProDOS will have no difficulties in finding the disk you want when you specify the volume name in one of the utilities that follows. But if all four volumes have the same volume name, ProDOS will be unable to determine which one you want simply from the volume name. You will have to provide other information (such as the slot and drive) to tell ProDOS where to look for the volume you desire. Otherwise, ProDOS will select the first volume that matches the path name. The one it finds depends on where the defaults for slot and drive (covered in the next few pages) point to. These defaults are set using the utilities described in this chapter; you can change them at any time.

Slots

ProDOS uses slot numbers in much the same way the post office uses state names. When you tell ProDOS to do something with a disk drive, for example, it needs to know where the disk drive is. Specifying the slot number gives it a place to look within the computer. Normally, the disk drives are connected to a disk controller card in slot 6. If you have more than two drives you will need a second disk controller card, which will probably be in slot 5.

Drive Numbers

Each disk drive on your Apple IIe is plugged into a disk controller card in expansion slot 6 or 5 inside the computer. The disk controller card has two plugs that are clearly labeled drive 1 and drive 2. You can think of these plugs as the city name of your disk drive. It is one step more specific than the slot number. Whichever drive is plugged into drive 1 is considered to be drive 1 by ProDOS. If you reverse the connections so that the former drive 1 is now plugged into drive 2, ProDOS will not notice the change until you try to read or write to one of the drives.

The reason ProDOS will not notice that you have changed the disk in the drive is very simple. Every time ProDOS reads a disk, it reads the directory to find the file it needs. So ProDOS does not

The ProDOS User's Disk Utilities

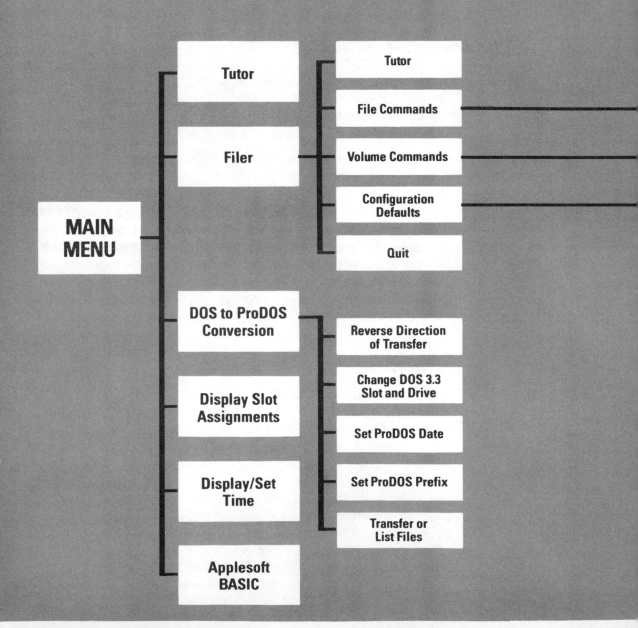

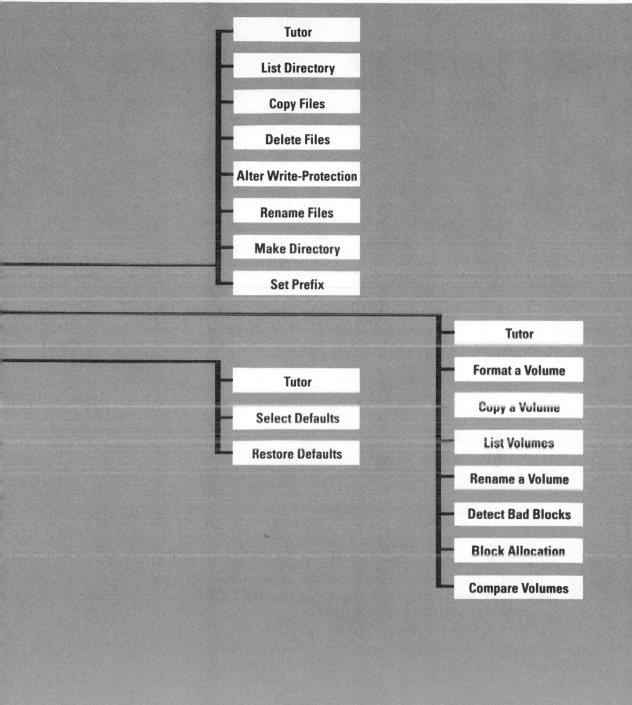

Tutor

List Directory

Copy Files

Delete Files

Alter Write-Protection

Rename Files

Make Directory

Set Prefix

Tutor

Format a Volume

Copy a Volume

List Volumes

Rename a Volume

Detect Bad Blocks

Block Allocation

Compare Volumes

Tutor

Select Defaults

Restore Defaults

care what you do to the drives in between its attempts to read the disk. This provides you with a lot of flexibility in relation to other systems. Many other operating systems read the directory of a disk into memory and must be notified about changes, or they will run into an error condition when they next try to read a drive that has been changed.

If you change the connections of the physical devices between operations, the next time ProDOS tries to read the disk it will treat whatever device is connected to the drive 1 plug as drive 1. While this procedure is not harmful, there is no particular reason to use it. If you have volumes with identical names, it might even cause some problems if you were deleting files or updating them.

Path Names

Path names tell ProDOS what route to travel to find the file or files you want. A path name always begins with a / and the volume (or disk) name. Following our analogy, you can think of the volume name as a street name. The rest of the path name consists of a string of directory names separated by the / character. The last part of the path name always consists of the name of the file you want to access.

For example, suppose you want to copy a file named MYFILE on a volume named PRODOS. That file is located inside another file (a directory file) called OURFILE. You will have to build a path name to tell ProDOS how to find MYFILE. In this case, the path name would be /PRODOS/OURFILE/MYFILE. The path name could get much longer if MYFILE is stored within a series of subdirectories within OURFILE. If MYFILE is located in the volume directory, the path name is simply /PRODOS/MYFILE.

The names of the volume, the directories, and the actual file give ProDOS the specific directions it needs to find the file you want. ProDOS follows this path in much the same way a person might follow directions to your house. If your directions are good, Pro-DOS will find what you want; if your directions are bad, ProDOS will come back and ask you for more.

Prefixes

Path names have their advantages, but the longer they are the more prone they are to error. It also becomes a chore to type in a long path name time after time. For these reasons, ProDOS allows you to store a prefix that will be attached to all your commands. Since you type it only once, you will be less prone to make a mistake in the path name. Also, because it is automatically placed in front of any path name you specify, it will save you a lot of extra typing.

For example, suppose you want to delete MYFILE from the directory OURFILE on the volume PRODOS. If the prefix is set to /PRODOS/OURFILE, you simply specify the file name MYFILE in the delete command. ProDOS automatically combines the prefix containing the path name with the file name you specify and locates the correct file. If no prefix is set or if the prefix points to a volume or directory other than /PRODOS/OURFILE, you have to specify the entire path name /PRODOS/OURFILE/MYFILE to delete the correct file.

Wild Cards

In a poker game a wild card can be used to represent any other card. A wild card in ProDOS acts in a similar way to represent any other character.

ProDOS has two wild-card symbols. The first of these is the = character. You can use the = to take the place of any characters in a name. For example, if you enter the file name BA=D, the command you are using will operate on all files in the correct path name that start with BA and end with D.

The ? is the second wild-card character. The ? works exactly the same way as the = except that ProDOS will ask you to hit Y or N for each file it finds before it performs the operation on that file. If you do not want the command to operate on that file, press N to go to the next file.

For example, if you wish to delete all the files beginning with BA and ending with D in the directory OURFILE on the volume PRODOS, specify the path name /PRODOS/OURFILE/BA=D. This automatically deletes all files in that directory fulfilling those requirements. This would mean that if that directory contained the files BARD, BAD.BOYD, and BARKED, they would all be deleted.

Because this can be a rather dangerous procedure, ProDOS has given you the ? character as an option. If you want to delete only the files BARD and BARKED in the example, you could use the ? instead of the = character, so that your path name reads /PRODOS/OURFILE/BA?D. ProDOS would then ask you to confirm each file name before deleting it. You would be able to skip over the file BAD.BOYD by typing the letter N when it is presented.

These wild cards will work only on the IIe version of ProDOS and only from within the Filer or Convert utilities. They cannot be used from the BASIC prompt or from within BASIC programs.

STARTING UP

In order to use ProDOS, you have to "boot" or load the operating system. This is a very simple thing to do. Take your ProDOS User's Disk and place it in drive 1 of your computer. Close the drive door and turn on the power to your Apple II. You will hear a whirring noise, the light on the disk drive will light up briefly, and the main menu will be displayed on the screen of your monitor.

THE MAIN MENU

Menus work very much the same on a computer system as they do in a restaurant. The waiter in a restaurant hands you a menu and waits for you to select what you want from the items available. The menu ProDOS gives you is displayed on the screen of your monitor. You tell ProDOS what you want by typing your choice on the keyboard. As shown in Figure 2.1, the menu on the ProDOS User's Disk provides a single character followed by a dash and a description of the item it represents. For example, the first item on the ProDOS menu reads

　？ – TUTOR: PRODOS EXPLANATION

If you want to use the Tutor, you simply press the ? key.

ProDOS uses a series of menus to allow you to access the utility programs. For example, when you select the Filer from the main menu, ProDOS will load the Filer menu into memory and present you with a second menu. This is done to make it easy for you to perform the variety of functions that are available to you. You will find that this approach will make the process of learning and using ProDOS much easier.

THE TUTOR

The Tutor is an option that appears on your menu at all levels of ProDOS. It is a feature that is becoming very popular in software today. Sometimes it is called Help or Explain rather than Tutor, but

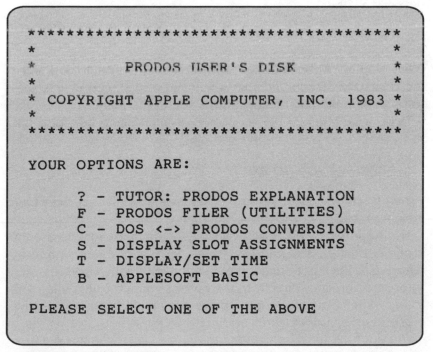

```
***************************************
*                                     *
*        PRODOS USER'S DISK          *
*                                     *
* COPYRIGHT APPLE COMPUTER, INC. 1983 *
*                                     *
***************************************

YOUR OPTIONS ARE:

     ? - TUTOR: PRODOS EXPLANATION
     F - PRODOS FILER (UTILITIES)
     C - DOS <-> PRODOS CONVERSION
     S - DISPLAY SLOT ASSIGNMENTS
     T - DISPLAY/SET TIME
     B - APPLESOFT BASIC

PLEASE SELECT ONE OF THE ABOVE
```

Figure 2.1: The Main Menu

the basic idea remains the same. It is designed to act as a quick reference card that you can access while you are using the ProDOS utilities.

In all cases, you get into the Tutor by pressing the ? key for a menu selection. The Tutor will clear the screen and show you a brief description of your options in that menu and a few hints on how to proceed. At the top of the screen you will see the display

TUTOR:

followed by the title of the screen. For example, if you press the ? key while you are in the Filer menu, the title will be

FILER MENU OPTIONS

There are only two commands you can use within the Tutor. If there is more information to be shown, the Tutor will display a message such as

PRESS <RET> TO CONTINUE: <ESC> TO EXIT

When you have this message on the screen, pressing the Return key clears the screen and shows you the next screen of information. Pressing the Escape key returns you to the menu.

If you have reached the last screen of information the Tutor has on this topic, you will see the message

PRESS <ESC> TO EXIT

No other command or keystroke will have any effect at this point. Pressing Escape returns you to the menu.

The Tutor will be especially valuable to you in learning to use the ProDOS utilities. You can very often solve a problem simply by referring to the Tutor. Remember that the information you see on a Tutor screen relates directly to the options you are using when you call it. When you are at one of the first menus, you will receive more general information about ProDOS. When you are in a menu such as the File Commands menu, you will see detailed information about only the commands available in that menu.

You should use the Tutor to get involved in ProDOS quickly. Start out by setting up a blank disk to work on. Try out your options. If you run into trouble or are unsure about what to do, ask the Tutor. Using the system while you are learning about it will help you learn better and faster.

THE FILER

When you enter the Filer by pressing F on the main menu, Pro-DOS will display the menu shown in Figure 2.2.

The Tutor

If you press the ? key the Tutor will come onto the screen and give you a brief explanation of your options from the Filer menu.

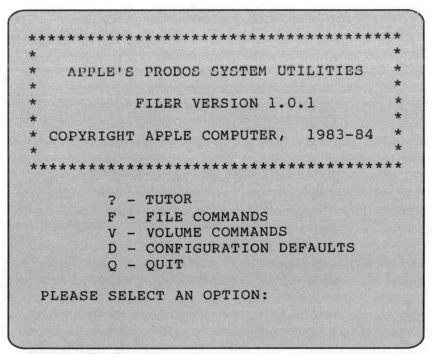

```
*****************************************
*                                       *
*    APPLE'S PRODOS SYSTEM UTILITIES    *
*                                       *
*          FILER VERSION 1.0.1          *
*                                       *
*  COPYRIGHT APPLE COMPUTER,  1983-84   *
*                                       *
*****************************************
            ? - TUTOR
            F - FILE COMMANDS
            V - VOLUME COMMANDS
            D - CONFIGURATION DEFAULTS
            Q - QUIT

     PLEASE SELECT AN OPTION:
```

Figure 2.2: The Filer Menu

The Tutor will display only information concerning the Filer if you call it from the Filer menu. Other than that, it operates exactly as described in the section on the Tutor.

File Commands

If you press the F key for File Commands, you will get a menu of all options for using the Filer on individual files. This menu is shown in Figure 2.3. The first of these is, of course, the Tutor. If you press the ? key at this point, the Tutor will give you a few hints on path names, file names, wild cards, and prefixes. These are described in Chapter 4 of this book.

The next command is L for List ProDOS Directory. This command will ask you to enter a path name to the directory you want listed. If you type in /PRODOS and press the Return key, you'll see

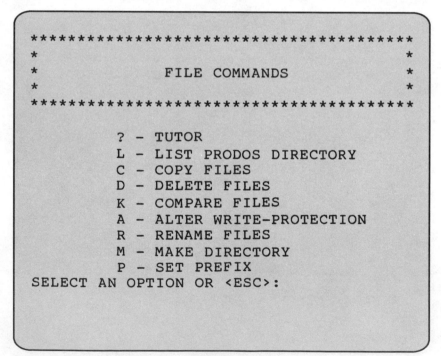

```
*****************************************
*                                       *
*            FILE COMMANDS              *
*                                       *
*****************************************


        ? - TUTOR
        L - LIST PRODOS DIRECTORY
        C - COPY FILES
        D - DELETE FILES
        K - COMPARE FILES
        A - ALTER WRITE-PROTECTION
        R - RENAME FILES
        M - MAKE DIRECTORY
        P - SET PREFIX
SELECT AN OPTION OR <ESC>:
```

Figure 2.3: The File Command Menu

something similar to the display shown in Figure 2.4. At the top of the screen is the word DIRECTORY followed by the name of the directory you are looking at. Underneath that is a line of headings followed by the names of the files in the directory and information about each.

If the name of a file has an asterisk before it, the file is locked or write protected. A file that is write protected cannot be deleted or changed. (We will discuss how to write protect a file in a few pages.)

In the column following the name of the file you will find a three-character code that describes what type of file it is. This can tell you whether you are looking at a program, a data file, or a system file. We will discuss the importance of file types in a later chapter.

The third column tells you how many blocks the file takes up on the disk. Each block is composed of 512 bytes. If you want to find

```
DIRECTORY:  /PRODOS

  NAME                 TYP   BLOCKS    MODIFIED
 *PRODOS               SYS      31     1-JAN-84
 *BASIC.SYSTEM         SYS      21    15-NOV-83
 *CONVERT              SYS      42     1-NOV-83
 *FILER                SYS      51    <NO DATE>
  STARTUP              BAS       7    14-DEC-83
 *BYE                  BAS       1    16-NOV-83
  TEST                 BAS       1    <NO DATE>
 *ABLE                 BIN       4    21-NOV-83
  WINDOW               BAS       1    21-FEB-84

  BLOCKS FREE:     121          USED:   159




 --PRESS <RET> TO BEGIN: <ESC> TO EXIT--
```

Figure 2.4: Sample Result of the List Directory Command

out exactly how many bytes a file occupies, simply multiply the number of blocks by 512.

The last column is the date on which the file was last modified. If the date was not set when you changed the file, this field will read

<NO DATE>

At the bottom of the display ProDOS shows you the number of blocks still free on the disk, as well as the number you have used.

Pressing the Return key takes you back to the beginning of the List command so you can specify a different directory. Pressing the Escape key returns you to the File Commands menu.

The Copy Files command allows you to copy a file from any directory on your disk drive to any other directory on the same or another drive. To do this you need to know the path name to the file you want to copy and the path name to the directory you want to copy it to. ProDOS will ask you for these path names and then prompt you to insert the disks and press the Return key. When the copy has been made, ProDOS will display the message

COPY COMPLETE

and return you to the first prompt within the Copy File command. If you want to copy another file, you can repeat the steps given above. If you don't want to copy any more files, you can press the Escape key to return to the File Commands menu.

The Delete Files command prompts you to provide the path name to the file you want deleted. When you hit the Return key, ProDOS looks in the directory you have specified and, if it finds the file, deletes it immediately. This is a very dangerous option— you should always check the path name you have provided before you hit the Return key. The Filer will not double-check with you before it deletes the file. Once the file is gone, you cannot call it back. The Delete Files command will not delete a directory or sub-directory file unless that file is empty (that is, it contains no other files). In this way ProDOS ensures that you won't delete a file that is your only access to a number of other files. If you want to delete a subdirectory or directory file, you must first individually delete each file that directory contains.

The Compare Files command checks whether two files are identical. You provide ProDOS with the path names of the files you want to compare. This command is useful when you want to check whether you have updated your backup file after making changes in your working file. If the two files are identical, the Filer will show you the message

COMPARE COMPLETE

If the two files are not identical, you will see the message

FILES DO NOT MATCH

This command will not show you where the two files differ; you will have to determine what the difference is and what you want to do about it.

The Alter Write-Protection command allows you to lock unprotected files or unlock protected files. A locked or write-protected file cannot be changed or deleted. You should develop the habit of using this feature to keep yourself from accidentally deleting important files.

The command first asks you for the path name to the file or files you want to change. After you have entered it and pressed the Return key, the Filer will ask you the question

LOCK FILES?(Y/N)

If you want to protect the file you have named, press Y for yes. This will update the directory and keep you from changing, deleting, or renaming the file until its status has been changed. The Filer will return the message

LOCK COMPLETE

when it is done. If you want to unlock a file, answer the question with an N for no. This allows you to do anything you want to the file. When it is done, the Filer will return the message

UNLOCK COMPLETE

You can use the wild-card characters with this command to alter the write-protection feature on more than one file at a time.

The Rename Files command allows you to change the name of a file without disturbing the contents of the file. This command first asks you for the existing path name and then for the new path name, both of which will end with the name of the file. The new path name, of course, ends with the new file name. When the Filer is finished changing the name, it displays the message

RENAME COMPLETE

and returns to the first prompt within the Rename Files command. As with all other commands from the menu, you can exit the Rename Files command by pressing Escape.

The Make Directory command allows you to create a new directory file. It asks you to provide a path name; the name should end with the name of the directory you are trying to create. Once you have entered the new path name and pressed Return, the Filer creates the directory and displays the message

MAKE DIRECTORY COMPLETE

The last command on the File Commands menu is Set Prefix. This command allows you to set a system prefix to save yourself extra typing when specifying path names. Simply enter the prefix you want to use and press Return. The Filer returns the message

SET PREFIX COMPLETE

when the prefix is set. Once this is done, the Filer automatically tacks the new prefix onto any path name you enter. You can return to the File Commands menu by pressing the Escape key.

Be careful when using the Set Prefix command. If for some reason you have two very similar volumes in your drives and you specify a prefix that affects the wrong one, you are in danger of making some far-reaching mistakes. If you are deleting files, for example, you can wipe out the wrong one because you have set the prefix to point to the wrong disk. The same sort of mistake can happen with identical files in different directories of the same volume. If you are working in a particular subdirectory, you can set the prefix to point to that one and then use the List ProDOS Directory command to make sure you are in the right subdirectory before you cause any damage.

Volume Commands

If you press V for Volume Commands from the Filer menu, you will get a menu of all your possible options for using the Filer on entire disks. The Volume Commands menu is shown in Figure 2.5. The first option on the menu is, of course, the Tutor. At this point, the Tutor will give you a few hints on slots, drives, and volume names. These are described in the beginning of this chapter.

The Format a Volume command prepares a disk for use. This command divides the surface of the disk into blocks so that ProDOS can store, find, and read information. First ProDOS asks you for the slot and drive number of the disk you want to format. Once

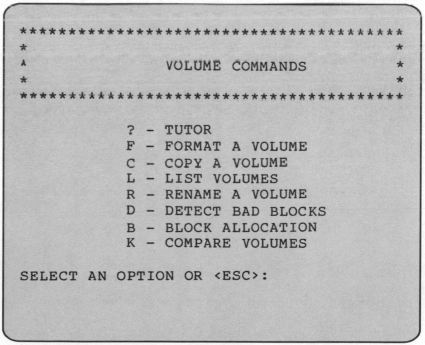

```
*********************************************
*                                           *
A               VOLUME COMMANDS             *
*                                           *
*********************************************


          ? - TUTOR
          F - FORMAT A VOLUME
          C - COPY A VOLUME
          L - LIST VOLUMES
          R - RENAME A VOLUME
          D - DETECT BAD BLOCKS
          B - BLOCK ALLOCATION
          K - COMPARE VOLUMES


  SELECT AN OPTION OR <ESC>:
```

Figure 2.5: The Volume Commands Menu

you have entered that information, it asks you for the new volume name. Figure 2.6 shows a sample screen for the Format a Volume command. If you do not want to give the disk a name when you format it, you can simply hit the Return key and the Filer will assign a name beginning with /BLANK followed by a two-digit number. Formatting takes a little time, and during this time the Filer displays the message

FORMATTING

When the formatting is complete, the message

FORMAT COMPLETE

appears and the program returns to the first prompt.

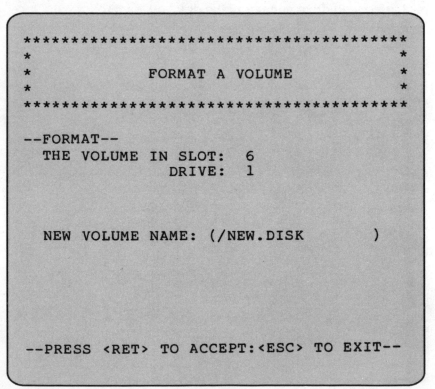

```
*****************************************
*                                       *
*            FORMAT A VOLUME            *
*                                       *
*****************************************

--FORMAT--
  THE VOLUME IN SLOT:  6
                DRIVE:  1



  NEW VOLUME NAME: (/NEW.DISK          )




--PRESS <RET> TO ACCEPT:<ESC> TO EXIT--
```

Figure 2.6: The Format a Volume Command

The Copy a Volume command allows you to copy one volume to another. This command will allow you to copy only volumes that are exactly alike. This means that you cannot use this command to copy the contents of a hard disk to a floppy disk or vice versa, because the two disks are not the same size. You can use the Copy Files command in the Filer to transfer from one to the other. You should use the Copy a Volume command with care—the previous contents of the destination disk will be destroyed in the process of the copy operation.

The Copy a Volume command first asks you for the slot and drive numbers of the volume you want to copy and the volume you will make the copy on. ProDOS then prompts you to insert the disks and press the Return key when you've done so. Next ProDOS asks you for the new volume name. You can accept the default name, which is /PRODOS, or change it to anything you wish. When the copy is complete, ProDOS displays the message

COPY COMPLETE

and returns to the first prompt within the Copy a Volume command.

If you are using a one-drive system, the slot and drive numbers of the volume you want to copy and the volume you want to place the copy on will be the same. The problem with using one-drive systems is that you have to switch the disks several times to complete the copy. ProDOS first tells you to

INSERT SOURCE DISK AND PRESS <RET>

Then ProDOS tells you to

INSERT DESTINATION DISK AND PRESS <RET>

After you do this, ProDOS will ask you if it should destroy the volume it finds on the destination disk. If you say no, it will return to the first prompt within the Copy a Volume command. If you say yes, it will continue with the copying and prompt you for each change of the floppy disk. When you are done copying, you can return to the Volume Commands menu by pressing the Escape key.

The List Volumes command will show you a list of all the volumes in the drives currently connected to your system. A sample screen showing the result of a List Volumes command appears in Figure 2.7. As you can see, the list also shows you the slot and drive of each volume. You can change the floppy disks in the drives and press Return to display another list.

The Rename a Volume command will ask you for the slot and drive of the volume you want to rename. It will then ask you for the new volume name while showing you the old one, as Figure 2.8 illustrates. If you decide not to change the name, you can simply hit the Return or Escape key. Otherwise, type in the new name (which will replace the old name) and press Return. ProDOS will display the message

RENAME COMPLETE

and return to the first prompt after it has changed the name.

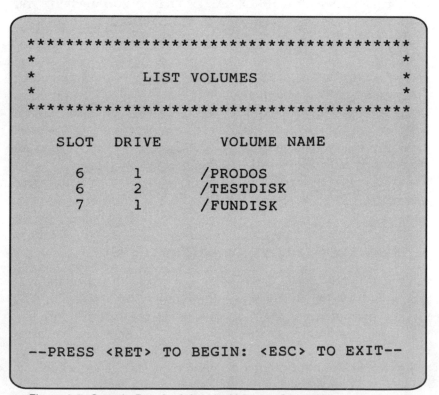

```
*****************************************
*                                       *
*              LIST VOLUMES             *
*                                       *
*****************************************

   SLOT    DRIVE        VOLUME NAME

     6       1        /PRODOS
     6       2        /TESTDISK
     7       1        /FUNDISK




   --PRESS <RET> TO BEGIN: <ESC> TO EXIT--
```

Figure 2.7: Sample Result of the List Volumes Command

The Detect Bad Blocks command checks to see if there are any damaged or unreadable sections on a volume. When you issue this command, ProDOS asks you for the slot and drive number of the volume you wish to check. As soon as you answer these questions, it begins reading and checking the volume. When it is finished, it displays a message showing you the numbers of any bad blocks on the volume and returns to the first prompt. If there are no bad blocks on the volume, the message will read

0 BAD BLOCKS

If you discover a volume with bad blocks, do not take any chances. Copy all the files on the volume to another volume immediately. You may be unable to copy some files because

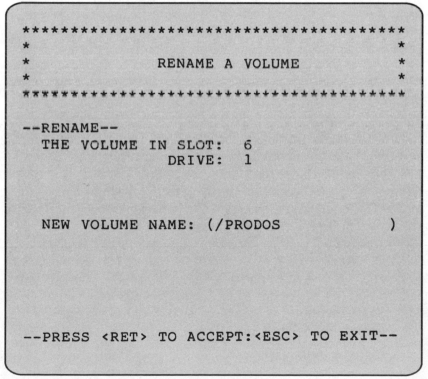

```
* * * * * * * * * * * * * * * * * * * * * * * * * * * * * * * * * * * * * *
*                                                                       *
*                      RENAME  A  VOLUME                                *
*                                                                       *
* * * * * * * * * * * * * * * * * * * * * * * * * * * * * * * * * * * * * *

--RENAME--
   THE  VOLUME  IN  SLOT:    6
                   DRIVE:    1



   NEW  VOLUME  NAME:  (/PRODOS                          )




--PRESS  <RET>  TO  ACCEPT:<ESC>  TO  EXIT--
```

Figure 2.8: The Rename a Volume Command

of the bad blocks; in this case, you will get the message

I/O ERROR

and will have to abandon those files. Once you have copied all the recoverable files, reformat the original volume and check it again.

If there are still bad blocks listed after you reformat the disk, the disk should be treated as unreliable. The best course of action with a damaged disk is to avoid using it (throw it away). If you must use it, be very careful. Do *not* store any files on it that you cannot recover from somewhere else.

If the volume you discover the bad blocks on is a ProFile or other hard disk system, you have a bigger problem. Back up as much as you can and contact your dealer or the manufacturer right away.

If you find that several of your disks have bad blocks on them, you should check to see what is causing the problem. Your disk drive may be the culprit. Try switching the brand of disk you are using to see if the bad blocks still occur. If they do, your drive probably needs servicing or replacement.

The Block Allocation command will show you how many blocks are used, how many are free, and how many total blocks there are in a volume. When you issue the command, ProDOS asks you for the slot and drive numbers of the volume you want to check. As soon as you enter this information, ProDOS shows you the figures and returns to the first prompt, as Figure 2.9 illustrates. The data will remain on the screen until you either enter another slot number or press Escape to get back to the Volume Commands menu. This command is an easy way of checking how much space you have left before you copy anything new to a disk.

The Compare Volumes command allows you to compare two different volumes to see if they are exactly alike. The main use of a command like this is to check whether you have updated your backup copy of a working disk. Again, ProDOS asks you for the slot and drive numbers of the volumes you want to compare. If the two volumes are identical, the message

COMPARE COMPLETE

will appear on the screen. If there is a difference between the two volumes, you will see a message such as

BLOCK NUMBERS DO NOT MATCH:

with the numbers of the blocks that are not identical underneath it.

Configuration Defaults

The next option on the Filer menu is the Configuration Defaults option. When you press D from this menu, you will get a menu of all options for configuring the system defaults, shown in Figure 2.10. The first of these options is, as usual, the Tutor. At this point, the Tutor will give you a few hints on slots, drives, and volume names.

The Filer assumes that you have two disk drives attached to a card in slot 6, that you want drive 1 to be your source disk drive and drive 2 to be your destination disk drive, and that you want all

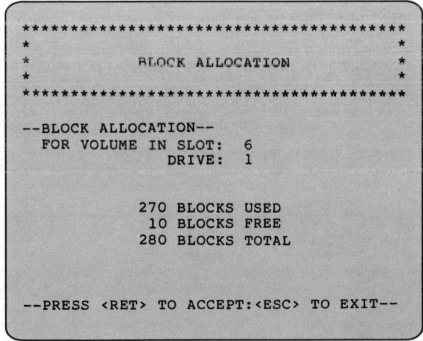

```
**********************************************
*                                            *
*            BLOCK ALLOCATION                *
*                                            *
**********************************************

--BLOCK ALLOCATION--
   FOR VOLUME IN SLOT:   6
                 DRIVE:  1


             270 BLOCKS USED
              10 BLOCKS FREE
             280 BLOCKS TOTAL



--PRESS <RET> TO ACCEPT:<ESC> TO EXIT--
```

Figure 2.9: Sample Result of the Block Allocation Command

output sent to the monitor. These are what are called the configuration defaults; they represent assumptions about how your system is set up. The Configuration Defaults option allows you to set up new values as you wish or to restore the original values.

The Select Defaults command will ask you for the source slot and drive, the destination slot and drive, and the default output device. By using this command you can set the default so that all output is routed simultaneously to both the printer and the monitor. If you have a single-drive system, you will want to make the source and destination drives and slots identical. Once you have selected all the defaults, the Filer returns you to the first prompt on the screen and allows you to repeat the process or return to the Configuration Defaults menu by pressing Escape. A sample screen

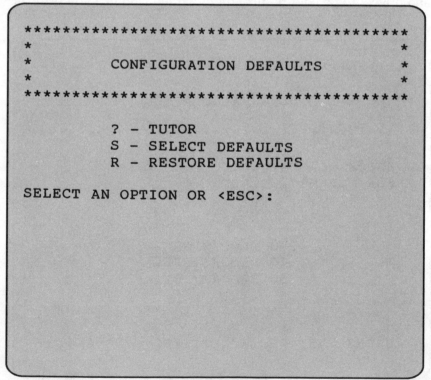

```
*****************************************
*                                       *
*          CONFIGURATION DEFAULTS       *
*                                       *
*****************************************


        ? - TUTOR
        S - SELECT DEFAULTS
        R - RESTORE DEFAULTS

SELECT AN OPTION OR <ESC>:
```

Figure 2.10: The Configuration Defaults Menu

showing the options this command offers appears in Figure 2.11.

This command becomes very useful if you have a system with more than two drives, or if you want to produce quickly a printed listing of what you are seeing on the monitor. In a system that has three or four drives, you can use this command to specify the one you normally want used as the source or destination drive and then zip through the Filer's prompts by pressing Return. If you want to "echo" to the printer everything that appears on the screen, you just set the output device to P for printer and monitor instead of M for monitor only. Once you have done this, ProDOS will attempt to send everything that is displayed to both the screen and the printer. This can save you hours of time when you need them most, because you can use this feature to keep an exact

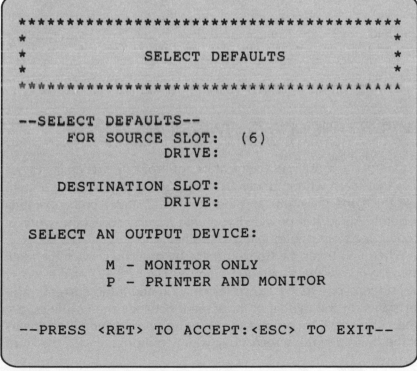

```
* * * * * * * * * * * * * * * * * * * * * * * * * * * * * * * * * * * * * * * *
*                                                                          *
*                      SELECT DEFAULTS                                     *
*                                                                          *
* * * * * * * * * * * * * * * * * * * * * * * * * * * * * * * * * * * * * * * *


--SELECT DEFAULTS--
      FOR SOURCE SLOT:    (6)
                  DRIVE:

      DESTINATION SLOT:
                  DRIVE:

   SELECT AN OUTPUT DEVICE:

          M - MONITOR ONLY
          P - PRINTER AND MONITOR


--PRESS <RET> TO ACCEPT:<ESC> TO EXIT--
```

Figure 2.11: The Select Defaults Command

printed record of every step you take in complicated situations. If there is a foul-up, you can see exactly what happened to cause it.

The Restore Defaults command shows you the standard system defaults and allows you to reset anything you have changed. If you do wish to restore the system defaults, simply press the Return key; otherwise, press the Escape key to exit. Once you press either of these keys, the Filer returns to the Configuration Defaults menu.

Quit

The last option on the File menu is Quit. The Quit command asks you for the path name to the next program and displays a default value. You can type in a new path name or simply press Return to accept the default. When you first boot ProDOS on your system the Quit program default is BASIC.SYSTEM. Once you specify a different program, that program remains the default until you either change it again or reboot ProDOS. Pressing Escape returns you to the main menu.

DOS TO PRODOS CONVERSION

One of the most important features of ProDOS is its ability to use files that were written under DOS 3.3. You will usually be able to use the same programs and the same data under both operating systems. Apple has provided you with a utility to do the work of converting from one format to the other.

When you enter the Convert utility by pressing C from the main menu, you will be shown the menu in Figure 2.12. At the top of the screen you will be shown information about the current transfer status. In the middle of the screen, between the two lines, are your choices. The prompt for entering your command appears at the bottom of the screen along with two more choices, the Tutor or Quit.

Transfer Information

The first item of information about the transfer is the direction. When you first enter the Convert menu, the transfer is set from DOS 3.3 to ProDOS, with the DOS disk in drive 2 and the ProDOS disk in drive 1. ProDOS indicates this to you with the message

DOS 3.3 S6,D2 --> ProDOS

The slot number of the DOS disk is 6, as indicated by the S6, and the drive number is 2, as indicated by the D2. This message will change to reflect any alterations you make in the direction of transfer.

The second line shows you the date that will be used to time-stamp the file when you transfer it. If you do not have a clock card

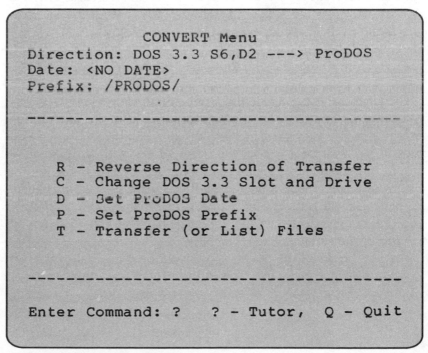

```
                    CONVERT Menu
   Direction: DOS 3.3 S6,D2 ---> ProDOS
   Date: <NO DATE>
   Prefix: /PRODOS/


   ------------------------------------------


       R - Reverse Direction of Transfer
       C - Change DOS 3.3 Slot and Drive
       D - Set ProDOS Date
       P - Set ProDOS Prefix
       T - Transfer (or List) Files


   ------------------------------------------


   Enter Command: ?    ? - Tutor,  Q - Quit
```

Figure 2.12: The Convert Menu

and have not set the ProDOS date, this field will read <NO DATE>. If you have a clock card or if you have already set the date, it will be displayed here in the form 20-MAR-85. This field will be updated every time you change the date.

The third piece of information about the transfer setup is the prefix you are currently using. ProDOS will show this to you with a message such as /PRODOS/. This would indicate that the transfer is going to a volume named PRODOS. This message will change to indicate the current prefix you are using any time you use the Set ProDOS Prefix option.

Convert Menu Options

The Reverse Direction of Transfer option tells ProDOS that you want to move in the opposite direction. ProDOS begins by assuming that you want to move files from DOS 3.3 over to a ProDOS disk. If you press the R key from the Convert menu, the information listed on the direction line at the top of the screen will change. Press the R key again to change it back to the original direction. The direction message at the top of the screen will always tell you which way ProDOS is set up to transfer the files.

The Change DOS 3.3 Slot and Drive option allows you to specify where the DOS disk is. The Convert program uses the same terminology that the Filer program did for slots and drives. When you press C you will be asked for the DOS 3.3 slot and drive. You can accept the defaults that appear on the screen by hitting the Return key, or you can type in a new value if you want to make a change. Pressing Escape returns you to the Convert menu. Any changes you make are reflected in the information in the direction line at the top of the screen.

The Set ProDOS Date option allows you to set any date you wish to have stamped on the files to be transferred. This date will appear when you list a ProDOS directory; it is a useful tool for keeping track of which file has the latest information. If you have a clock card in your Apple, ProDOS will automatically check it to get the correct date and time when ProDOS boots. If you do not have a clock card, you will have to set the date manually either at this point or from the Date and Time option ProDOS provides from the main menu (discussed in a few pages). Any changes that you make here are reflected in the date field at the top of the screen. When no date has been set, ProDOS will use the phrase <NO DATE>. All files will be marked this way until you set a date. You can also use this feature to change the existing date after ProDOS has been booted. Pressing Escape at this point returns you to the Convert menu.

The Set ProDOS Prefix command allows you to do two things. The first of these is to set the path name to be followed when executing ProDOS commands. The second allows you to change the slot and drive of the ProDOS volume involved in the transfer.

If you choose to change the ProDOS prefix by typing in a new path name, press P and then type in exactly the path name you wish ProDOS to follow. Sometimes you will not know the exact path name. It is very likely that you will want to transfer the files to a blank ProDOS volume. In this case, you can simply insert the blank formatted disk in the drive and tell the Convert program what slot and drive it resides in. ProDOS will read the disk, get the volume name, and change the prefix to agree with it. Any changes you make will be shown to you in the prefix field at the top of the screen.

The Transfer or List Files option allows you to move files between DOS and ProDOS. You can also use this command to list the files on a disk. When you press T from the Convert menu, you will be asked which files you wish to copy. If you already know the name of the file you want to copy, you can simply enter it here. If you are not sure of the exact name of the file you want to copy, pressing the Return key will provide you with a list of the files on the source disk. The name of one of the files will be highlighted in reverse video. If you hit the ↓ key, the highlighting will move to the next file. If you hit the ↑ key, it will move back to the previous file. You will be unable to move past the beginning or the end of the list. By using the cursor keys to move the highlighting to the file you wish to transfer and then hitting the Space bar, you can mark each file you wish to be copied. If you mistakenly highlight a file, you can move the highlighting back to the name of the file and hit the Space bar again. This will remove the file from the list to be transferred. Each file you select will be marked by an arrow to the left of the file name. When you are finished selecting files to be transferred, press the Return key to begin the process of copying the files from one disk to the other. Pressing the Escape key allows you to backtrack to the Convert menu.

If an error is encountered in transferring a file, an error message will appear at the bottom of the screen and the word ERROR will appear to the left of the file name that caused the problem. You will then have to correct the problem before attempting to copy the file again. Pressing Escape will return you to the main menu.

SLOT ASSIGNMENTS

When you select this option from the main menu, ProDOS will tell you the name of the disk you used to start the system. It will also tell you whether you are using an Apple II+ or IIe (it mistakenly tells you that you are using a IIe when you run the User's Disk on a IIc), how much memory you have available, and whether you have Applesoft in ROM. Then it will show you a list of all the peripheral cards that are currently in the expansion slots of your system.

Most of the time ProDOS will know exactly what type of card you have in each slot and will tell you what that card is. If there is no card plugged into a slot, it will tell you that the slot is empty. If there is a card in a slot and ProDOS does not know what type of card it is, you will see the message USED.

DATE AND TIME

This option is used to set the date and time for ProDOS if you do not have a clock card in your system. ProDOS looks for the clock card and automatically gets the date and time from it if it is there. This information is used primarily for time-stamping files when you copy or update them.

When ProDOS does not find a clock card, the date field will display <NO DATE>. This will also appear in your directory listings.

There are two main reasons why you would want to time-stamp a file. The first is that you might want to compare different versions of a file to see which one was changed last. The second is to maintain a record of when an activity was performed, such as making a backup copy of a file.

BASIC

When you select the BASIC option from the main menu, you are in direct contact with ProDOS. This means that you do not have to go through the menu structure to issue the ProDOS commands you need. These commands and their formats are discussed in Chapter 4. On the left side of the screen, next to the cursor, you will see the ⌐ character. This is known as the BASIC prompt; it means that ProDOS is waiting for you to type in a command. In addition to allowing you to use the ProDOS commands that are not accessible from the menus, this option allows you to program in BASIC. Programmers will select this option to write and run their programs. Since several of the later chapters in this book will deal with programming under ProDOS, we will not discuss it here.

You can also start up an application program at this point. Many software packages, however, do not need the ProDOS User's Disk to be run. They will run from a menu when you boot the system from the disk containing the program.

To return to the main menu, simply type RUN STARTUP and press Return with the User's Disk in the drive.

Using ProDOS from the System Utilities Disk

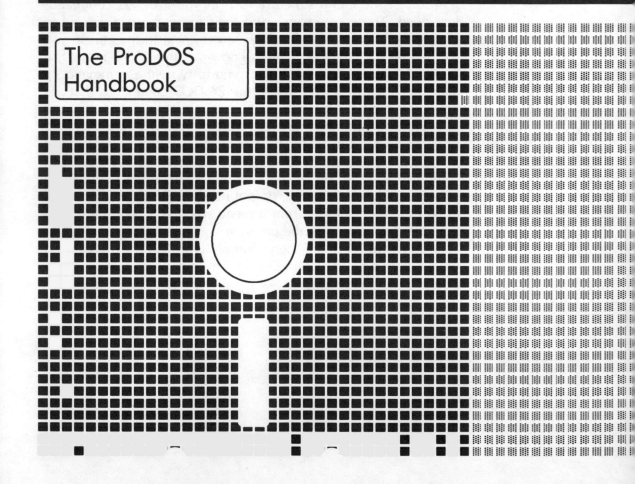

The ProDOS
Handbook

THREE

This chapter will show you how to use the standard options available from the ProDOS System Utilities menu on an Apple IIc. These options are different in several ways than the options that are available on a IIe with the ProDOS User's Disk. The two versions will be called the IIc and the IIe versions in the discussion that follows.

It can be difficult to understand why the same operating system appears differently in the two versions. ProDOS itself is exactly the same. What is different is not the operating system but the utility programs that Apple has provided to use the features of ProDOS.

If you compare the IIc and IIe computers, you will notice that they are substantially different. The IIc is a much smaller machine.

It has no room for expansion slots on the inside, as the IIe does. (In fact, opening the top of an Apple IIc invalidates the machine's warranty.) Instead, the IIc has ports (places to plug devices into) on the back of the machine. In order to achieve the compactness of the IIc, Apple's designers had to make trade-offs to save space while still retaining the essential functions of an Apple II computer.

The System Utilities menu on the IIc reflects these differences while it retains many of the functions of ProDOS on the IIe. The IIc version is generally simpler to use, it offers fewer functions, and it is thus more appropriate for the casual user. As we will explain later in this chapter, the System Utilities disk will not run on any other Apple II, but the ProDOS User's Disk will run on a IIc with only a few difficulties.

TERMS AND DEFINITIONS

The following terms and definitions form an important base for understanding the use of ProDOS with your Apple. They will be used frequently in this chapter and the ones that follow, so it would be a good idea to spend some time familiarizing yourself with them before continuing to the rest of the book. The use of terms is sometimes different between an Apple IIc and a IIe or II+, and we have noted the difference where it occurs.

Volumes

In the eyes of ProDOS, a volume is a disk. A volume may be either a floppy disk or a hard disk such as the ProFile. (At the present writing, Apple does not provide a way to connect a ProFile to the IIc.) Each volume has a volume name that is assigned during the format process described in this chapter. ProDOS uses this name to recognize the disk you have in the drive and to try to find things when you give it a command. (To make things a little easier for you, the System Utilities allow you to specify either a drive or a volume name when you give a command.)

Ports, Drives, and Slots

An Apple IIc does not have expansion slots like the Apple IIe's or II+'s. Instead, it has ports built into the rear of the machine for connecting particular devices. For programming purposes, these ports correspond to certain slots in other Apple II computers. The correspondence is shown in Table 3.1.

ProDOS uses slot numbers in much the same way the post office uses state names. When you tell ProDOS to do something with a disk drive, for example, it needs to know where the disk drive is. Specifying the slot number gives it a place to look within the computer. Although you do not need to use slot numbers while you are using the menu functions on the System Utilities disk, you will have to be aware of the port-to-slot relationship to use ProDOS commands from BASIC. Also, some programs that are written for a IIe version of ProDOS may ask you to supply slot and drive numbers.

As you can see from Table 3.1, the IIc treats the internal drive as slot 6, drive 1. Any drive connected to the external drive port is treated as slot 6, drive 2. There is an exception to this rule. The PR# command (described later in this book) is unable to access the external drive under this arrangement. This would become important if the internal disk drive became inoperable, since you would be unable to start up ProDOS because of the problem with the internal disk drive. On a IIe you could simply switch the cable connections of your drives if you suspected a problem with the drive

Apple IIc	Apple IIe, II+, II
Port 1	Slot 1
Port 2	Slot 2
Built-in 80-column card	Slot 3
Joystick port	Slot 4
Built-in disk drive	Slot 6, drive 1
External disk drive	Slot 6, drive 2

Table 3.1: Apple IIc/IIe Port/Drive Comparison

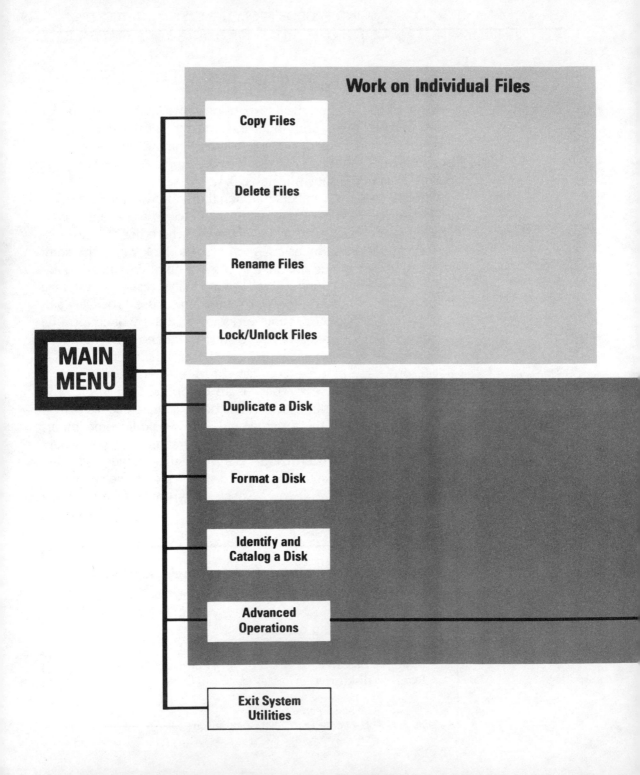

Work on Individual Files

Copy Files

Delete Files

Rename Files

Lock/Unlock Files

MAIN MENU

Duplicate a Disk

Format a Disk

Identify and Catalog a Disk

Advanced Operations

Exit System Utilities

The ProDOS System Utilities on the Apple IIc

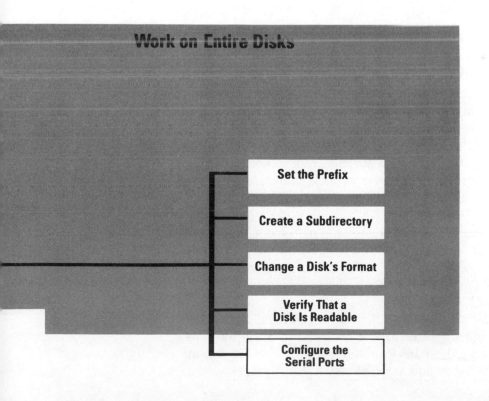

Work on Entire Disks

Set the Prefix

Create a Subdirectory

Change a Disk's Format

Verify That a
Disk Is Readable

Configure the
Serial Ports

itself. This would allow you to boot from the second drive, which would then be connected as drive 1. But on a IIc you don't have this flexibility.

To prevent this impasse, Apple has provided the following procedure:

1. Put your System Utilities disk in the external drive.
2. Simultaneously press the Control and Reset keys on your IIc.
3. Type PR#7 and press Return.

This procedure forces your IIc to boot the disk in the external disk drive and makes it possible for you to use your IIc when the internal disk drive is not working. In effect, your IIc has translated the PR#7 command (which would refer to slot 7 on a IIe system) to read as slot 6, drive 2.

Path Names

Path names are used in exactly the same manner and perform exactly the same function on all Apple II ProDOS systems. Path names tell ProDOS what route to travel to find the file or files you want. A path name always begins with a / and the volume (disk) name. The rest of the path name consists of a string of directory names separated by the / character. The last part of a path name always consists of the file name you actually want to access.

For example, suppose you want to copy a file named MYFILE on a volume named PRODOS. That file is located inside another file (a directory file) called OURFILE. You will have to build a path name to tell ProDOS how to find it. In this case, the path name would be /PRODOS/OURFILE/MYFILE. The path name could get much longer if MYFILE is stored within a series of subdirectories within OURFILE. If MYFILE is located in the volume directory, the path name is simply /PRODOS/MYFILE.

The names of the volume, the directories, and the actual file give ProDOS the specific directions it needs to find the file you want. ProDOS follows this path in much the same way a person might follow directions to find your house. If your directions are good, ProDOS will find what you want; if your directions are bad, ProDOS will come back and ask you for more.

Prefixes

Path names have their advantages, but the longer they are the more prone they are to error. It also becomes a chore to type in a long path name time after time. For these reasons, ProDOS allows you to store a prefix that will be attached to all your commands. Since you type it only once, you will be less prone to make a mistake in the path name. Also, because it is automatically placed in front of any path name you specify, it will save you a lot of extra typing. Prefixes, like path names, are used in exactly the same manner and perform exactly the same function on all Apple II Pro-DOS systems.

Suppose you are working with the files contained within a subdirectory file named DIRECTORY 2. The path name for that file is /UTILITIES/DIRECTORY1/DIRECTORY2. If the prefix is set to this path name and you want to catalog the subdirectory file DIRECTORY3 in DIRECTORY2, all you have to do in the Identify and Catalog a Disk option, for example, is to type DIRECTORY3 in response to the ProDOS Pathname option. ProDOS adds the prefix to the file name to make the path name.

Multiple-File Selection

Wild-card characters do not exist in the IIc version of ProDOS. The IIe version allows their use in the Filer and Convert utilities to allow you to specify a string of characters that will match more than one file name in an operation. The approach used in the IIc version is to display the file names on the screen. You must then mark individually the file names you want to affect with one of the menu functions. Alternatively, you can indicate that all files on the disk or directory you have chosen should be affected by the menu function you are using. This process will be demonstrated in the Copy Files section below.

STARTING UP

In order to use ProDOS, you have to "boot" or load the operating system. This is a very simple thing to do. Take your System Utilities disk and place it in the internal drive of your computer. Close the drive door and turn on the power to your Apple IIc. You will hear a whirring noise, the Disk Use light on your computer will light up, and the main menu will be displayed on the screen of your monitor.

THE MAIN MENU

Menus work very much the same on a computer system as they do in a restaurant. The waiter in a restaurant hands you a menu and waits for you to select what you want from the items available. Instead of being in a cardboard folder, the menu ProDOS gives you is displayed on the screen of your monitor. You tell ProDOS what you want by typing your choice on the keyboard.

The System Utilities menu is different than the one you will see if you are using the IIe version of ProDOS. It includes functions that can be used only on the IIc, and it lacks some functions available on the IIe version. As a result, the choices offered to you on the menu (which are described in the following pages) are different. Figure 3.1 shows the IIc main menu.

The means of using the menus on the IIc is also slightly different than it is on the IIe version. The IIc menu allows you to select your option by using the ↓ and ↑ keys on your keyboard. The current selection is indicated by changing that line of the screen display to uppercase (capital letters) and placing the symbols < and > before and after the option description. When you first bring up a menu, item 1 will be the current selection, as represented in Figure 3.1.

If you press the ↓ key, the current selection will change from item 1, Copy Files, to item 2, Delete Files. Press ↓ again and the current selection will change to item 3. Changing the choice to item 5, Duplicate a Disk, would cause the screen to change as shown in Figure 3.2. This will continue until you reach item 9, which is the last item on the menu. If you press the ↓ key one more time, the selection will loop back to item 1. You can keep this up indefinitely, looping around in a circular fashion every time you reach the end of the list. The ↑ key will have the same effect, except that the direction of travel is reversed.

You can also move directly to a menu item by typing the number that appears to the left of your choice on the screen. For example, if you want to select item 6, Format a Disk, you can simply type the number 6 on the keyboard. The screen would change to indicate your selection exactly as if you had selected it with the arrow keys.

When you have made your selection and want to execute it, press the Return key. This tells your Apple that you have decided and gives it the signal to continue to the procedure you have selected.

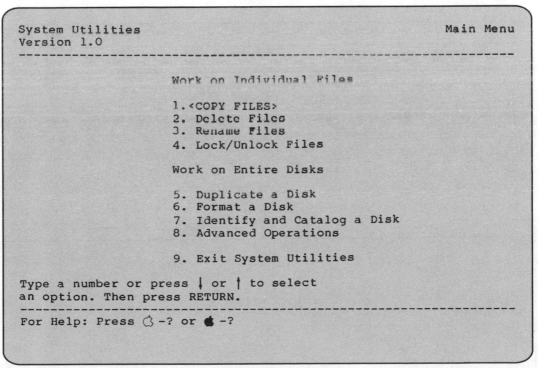

```
System Utilities                                    Main Menu
Version 1.0
-------------------------------------------------------------
                    Work on Individual Files

                    1.<COPY FILES>
                    2. Delete Files
                    3. Rename Files
                    4. Lock/Unlock Files

                    Work on Entire Disks

                    5. Duplicate a Disk
                    6. Format a Disk
                    7. Identify and Catalog a Disk
                    8. Advanced Operations

                    9. Exit System Utilities

Type a number or press ↓ or ↑ to select
an option. Then press RETURN.
-------------------------------------------------------------
For Help: Press ⌃-? or  -?
```

Figure 3.1: The Apple IIc ProDOS System Utilities Menu

Certain items on the main menu present you with additional menu choices. These subordinate menus follow the same rules as the main menu, with one major addition. This new feature is the use of the Escape key to return to the function or menu you were most recently using. This option is always indicated by a brief message in the upper right corner of the screen that tells you where the use of the Escape key will take you. For example, when you are in the Copy Files function, the upper right corner of the screen includes the message

   ESC: Main Menu

This means that if you press the Escape key at this point you will return to the main menu. The Escape key can be used to exit any of the functions that have been accessed from the main menu, but it cannot be used to leave the main menu itself.

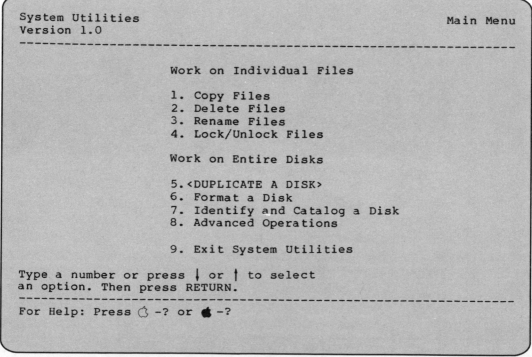

```
System Utilities                                        Main Menu
Version 1.0
-----------------------------------------------------------------

                    Work on Individual Files

                    1. Copy Files
                    2. Delete Files
                    3. Rename Files
                    4. Lock/Unlock Files

                    Work on Entire Disks

                    5.<DUPLICATE A DISK>
                    6. Format a Disk
                    7. Identify and Catalog a Disk
                    8. Advanced Operations

                    9. Exit System Utilities

Type a number or press ↓ or ↑ to select
an option. Then press RETURN.
-----------------------------------------------------------------
For Help: Press ○ -? or  -?
```

Figure 3.2: Changing the Current Selection in the Menu

HELP

ProDOS on the IIc has a Help feature that can be called from anywhere within the System Utilities programs. This feature takes the place of the Tutor program found in the IIe version of ProDOS. It is designed to act as a quick reference card that you can access while you are using the system. It is accessed by simultaneously pressing either the Open Apple or Closed Apple keys together with the ? key on your keyboard.

The Help feature will open a window on the screen and show you a brief description of your options in that situation and a few hints on how to proceed. This window or box will always contain the phrase "Press RETURN to continue." You can continue operations by pressing any key at all, however—you do not have to use the Return key to end the Help feature.

The contents of the Help window change according to the function or menu you are in. For example, when you are at the main menu and the current selection is Copy Files, the window contains a description of what that function does. If you change the current selection to Rename Files, a description of the Rename Files function appears when you ask for help. The use of the Help feature is not limited to the main menu. You can use it at any point within the System Utilities to aid you in your use of ProDOS.

You should use the Help feature to get involved in ProDOS quickly. Start out by setting up a blank disk to work on. Try out your options. If you run into trouble or are unsure about what to do, use the Help feature. Using the system while you are learning about it will help you learn better and faster.

WORK ON INDIVIDUAL FILES

The first four options on the main menu all consist of operations that affect files on an individual basis:

1. Copy Files
2. Delete Files

3. Rename Files

4. Lock/Unlock Files

We will discuss them here one by one. These same functions are performed on the IIe version of ProDOS from the File Commands menu within the Filer.

Copy Files

The Copy Files function allows you to copy a file from any directory on your disk drive to any other directory on the same or another drive. It performs the same duties as the Copy Files command in the IIe version. The only difference between the two is the way in which you choose the files you want to copy.

To use the Copy Files function, first select option 1 for Copy Files from the main menu and press Return. You will be presented with a menu for selecting the source disk or path name where the copy will originate. You can simply choose the drive of the originating disk, or you can choose to provide a path name to the correct directory, as shown in Figure 3.3. Select the option that is appropriate and press Return. The path name must always point to a directory. You will be presented with a similar menu for selecting your destination disk or path name. Once again, make the appropriate choice and press Return. If you wish to specify a subdirectory, you must select the path name option. The disk options will always point to the volume directory of the disk in that drive.

You will then be asked whether you want to copy some or all of the files on the source directory to the destination directory. The Copy Files option will copy all the files on a disk, but it will do it less efficiently than the Duplicate a Disk option, which is also available from the main menu. This option of copying all the files is useful, however, when you want to copy all the files contained in a particular subdirectory. If you choose to copy only some of the files on your source directory, the names of the files in that directory are loaded and displayed on the screen. Follow the instructions at the bottom of the screen to select files with the arrow keys. Files that are marked to be copied will have a check mark appear to the left of the file name. When you have marked all the files you wish to copy, press the Return key to signify you have finished.

If you are using a two-drive system and are copying from one drive to the other, ProDOS will simply copy all the files from the source disk to the destination disk one by one. If your source and destination drives or path names are the same, ProDOS will prompt you to change the disk in the drive and press Return every time it is necessary. This will also happen if you are copying between directories on the same disk. If a file you are copying already exists on the destination directory, ProDOS will ask you if it is okay to erase the old file before copying the new one into its place.

When all copying is complete, you will be shown a message at the bottom of the screen and asked to press Return to continue (at which point you can copy other disks or files) or to press Escape to get back to the main menu.

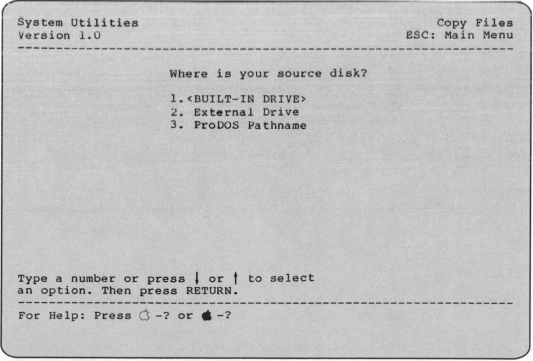

```
System Utilities                                    Copy Files
Version 1.0                                       ESC: Main Menu
----------------------------------------------------------------

                    Where is your source disk?

                    1.<BUILT-IN DRIVE>
                    2. External Drive
                    3. ProDOS Pathname








Type a number or press ↓ or ↑ to select
an option. Then press RETURN.
----------------------------------------------------------------
For Help: Press ⌃ -? or ⌘ -?
```

Figure 3.3: Initial Menu of the Copy Files Function

Delete Files

The Delete Files function allows you to delete a file from any directory on any of your disk drives. It performs exactly the same function as the Delete Files command in the IIe version. Again, the only difference between the two is in the way you choose the files you want to delete.

To use the Delete Files function, first select option 2 for Delete Files from the main menu and press Return. You will be presented with a menu for selecting the disk where the deletions will be made. Once again, you can specify the drive or you can choose to provide the path name to the directory you want. Select the option that is appropriate and press Return.

You will then be asked whether you want to delete some or all of the files on the disk or directory. If you choose to delete only some of the files, the names of the files on the volume directory or sub-directory you have specified are loaded and displayed on the screen. Select the appropriate files with the arrow keys; files that are marked to be deleted will have a check mark appear to the left of the file name. When you have marked all the files you wish to delete, press the Return key. Before you delete a subdirectory file, you must first delete all the files in it.

When all deleting is complete, you will be shown a message at the bottom of the screen and asked to press Return to continue (at which point you can delete other files from other disks or directories) or to press Escape to get back to the main menu.

When you delete files, ProDOS looks in the directory you specified and, if it finds the file, deletes it immediately. This is a very dangerous option, and you should always double-check your file names before hitting Return. Once the file is gone, you cannot retrieve it.

Rename Files

The Rename Files function allows you to change the name of a file without disturbing the contents of the file. Although you choose the files you want to rename differently, this function performs the same operation as the Rename Files command in the IIe version.

To use the Rename Files function, select option 3 for Rename Files from the main menu and press Return. You can then either specify the drive or choose to provide the path name for the directory where the name changes will be made. Select the option that is appropriate and press Return.

You will then be asked whether you want to rename some or all of the files on the disk. If you choose to rename only some of the files, the names of the files on your directory will be loaded and displayed on the screen. Select the files you want to rename with the arrow keys; those files will have a check mark appear to the left of the file name. When you have marked all the files you wish to rename, press the Return key.

ProDOS will prompt you to enter a new file name for each file that has been marked for renaming. Simply type in the new name you wish to give the file and press Return. If you try to rename a file to a name that already exists for another file in that directory, ProDOS will ask if it is okay to erase the already existing file. When all renaming is complete, you will be shown a message at the bottom of the screen and asked to press Return (if you want to continue to rename files on other disks) or to press Escape to get back to the main menu.

Lock/Unlock Files

The Lock/Unlock Files function is equivalent to the Alter Write-Protection command in the IIe version. This function allows you to mark a file so that it cannot be changed or deleted and to change that mark so that the file can be changed or deleted. You should develop the habit of using this feature to keep yourself from accidentally deleting files.

To use the Lock/Unlock Files function, select option 4 for Lock/Unlock Files from the main menu and press Return. You can either specify the drive or choose to provide the path name for the directory where the write-protection changes will be made. Select the option that is appropriate and press Return.

You will then be asked whether you want to lock or unlock files. Make your selection and press Return. You can choose whether you want to affect some or all of the files in the directory. If you choose to lock or unlock only some files, the names of the files in your directory will be loaded and displayed on the screen. Select the files you want to affect with the arrow keys. Files that are to be locked or unlocked will have a check mark appear to the left of the file name. When you are done selecting files, press the Return key.

When all changes are complete, you will be shown a message at the bottom of the screen and asked to press Return (if you want to continue locking or unlocking files on other disks or directories) or to press Escape to get back to the main menu.

WORK ON ENTIRE DISKS

The second group of options on the main menu consists of operations that affect an entire disk in a single function. Once again, Apple has provided the IIc user with four functions to do this work:

5. Duplicate a Disk
6. Format a Disk
7. Identify and Catalog a Disk
8. Advanced Operations

The Advanced Operations option will present you with a second menu of functions. These functions are less frequently used than the other options on the main menu and require a little more knowledge of ProDOS and your Apple to use. They can, however, be used by anyone who is prepared to spend a little time and thought in learning them. We will discuss this group of functions here one by one.

Duplicate a Disk

The Duplicate a Disk function is equivalent to the Copy a Volume command in the Filer program of the IIe version (under the Volume Commands option). This function allows you to copy the contents of an entire disk to a second disk in a single operation.

To use the Duplicate a Disk function, first select option 5 for Duplicate a Disk from the main menu and press Return. You will be presented with a menu for selecting the drive where the source disk will be. Select the option that is appropriate and press Return. You will then be presented with a menu for selecting the drive where the destination disk will be. Select the option that is appropriate and press Return.

ProDOS will prompt you to change the source and destination disks if they are specified as the same drive. If they are different drives, ProDOS will copy the source disk to the destination disk without interruption until it is finished.

When all copying is complete, you will be shown a message at the bottom of the screen and asked to press Return (if you want to continue copying other disks) or to press Escape to get back to the main menu.

Format a Disk

The Format a Disk function prepares a disk for use. This program divides the surface of the disk into blocks so that ProDOS can store, find, and read information. This function is similar to the Format a Volume command in the IIe version, but the IIc version can also format DOS 3.3 and Pascal disks. It can even determine what format a disk is when you are unsure of its type.

To use the Format a Disk function, select option 6 for Format a Disk from the main menu and press Return. You will be presented with a menu for selecting the drive where the disk will be. Select the option that is appropriate and press Return.

You will then be asked to select the operating system that you wish to use to format this disk. Your choices are ProDOS, DOS 3.3, and Pascal. If you don't know how a disk is formatted, you can select option 4, the "I don't know which one to use" option. Pro-DOS will then prompt you to place the disk in the drive and press Return. It will read the disk and determine how to format it based on how that disk is currently formatted. (Of course, if the disk is unformatted or set up for some other operating system, ProDOS will be unable to identify it and will tell you so.)

ProDOS will then prompt you to enter the name you wish to give the new volume. If you simply press Return, ProDOS will assign a name beginning with Blank followed by a two-digit number.

If the disk has already been formatted, you will be asked if it is okay to destroy the existing volume. If you say no, you will be returned to the beginning of the process.

When all formatting is complete, you can press Return (if you want to continue formatting other disks), or you can press Escape to get back to the main menu.

Identify and Catalog a Disk

The Identify and Catalog a Disk option is similar to the IIe List Directory command in the Filer's File Commands menu. This command will show you all the files on a particular disk or within a ProDOS subdirectory file. It identifies the disk by displaying the disk's name and format. An example of a listing of your System Utilities disk is shown in Figure 3.4.

It takes only three steps to catalog a disk with the IIc version:

1. Select option 7 from the main menu.
2. Specify the drive or provide the path name to the directory you want to look at.
3. You will be asked where you want the listing to appear. If you select Display, it will appear on the screen. If you select Printer, you will be asked which port your printer is connected to. Once you provide the port, the catalog of your disk will be sent to your printer.

The first column of the catalog contains the name of each file. If the name of a file has an asterisk before it, the file is locked or write protected. (A file that is write protected cannot be deleted or changed.)

In the Type column that follows the name of the file, there is a short description that tells you what type of file it is. This can tell you such things as whether you are looking at a program, a data file, or a system file. We will discuss the importance of file types in

Chapter 4. Unlike the IIe, on a IIc the type is not represented as a three-character code but as an actual description. This does not mean that the IIc is using different file types than the IIe or that it is storing extra information in the directory. The program that reads the disk to list the files is simply translating the code it finds into a more readable description. For example, a single file on a disk cataloged by the IIc System Utilities would show on the screen as a Binary file, while the Filer program on the IIe version would show it as a type BIN file.

The Size column tells us how many blocks of space the file takes up on the disk. Each block is composed of 512 bytes. If you want to find out exactly how many bytes long a file is, simply multiply the number of blocks by 512.

```
System Utilities                    Identify and Catalog a Disk
Version 1.0                                     ESC: Main Menu
---------------------------------------------------------------
Disk Name: /UTILITIES                   Disk Format : ProDOS
Filename                  Type              Size
*STARTUP                  ABasic             4
*SU                       ABasic            35
*SU1.OBJ                  Binary            27
*SU2.OBJ                  Binary            10
*SU3.OBJ                  Binary            61
*SU4.OBJ                  ABasicV           18
*ProDOS                   ProDOS            31
*BASIC.SYSTEM             ProDOS            21

8 Files Listed, 207 Blocks Listed, 66 Available




---------------------------------------------------------------
Listing complete; Press RETURN to continue; ESC to return to the
Main Menu.
```

Figure 3.4: Sample Result of the Identify and Catalog a Disk Option

At the bottom of the display ProDOS will show you the number of files listed, the number of blocks used by the files listed, and the number of blocks still free on the disk.

If there is more data than will fit on a single screen, press Return to continue to the next page of information. If there is only a single page of data, or if you have reached the last page, pressing Return will take you back to the beginning of the command, where you can specify a different directory or device. You can return to the main menu by pressing Escape.

Advanced Operations

The first two operations on the Advanced Operations menu concern only ProDOS disks and operations. The next two choices can be used with disks formatted for both ProDOS and DOS 3.3. The last option pertains directly to the Apple IIc and deals with the connection of hardware devices (such as printers and modems) to your computer. The options are shown in Figure 3.5.

Set the Prefix

The first option on the Advanced Operations menu allows you to change the system prefix to save yourself extra typing when specifying path names. As soon as you have done this, ProDOS will automatically tack the new prefix onto the beginning of any path name you enter. This option has the same effect as the Filer command Set Prefix in the IIe version.

Use the following steps to set the prefix with the IIc version:

1. Select option 1 from the Advanced Operations menu.
2. Identify the drive or choose to provide a path name.
3. If you have selected a drive in step 2, ProDOS will read the disk in the drive you selected and set the prefix to point to the volume directory on that disk. If you have selected the path name option, you will have to type in the exact path name you want to use. This is the only way you can set the prefix to point to a subdirectory.

Be very careful when using the Set the Prefix command. If for some reason you have two very similar volumes in your drives and you specify a prefix that affects the wrong one, you are in danger of making some big mistakes. This is because ProDOS will always select the first match it finds, which may not be what you intended. If you have two volumes on line that have the same volume name, ProDOS will look first at the drive from which the system was booted. (This will be the built-in drive on a IIc, unless you have booted from the external drive with the PR# command.) If you are deleting files, for example, you can wipe out the wrong one because you have set the prefix to point to the wrong disk. The same sort of mistake can happen with identical files in different directories of the same volume. If you are working in a particular subdirectory, you can set the prefix to point to that one and then

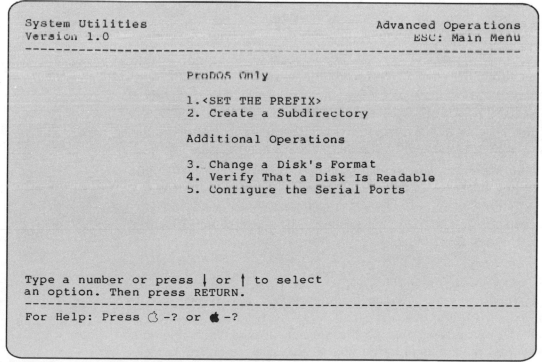

```
System Utilities                            Advanced Operations
Version 1.0                                     ESC: Main Menu
----------------------------------------------------------------
                    ProDOS Only

                    1.<SET THE PREFIX>
                    2. Create a Subdirectory

                    Additional Operations

                    3. Change a Disk's Format
                    4. Verify That a Disk Is Readable
                    5. Configure the Serial Ports




Type a number or press ↓ or ↑ to select
an option. Then press RETURN.
----------------------------------------------------------------
For Help: Press ⌃ -? or ⌘ -?
```

Figure 3.5: The Advanced Operations Menu

use the Identify and Catalog a Disk option to make sure you are in the right subdirectory before you cause any damage.

Create a Subdirectory

The Create a Subdirectory command allows you to create a new subdirectory file. Subdirectory files are used to hold other files, including other subdirectory files, so that you can have more files on a volume than can be contained in the volume directory. (The volume directory can contain only 55 files.) This command has the same effect as the command Make Directory in the IIe version's Filer program.

Use the following steps to create a subdirectory with the IIc version:

1. Select option 2 from the Advanced Operations menu.
2. Identify the drive or choose to provide a path name to the disk where you want the subdirectory created.
3. If you have selected the path name option, you will have to type in the exact path name you want to use. This is the only way you can create a subdirectory within a subdirectory. The path name you enter should point to the subdirectory in which you want the new subdirectory to be created.
4. Then ProDOS asks you to enter the new subdirectory name. Press Return when you've typed in the new name.
5. ProDOS will now create the file. When it has finished, you will see a message telling you that the file has been created. Pressing Return allows you to repeat the Create a Subdirectory function; the Escape key returns you to the Advanced Operations menu.

Change a Disk's Format

One of the most important features of ProDOS is its ability to use files that were written under DOS 3.3. You will usually be able to use the same programs and the same data under both operating systems. Apple has provided you with a utility to do the work of converting from one format to the other.

The IIc version is much less complicated to use than the IIe Convert program. It also offers the ability to convert DOS 3.2 files to DOS 3.3 (DOS 3.2 is the predecessor to 3.3 in the world of Apple operating systems).

To use the Change a Disk's Format command, first select option 3 from the Advanced Operations menu. Then select an option to identify the type of conversion you want to make from the menu shown in Figure 3.6.

You will be asked to choose either the built-in drive or the external drive as the location of your source disk. Select one and press Return. Then you will be asked to choose the location of your destination disk. Select one and press Return.

If you are making a copy involving both the built-in drive and the external drive, ProDOS prompts you to insert the source and destination disks in their proper drives. If you are making a conversion

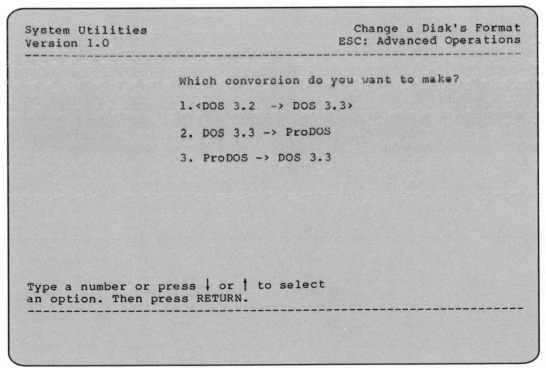

```
System Utilities                           Change a Disk's Format
Version 1.0                                ESC: Advanced Operations
-----------------------------------------------------------------

                    Which conversion do you want to make?

               1.<DOS 3.2   -> DOS 3.3>

               2. DOS 3.3 -> ProDOS

               3. ProDOS -> DOS 3.3




Type a number or press ↓ or ↑ to select
an option. Then press RETURN.
-----------------------------------------------------------------
```

Figure 3.6: Initial Menu of the Change a Disk's Format Option

where the source and destination drive is the same, you will be asked to insert only the source disk. Press Return to continue when you are ready. ProDOS will then read and load the file names from the source disk. If you are using a single drive, you will be prompted to place the destination disk in the drive.

At this point ProDOS asks for the name of the new volume. Enter it and press Return. If the disk has already been formatted, ProDOS asks if it is okay to destroy the existing volume. Make your selection and press Return. If you select No, you will be returned to the beginning of the process. If you select Yes, ProDOS will now format the disk.

Then ProDOS copies the files. If you are using a single drive, you will be prompted to switch the source and destination disks as necessary. When the process is complete, ProDOS will display the message

Update Complete

You can repeat the conversion process by pressing Return, or you can hit the Escape key to return to the Advanced Operations menu.

Verify That a Disk Is Readable

The Verify That a Disk Is Readable option checks to see if there are any damaged or unreadable sections on a volume. ProDOS does this by reading through every block on the disk to see if there are any problems. This option performs exactly the same function as the Detect Bad Blocks command in the Filer utility of the IIe version.

If there are any bad blocks, don't take any chances. Copy all the files on the volume to another volume immediately. You may be unable to copy some files because of the bad blocks; in this case you will have to abandon those files. Once you have copied all the recoverable files, reformat the original volume and check it again.

If there are still bad blocks listed after you reformat the disk, the disk should be treated as unreliable. The best course of action with a damaged disk is to avoid using it (throw it out). If you must use it, be very careful. Do *not* store any files on it that you cannot recover from somewhere else.

If the volume you discover the bad blocks on is a ProFile or other hard disk system, you have a bigger problem. Back up as much as you can and contact your dealer or the manufacturer right away.

If you find that several of your disks have bad blocks on them, you should check to see what is causing the problem. Your disk drive may be the culprit. Try switching the brand of disk you are using to see if the bad blocks still occur. If they do, your drive probably needs servicing or replacement.

Use the following steps to verify that a disk is readable with the IIc version:

1. Select option 4 from the Advanced Operations menu.

2. Select the drive that contains the disk you want to verify from the menu that appears.

3. ProDOS will read every block on the disk in the drive you have specified and report the result of its test. If there are any errors reported, you should follow the steps outlined above concerning unreliable disks.

4. You can return to step 2 by pressing the Return key or to the Advanced Operations menu by pressing Escape.

Configure the Serial Ports

The IIe version of ProDOS has no comparable option or command to the Configure the Serial Ports option. With this option you can set up the printer and modem ports on your Apple IIc to use devices other than the Apple Imagewriter printer and the Apple 300-baud modem. It really has nothing to do with ProDOS or with files or disks. It pertains only to the computer and to the other devices you may wish to connect to the computer. The IIc version offers this option because it has no expansion slots. Apple IIc computers have only these two serial ports available for expansion, and there are a limited number of ways these ports can be configured. To make the configuration process simpler, Apple has provided the Configure the Serial Ports option on the System Utilities disk.

Your Apple IIc is automatically configured to communicate with an Apple Imagewriter printer in port 1 and an Apple 300-baud modem in port 2. Before any other device can be used with the serial ports, it must be assigned a PIN (product identification number). This value tells your Apple the characteristics of the device so that the Apple can communicate with it. Each number in the PIN specifies a particular characteristic of the device. A complete description of each characteristic specified in the PIN number would be highly technical and is beyond the scope of this book. The information needed to determine the values in the PIN number is commonly included in the technical documentation you receive when you buy the device, usually in an easy-to-understand chart or table. If this is unavailable, you will have to contact the dealer who sold you the device or the manufacturer itself to determine how you should configure the port. Following is a brief description of what the values in the PIN number represent:

- Mode (printer or communications)
- Data bits and stop bits
- Baud rate (speed at which data is sent)
- Parity (used for error checking)
- Video echo (determines whether data sent to the port will also be sent to the screen)
- Linefeed (advance to the next line after a carriage return)
- Line width (number of characters to printed on a single line)

Apple has included a device list within this option that provides the information Apple needs (the PIN numbers) to communicate with four different devices: the Imagewriter, the Apple 300-baud modem, the Apple 1200-baud modem, and the Apple color plotter.

If you want to add other devices to this list (so that you can easily configure the ports to communicate with these devices), you can either replace the items listed as Your Device in the device list or change the devices Apple has provided. We'll explain how to do this a little later. But first we'll discuss the configuration process for a device that's already on the list.

Suppose you want to configure port 1 to communicate with the Apple color plotter. First select option 5 from the Advanced Operations menu. Then select option 1 from the menu shown in Figure 3.7 (you can simply press Return to accept the choice).

At this point you are asked to select the device that will be attached to the port from the menu shown in Figure 3.8. Choose option 4 for the Apple color plotter.

Now you will be asked if you want to save this configuration to disk. If you do not save it to disk, port 1 will be configured for the Apple color plotter only for this session with your computer. When you reboot your system, port 1 will be configured once again for the Imagewriter. If you do save the configuration to disk, the configuration for the color plotter is the one automatically implemented in port 1 upon rebooting.

Now let's suppose that you want to configure port 2 for a device that is not on the device list. From the menu shown in Figure 3.7, choose option 2. If you know the PIN value for the device you want to use, select option 8 from the menu in Figure 3.8. You will be asked to enter the new PIN value. Do so and press Return.

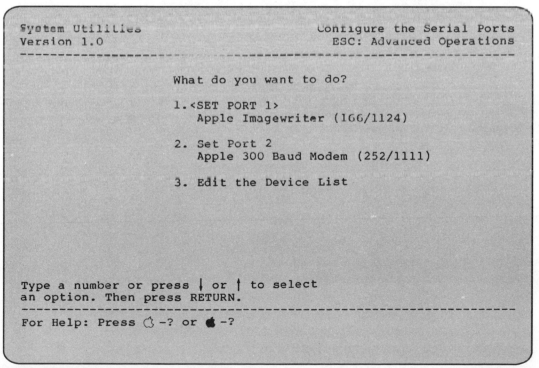

```
System Utilities                        Configure the Serial Ports
Version 1.0                             ESC: Advanced Operations
-----------------------------   --------------------------------------

                    What do you want to do?

                    1. <SET PORT 1>
                       Apple Imagewriter (166/1124)

                    2. Set Port 2
                       Apple 300 Baud Modem (252/1111)

                    3. Edit the Device List




Type a number or press ↓ or ↑ to select
an option. Then press RETURN.
--------------------------------------------------------------------
For Help: Press ⌂-? or ⌘-?
```

Figure 3.7: The Configure the Serial Ports Menu

Then you will be asked if the PIN is correct—a chance to double-check your typing.

If you do not know the PIN value for your device, select option 9. At this point you must answer a series of questions dealing with the characteristics of your device. When you haved answered each of them, ProDOS will present you with a list of the characteristics you have specified and show you the resulting PIN number. You will be asked to verify this information.

Then you will be asked if you want to save this new configuration to disk, making it the default configuration for port 2. You should be aware that saving this new configuration to disk does *not* add the device to the device list. If you want to be able to change the port configurations easily (and use this new device frequently), you should edit the device list to include the device.

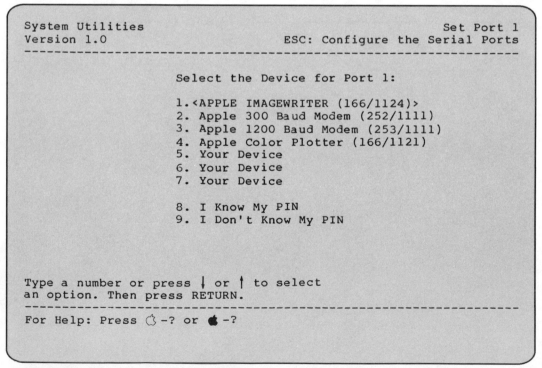

```
System Utilities                                         Set Port 1
Version 1.0                          ESC: Configure the Serial Ports
--------------------------------------------------------------------
                     Select the Device for Port 1:

                     1.<APPLE IMAGEWRITER (166/1124)>
                     2. Apple 300 Baud Modem (252/1111)
                     3. Apple 1200 Baud Modem (253/1111)
                     4. Apple Color Plotter (166/1121)
                     5. Your Device
                     6. Your Device
                     7. Your Device

                     8. I Know My PIN
                     9. I Don't Know My PIN




Type a number or press ↓ or ↑ to select
an option. Then press RETURN.
--------------------------------------------------------------------
For Help: Press ♢-? or  -?
```

Figure 3.8: Selecting a Device to Configure

To edit the device list, select option 3 from the menu shown in Figure 3.7. After you select the device to replace from the menu shown in Figure 3.9, you will be asked to enter the new device name. Type it in and press Return. Then you will be asked if you know what PIN to use. If you answer Yes, you will be asked to enter the new PIN value. Type it in and press Return. You will then be asked if this is correct. Make your selection and press Return.

If you don't know the PIN number, you must answer the questions that characterize the device so that the Apple can construct the PIN number. Once again, you will be asked to verify the information at the end of the process. When you do, the device is added to the list.

EXIT SYSTEM UTILITIES

The last option on the System Utilities disk allows you to leave the menu structure of the System Utilities and issue direct commands to your Apple through Applesoft BASIC. When you choose this option you are asked to verify that you really want to leave the System Utilities. If you answer yes, you will be transferred to the BASIC prompt. If you answer no, you will be returned to the main menu.

When you execute the Exit System Utilities option from the main menu, you are in direct contact with BASIC. You can use individual ProDOS commands from within BASIC, as we will describe in the next several chapters of this book. On the left side of the screen, next to the flashing cursor, you will see the ⊐ character. This is known as the BASIC prompt; it means that your Apple is waiting for you to type in a command. Programmers will select this option to write and run their programs. Since several of the later chapters in this book deal with programming under ProDOS, we will not discuss it here.

You can also start up an application program at this point. Many software packages, however, do not need the System Utilities disk to be run. They will run from a menu when you boot the system from the disk containing the program.

To return to the main menu, simply type RUN STARTUP and press Return with the System Utilities disk in the drive.

THE SYSTEM UTILITIES DISK
AND THE PRODOS USER'S DISK

The IIc's System Utilities disk will not boot and run correctly on other Apple II computers. This is because of the difference in the IIc's hardware. The System Utilities disk expects to find the rigid and unchanging internal setup of an Apple IIc—on any other Apple it will be unable to find the devices it expects.

The ProDOS User's Disk, on the other hand, will boot up and run on an Apple IIc. There are two minor bugs that we know of

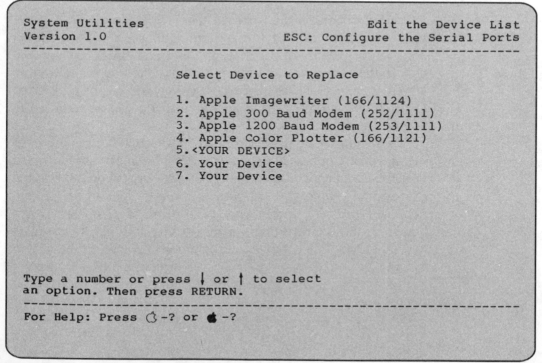

```
System Utilities                              Edit the Device List
Version 1.0                          ESC: Configure the Serial Ports
-------------------------------------------------------------------
                    Select Device to Replace

                    1. Apple Imagewriter (166/1124)
                    2. Apple 300 Baud Modem (252/1111)
                    3. Apple 1200 Baud Modem (253/1111)
                    4. Apple Color Plotter (166/1121)
                    5.<YOUR DEVICE>
                    6. Your Device
                    7. Your Device




Type a number or press ↓ or ↑ to select
an option. Then press RETURN.
-------------------------------------------------------------------
For Help: Press ⌃-? or ⌘-?
```

Figure 3.9: Editing the Device List

which occur when using this version of ProDOS on a IIc. The first is that the Display Slot Assignments option does not recognize that it is dealing with a IIc and will report that it is dealing with a IIe instead. The second occurs when using the Convert program. While this program will operate properly, the highlighted display of the file name you are currently on will be rendered unreadable. This is a result of changes Apple made when designing the Apple IIc. What is happening is that the program is attempting to display a special characteristic that is not available on the Apple IIc. This causes the characters that are being displayed to become indecipherable. There is no way to correct this problem.

The IIc utilities are generally smoother in appearance and use than those on the IIe ProDOS User's Disk. The IIc utilities, however, are more powerful and versatile. They contain a number of features that are not available with the IIc System Utilities. These include the following capabilities:

- Set the time and date
- Rename a volume
- List all the volumes that are in the disk drive
- Compare two volumes
- Set the configuration defaults
- Display slot assignments
- Check the space used on a disk with block allocation

If you wish to learn more about the IIe ProDOS User's Disk utilities, refer to Chapter 2.

Directories and ProDOS Files

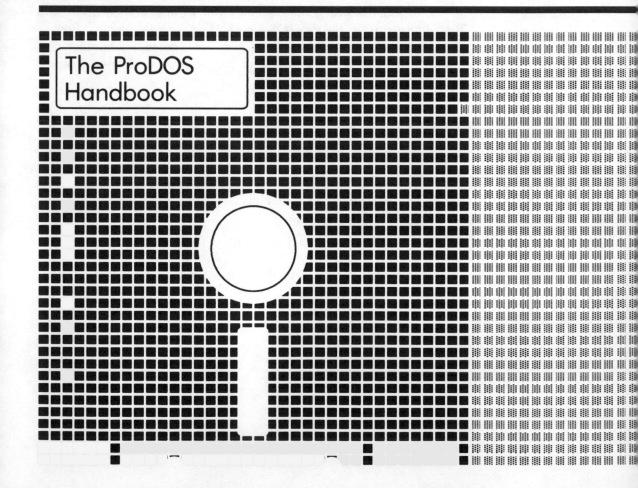

The ProDOS
Handbook

FOUR

This chapter begins a different approach to ProDOS. The previous chapters stressed using the utility programs available on the IIe and IIc versions of ProDOS. From this point on, we will be examining the structure of ProDOS, its use from within BASIC programs, and finally the Machine Language Interface of ProDOS. If you are a casual user with little or no intention of programming, read through these chapters, but skim over the sections you find too technical and concentrate on getting a feel for how ProDOS works. If you intend to do a moderate amount of BASIC programming, you should definitely read this and the following chapters with an eye to making full use of the features ProDOS offers. Even as a BASIC programmer, you may find that an occasional section within this part of the book is too technical for your needs, such as the detailed information on the directory headers and file entries in this chapter. When this is the case, feel free to skim over it or skip ahead to the next section. You can always come back when you need to. The truly advanced programmer can reverse this procedure, skimming through the material to find the parts that will have particular appeal to him, such as the chapter on ProDOS's Machine Language Interface and the detailed information on the contents of directories and file structures available in this chapter.

This chapter examines the structure of ProDOS and the way it files information. We will discuss in detail the concept of a volume, the formatting of volumes, and how ProDOS organizes files into directories and subdirectories. These are important concepts; a clear understanding of what they are and how they work will make it much easier for you to use ProDOS.

PRODOS AND DISK FORMATTING

As we mentioned in Chapter 1, you can compare the disks in your disk drive to the cabinets in a filing room and ProDOS to a top-notch filing clerk. In order for ProDOS to find things when you need them, it must follow certain rules when it puts things away. The first of these rules is called formatting.

The best filing cabinets are neat and orderly. You will not discover disorganized piles of folders, misfiled records, or missing information in a good filing system. The cabinets are arranged so that they can be easily used, and the drawers are not overstuffed.

Just as someone designing a new filing system in an office would take care of the details of organization, the designers of ProDOS have done the same. Before you can use a disk with ProDOS, you must format it. Formatting is the process of organizing the space on the disk to make it usable.

ProDOS thinks of space on a disk as a volume. If you have a Disk II with a floppy disk in it, ProDOS will think of that disk as one volume. ProDOS will also think of a ProFile (which is 40 times the size of the floppy disk) as a single volume. If you have two or more drives connected to your system, ProDOS will think of the disks contained in those drives as separate volumes. This may seem a little unusual, but we see the same thing in a filing room. A small metal box used to store index cards is just as much a filing cabinet as a six-foot-tall, four-drawer cabinet is.

To keep track of the volumes, ProDOS gives each volume a name. All volume names must follow a set of rules. First, all volume names must begin with a slash and a letter. Second, the only legitimate characters you can use in the name are letters, numbers, and periods. There cannot be any spaces or punctuation characters (other than the period) in the name. Third, the maximum name length is 15 characters plus the slash. Here are some examples of valid ProDOS volume names:

/YOUR.DISK
/FUN.AND.GAMES
/DOCUMENTS

Here are some names that are unacceptable in ProDOS:

/BILL AND TONY'S DISK
/THE.SUN.ALSO.RISES.
/400.GAMES

The first example is invalid for three reasons: the name includes spaces, it includes an apostrophe, and it has more than 15 characters. The second entry is simply too long. The third is unacceptable because it starts with a number; the only valid character for the first position is a letter. If you forget and try to enter an invalid name, ProDOS will give you an error message.

Like many other operating systems, DOS 3.3 deals with disks in terms of the physical tracks and sectors that exist on them. A track can be pictured as a ring on the surface of the disk. A sector is a piece of this track. A typical disk has a number of tracks, each longer than the other, starting at the central hole and growing longer as they approach the edge of the disk. Under DOS 3.3, each of these tracks is made up of 16 sectors.

ProDOS does not work this way. ProDOS reads and writes all information to and from the disk in 512-byte blocks. The conversion from ProDOS blocks to disk sectors is handled automatically. This feature makes ProDOS independent of all physical limitations of a single disk type or size.

This is an important advantage of ProDOS over DOS 3.3. Under DOS it is very difficult to make full use of the space available on anything other than a Disk II, because there is only one format. A 5-megabyte hard disk must be treated as a series of forty 140K floppy disks. This limits the size of a single file to the size of a single floppy disk, making it harder to find the information you want.

ProDOS, however, simply sends a request to the device driver for a block of information. The device driver, which is a small machine-language routine loaded into your system along with ProDOS, takes care of all the work involved in getting that information from the disk. If the disk is formatted with 128 bytes per sector, the driver will read four sectors to fill out the block; if it is formatted with 256 bytes to a sector, the driver will read only two sectors. ProDOS works independently of the organization of the disk, so it can deal with drives of many different capacities.

When ProDOS formats a volume, it places the information it needs to read that volume in specific locations on the disk so that it knows where to look for that information later. This information includes a loader program to enable you to boot ProDOS from that volume, the volume directory, and the volume bit map. (Note: the loader program will allow you to boot ProDOS from that volume only if the files PRODOS and BASIC.SYSTEM are also on that volume.)

The loader program is a small machine-language program with a single purpose. When you boot a disk in a drive, the loader program is transferred from the disk into memory. It then performs its function of loading the BASIC.SYSTEM program from the disk into memory.

The volume directory serves as the table of contents for the volume. We'll discuss it in more detail in the next two sections.

The bit map keeps track of which blocks in the volume are currently in use. When you create a new file or add information to an existing file, the system first checks the bit map to find an available block to use in expanding the file. It is called a bit map because each block on the volume is represented by a single bit in the map. If the bit is set to 0 the block is unused; if it is set to 1 the block is in use.

THE ORGANIZATION OF THE VOLUME

Just as a good filing clerk keeps and follows a system for storing information, ProDOS organizes all the information on a volume for quick and easy access. All information is stored in files and labeled in a specific way to aid in identifying the contents. Files can be date- and time-stamped to keep track of changes. Files can also be protected from change.

ProDOS is organized as a hierarchical filing system. This means that the system is arranged in a series of layers or levels. This is not a concept unique to computer science; it has been in use for thousands of years in almost every human society.

A hierarchy is usually compared to the structure of an upside-down tree. The tree has one root. As we move down the trunk of the tree, it splits and branches out into an ever larger number of twigs and leaves. Nourishment to the twigs and leaves must arrive through the trunk. A hierarchy looks much like this upside-down tree. Each level is subordinate to the level above it in importance.

ProDOS thinks of each disk as one volume (the root of the tree). Each ProDOS volume has a single volume directory that acts as a table of contents for the disk. Everything you store on a disk is stored as a file, and each file has an entry in the volume directory. These files can be identified as subdirectories that can contain yet other file entries or subdirectories. ProDOS allows 64 levels of files and subdirectories, making it practically impossible to exhaust the number of files available for use.

For example, suppose you have a ProDOS disk with ten levels of directories on it. The first level is the volume directory and is limited to a maximum of 51 files. Ten of those files are subdirectory files, and each of these contains ten other subdirectories, each of which in turn contains ten other subdirectories, and so on up to ten levels. The total number of files on that disk with ten levels of directories is 11,111,111,151. The number of files that can be in any individual subdirectory is limited only by the amount of space available and the ProDOS file size limitations.

THE VOLUME DIRECTORY

Each volume has a single volume directory that serves as a table of contents for the disk. The volume directory is limited to 51 entries. Each of these entries may be a directory file or a standard file. When a disk is first formatted, the volume directory is empty. The volume directory file contains two kinds of entries: the header entry and file entries. We will discuss these entries and the information they contain in the following sections.

The Header Entry

The header entry of a volume directory contains all the vital information about that volume. There is only one header entry per volume. The name of the volume as well as the date on which the volume was created are stored here. Information on which version of ProDOS was used to create this volume is also recorded so that later versions will know how to access it. The header entry contains the number of entries in the directory, the number of entries per block in the volume directory file, and the total number of blocks available on the volume. It also contains the block address of the volume's bit map.

All of this information is necessary for the efficient operation of ProDOS. Simply by reading this block from a disk, ProDOS has enough information to perform any operation you want it to on that volume. The address of the volume's bit map (called the bit map pointer) makes it easy for ProDOS to find the first available block of free space. The volume name allows ProDOS to recognize path names that refer to this volume. The creation date is provided to allow you to keep track of when you do things. There is also a single byte of information that ProDOS uses to record whether you want the volume protected to prevent accidental loss of information. All told, the header entry is composed of 39 bytes of information. These bytes of information are divided into the following fields.

Storage Type and Name Length (1 Byte)

The first byte of the header entry is divided into two 4-bit fields. The high four bits are all set to ones and indicate that this is the key block of the volume directory file. This storage information is used internally by ProDOS and should never be changed. The low four bits contain the length of the volume's name, stored as a binary number. This value should be updated if you change the contents of the File Name field without using the ProDOS commands to do it.

File Name (15 Bytes)

The next 15 bytes of the header entry contain the volume's name. This is the maximum length allowed. The data stored in the field may take less space than this (for example, MYFILE requires 6 bytes). The Name Length field discussed above tells you how many of these bytes contain the actual file name as ProDOS will see it. If you change the file name without using a ProDOS command, be sure to adjust the Name Length field to match.

Reserved (8 Bytes)

The next eight bytes have no current use and are reserved for future expansion by Apple.

Creation (4 Bytes)

The four bytes following the Reserved field contain the date and time at which the volume was initialized by ProDOS.

Version (1 Byte)

The next byte contains the version number of ProDOS that was used to initialize the volume.

Minimum Version (1 Byte)

This byte specifies the minimum version number of ProDOS needed to access information on this disk.

Access (1 Byte)

This field is used to determine whether a volume has been protected from being written to, destroyed, or renamed.

Entry Length (1 Byte)

This byte contains a binary number representing the length in bytes of each entry within the directory, including the volume directory header. All entries in the directory have the same length.

Entries per Block (1 Byte)

The number of entries stored in each block of the directory file is represented here as a binary number.

File Count (2 Bytes)

This field contains the number of active file entries in this directory. An active file is one whose storage type does not equal zero. This means that all files (standard or subdirectory) are included in this count.

Bit Map Pointer (2 Bytes)

This field contains the address of the first block of the volume's bit map. The bit map always occupies consecutive blocks, one block for every 4,096 blocks or portion of that number available on the volume. (A typical floppy disk uses a single block for a bit map. If that floppy had 4100 blocks, it would use two blocks for the bit map: one for the first 4096 blocks and one for the next four blocks.) The bit map pointer tells you where the volume bit map actually begins on the disk.

Total Blocks (2 Bytes)

This field contains a binary number representing the total number of blocks available on the volume.

The File Entries

The second type of entry in the volume directory file is called a file entry. There is one file entry for every file within the directory. The file entries contain information that allows ProDOS to find any file you want, much like the building directory in an office building.

Each file entry is made up of the following fields of information. Most of these fields appear when you use the Filer to list a ProDOS directory or when you use the CAT or CATALOG commands from the BASIC prompt. The information you do not see when you list a ProDOS directory is used by ProDOS internally and will not affect you unless you are writing your own advanced programs using the Machine Language Interface. If you are not interested in this, you can skip to the section entitled "Subdirectory Files."

Name Length and Storage Type (1 Byte)

The first four bits of the file entry contain the length of the file's name. The last four bits of this byte contain a value specifying what type of file this is. These are the valid file type codes (the $ sign indicates that the code is written in hexadecimal notation):

Code	File Type
$1	Standard seedling file
$2	Standard sapling file
$3	Standard tree file
$D	Subdirectory file

The subdirectory files have a similar format to the volume directory file. They will be discussed shortly. All other files are standard files; their structure is explained under that heading in this chapter.

File Name (15 Bytes)

The next 15 bytes contain the name you assigned when you created the file. The file name must follow the same rules for a valid name as those used by a volume name. The Name Length field discussed above must always reflect the actual length of the file name. If Name Length is 6 and there are eight characters in the file name, only the first six would be used. (For example, OURFILES would become OURFIL.) When you change a file's name through the ProDOS commands, ProDOS adjusts the Name Length field for you.

File Type (1 Byte)

This byte contains ProDOS's shorthand for the three-character file type you see when you list a directory. For a complete list of file types, see Appendix A.

A single byte is composed of eight bits and can contain a binary value between 0 and 255 inclusive. ProDOS encodes this information to save space on the disk. ProDOS knows, for example, that a value of 252 (FC in hexadecimal notation) represents an Applesoft BASIC file.

Key Pointer (2 Bytes)

The eighteenth and nineteenth bytes of the file entry contain the block address ProDOS uses to locate the file described in this entry, expressed as a binary number.

Blocks Used (2 Bytes)

The next two bytes tell you the total number of blocks used by the file being described. For a standard file, this is the actual length of the file and everything it contains. For a subdirectory file, this includes only the length of the subdirectory, not the length of all the files contained in that subdirectory.

EOF (End of File) (3 Bytes)

These three bytes represent the total number of bytes ProDOS can read from the file. This number is stored as a binary value.

Note that in some special cases (sparse files) this number may be greater than the actual length of the file. Sparse files are never created by the normal operations of the operating system. They are oddities created by a program that directly alters information in a file directory. They are an abnormal form of standard files and will be discussed in that section of this chapter.

Creation (4 Bytes)

Bytes 25 through 28 of the file entry contain the date and time the file was created, stored as a binary number. This field is composed of two smaller fields. The first two bytes contain a binary integer representing the year, month, and day. The data is stored in these two bytes as illustrated in Figure 4.1. Notice that the month spans the lowest bit of byte 26 and the highest three bits of byte 25.

The time field occupies the next two bytes. Byte 27 contains the minutes and will always have zeros in bits 7 and 6. Byte 28 contains the hour; it always has zeros stored in bits 5, 6, and 7. This is illustrated in Figure 4.2.

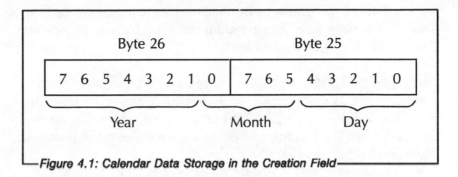

Figure 4.1: Calendar Data Storage in the Creation Field

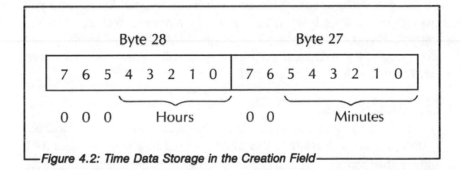

Figure 4.2: Time Data Storage in the Creation Field

Version (1 Byte)
The next byte contains the binary value that represents the version number of ProDOS used to create this entry. Newer versions of ProDOS can check this byte and make adjustments as necessary.

Minimum Version (1 Byte)
This byte contains the minimum version number of ProDOS that can read this file. This allows older versions of ProDOS to determine if they can read files created by newer versions.

Access (1 Byte)
This field of the file entry is used primarily to determine whether a file is write protected. It also contains a bit that can be set to indicate whether a backup copy of the file has been made. If you are

writing backup programs using the Machine Language Interface, you should make sure your program sets bit 5 to zero to indicate that the file has been backed up.

Aux_Type (2 Bytes)

Programs can store additional information about a file in this field. The ProDOS BASIC.SYSTEM program uses this oddly named field to record the loading address of a binary file or the length in records of a text file.

If you are writing machine-language or assembly-language programs, the contents of this field may be used for any purpose you desire. You may, however, be unable to run or load properly a binary file without specifying an address in this field, and you will no longer be able to trust the length information displayed in the catalog if you do not place that information there yourself. If you do not save the information on disk, you will have to write it down or remember it when you need it later.

Last_Mod (4 Bytes)

This field records the last time the file was updated or modified; it uses the same format as the creation field to store the data as a binary number.

Header Pointer (2 Bytes)

This field contains the address ProDOS uses to access the directory that owns this file. In short, ProDOS can use this field to return to the parent directory of this file.

SUBDIRECTORY FILES

ProDOS subdirectory files are files that can be used to contain other files. This does not mean that a file's actual data are contained inside a subdirectory file. Like the volume directory, the subdirectory contains a file entry for each file that has been set up within that subdirectory. When ProDOS is searching for a file, it follows the path name from the volume directory through each subdirectory until it reaches the actual file it is seeking. At each level of the search, Pro-DOS reads a file from the directory or subdirectory to determine where to go next.

For example, suppose ProDOS were following the path name /PRODOS/DIRECTORY.ONE/TESTFILE. The following steps would occur:

1. ProDOS would read the volume directory to obtain the file entry for DIRECTORY.ONE.

2. Using the information obtained in step 1, ProDOS would read the subdirectory file DIRECTORY.ONE to obtain the file entry for TESTFILE.

3. Using the information obtained in step 2, ProDOS would be able to perform whatever operation was requested (assuming it was a legal ProDOS command) on TESTFILE.

Each subdirectory file has a single subdirectory header record and one file entry record for each file it contains. The file entry records share an identical format with the volume directory file entry records. The subdirectory header record format is similar but not identical to the volume directory header. Following is a discussion of the elements of the subdirectory header record, where you can see how it differs from the volume directory header.

The Storage Type and Name Length byte is composed of two 4-bit fields. The high four bits are set to $E (1110 in binary) and indicate to ProDOS that this is the key block of the subdirectory file. The low four bits contain the length of the volume's name.

The File Name field (15 bytes long) contains the subdirectory file's name. As with the File Name field in a volume directory header or a file entry, the Name Length field must always be adjusted to reflect any changes in this field.

Then follows a Reserved field (8 bytes long) that has no current use and is reserved for future expansion by Apple.

The Creation field (4 bytes long) contains the date and time at which the subdirectory was initialized by ProDOS.

The Version byte contains the version number of ProDOS which was used to create this subdirectory.

The Minimum Version byte specifies the minimum version number of ProDOS needed to access information in this subdirectory.

The Access field (1 byte) is used to determine whether this subdirectory has been protected from being written to, destroyed, or renamed.

The Entry Length field (1 byte) is a binary number representing the length in bytes of each entry within the subdirectory, including the subdirectory header. (All entries are the same length.)

The Entries per Block field (1 byte) stores the number of entries in each block of the subdirectory file, represented here as a binary number.

The File Count field (2 bytes long) contains the number of active file entries in this subdirectory. An active file is one whose storage type does not equal zero. All standard and subdirectory files are included in this count.

The Parent Pointer field is two bytes long and contains the block address of the directory file block to which this subdirectory belongs. The parent directory may be either the volume directory or another subdirectory.

The Parent Entry Number byte contains the entry number of this subdirectory within the block pointed to by the parent pointer. For example, if this subdirectory were the fifth file in the parent directory, this field would contain a value of 5.

The Parent Entry Length field (1 byte long) contains the length of each entry in the parent directory. (All entries are the same length.)

STANDARD FILES

Standard files under ProDOS are all those files that are not directory files. All standard files begin as seedling files and have the ability to expand into sapling files and then into tree files. A seedling file is naturally the simplest type of file; it occupies exactly 512 bytes (1 block) of space.

As soon as a file is expanded to more than 512 bytes, it becomes a sapling file. While a seedling file consists of only one data block, a sapling file consists of one index block and at least two data blocks. The index block is used to store the locations of the data blocks that make up the file. This arrangement explains why you will not find any standard files composed of only two blocks of disk space. If there is only one block or less worth of data to be stored, the file is stored as a seedling file. If the file contains more data than can be stored in one block, there is always an index block included in the file with the two or more data blocks.

Sapling files can contain up to 256 data blocks, for a total of 128K of data. When a file is bigger than this, a single index block cannot keep track of all the data blocks. This file then grows into a tree file. A tree file has a master index block that can point to 128 index blocks, which can each point to 256 data blocks. This is a total of 16 megabytes of disk storage, less one byte. This last byte is unavailable because ProDOS will not allow the end of file (EOF) to be greater than 16,777,216. ProDOS will keep track of the allocation and deallocation of blocks automatically; you need never concern yourself with this detail.

A sparse file is an abnormal type of standard file; it is a sapling or tree file that has been modified for a particular purpose. Sparse files have the unusual property that more bytes of data can be read from them than are physically stored in the file on disk.

They are created by directly modifying the information stored in the file entry. What you do is to change the end-of-file marker of an already allocated file so that ProDOS will think the file is bigger than it actually is. If you do this to a seedling file and make the end-of-file marker large enough that ProDOS must allocate additional space for an index and data block, it will do so *only* if you write data to the end of the file. For example, if you make a seedling file's EOF large enough to require five data blocks and then write data to the fifth block, ProDOS will allocate the fifth block and place data in it. The second, third, and fourth data blocks will not have been allocated, but ProDOS will respond to any attempt to read data from those blocks by returning a null character (ASCII 0). This gives the appearance of reading data that do not exist.

While interesting, this technique is not recommended for inexperienced programmers. One of its difficulties lies in the unexpected effects of reading this file with a program and writing it back to disk. This results in the output file being much larger than the input file, because all of those null characters are actually written to the disk. You can, however, use the Filer program to preserve the structure of sparse files while copying.

Sparse files might be useful in special situations. If you need to maintain an exceptionally large array of data, sparse files might be the only way to get around memory or disk space limitations. They would allow you to write out only the pertinent information and return a null value for any unused space. Remember that using one byte of space in a block means that the entire block is allocated on the disk.

This chapter has covered a very important topic on which the entire ProDOS system is based—the directory and file structure by which ProDOS stores and retrieves information. The most important idea to carry away with you from this chapter is the organization of the ProDOS directory structure. This structure is the key to the effective use of the power of ProDOS. Once you understand it and know how to use prefixes and path names to access files, you are on the road to mastering ProDOS. If you do not feel that you understand the directory structure, you should immediately reread the sections on disk formatting and the organization of the volume before continuing.

ProDOS Commands

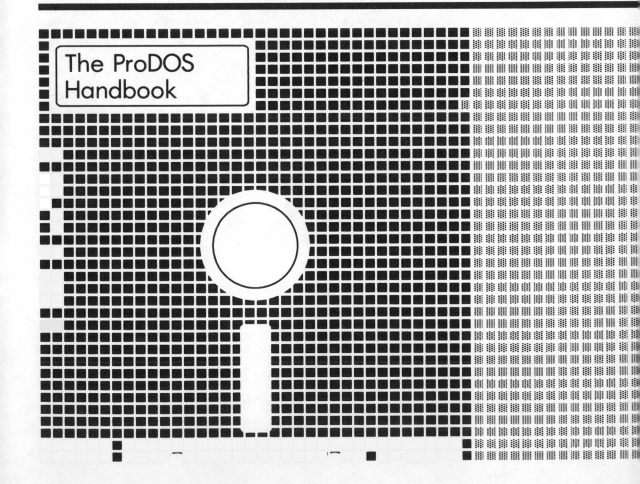

The ProDOS
Handbook

In this chapter we will briefly describe the command functions available to you through ProDOS. ProDOS commands fall into two groups. The first of these is composed of updated DOS 3.3 commands; the second is composed of new commands used only by ProDOS. We will also briefly describe the DOS commands that are no longer available under ProDOS. Finally, we will discuss changes in the use of Applesoft commands required by the change from DOS to ProDOS.

These ProDOS commands are used from within BASIC, either by typing them in directly (in immediate mode) or by embedding them in a BASIC program. (Some of these commands will not work in immediate mode. We have indicated the commands where this is the case.) Some of the functions provided by these commands are also implemented through the ProDOS utilities, such as the Filer, for your convenience. But most of these functions are not available through the utilities because they would not be useful from a menu structure. They are really intended for use from within programs.

UPDATED COMMANDS

The following commands existed under DOS 3.3, but many of them have been enhanced under ProDOS. DOS programs that use these commands will work under ProDOS, but ProDOS programs written to use the newer features of these commands will not work under DOS 3.3.

APPEND

The APPEND command allows you to add data to the end of a file. Under DOS this command allowed you to append data only to sequential text files; under ProDOS it will append data to any file. The APPEND command will not work in immediate mode. Because it applies to all file types, we will be discussing APPEND thoroughly in Chapters 7 and 8.

BLOAD

The BLOAD command is used primarily to transfer binary data from a disk file to memory. However, under ProDOS it can be used with any file type to load the contents of the file to a desired location in the Apple's RAM memory. ProDOS has also made it possible with this command to load only a portion of a file into memory. We will discuss the BLOAD command in detail in Chapter 8.

BRUN

The BRUN command transfers the contents of a binary file (type BIN) into memory and attempts to run it as a machine-language program. As with BLOAD, ProDOS has made it possible to run any portion of a binary file with BRUN. The BRUN command cannot be used to run nonbinary files, however. Since this command is intimately involved with the discussion of binary files, we will delay discussing it in detail until Chapter 8.

BSAVE

The BSAVE command transfers information from memory to a file on a disk. This information is stored as binary data. Binary data is commonly used to store machine-language programs, graphics, and the contents of memory for quick loading and unloading. For example, you could save the binary representation of a graphics image from memory into a disk file. This would allow you to make the code for your program shorter because you would not have to include the lines of code to generate the graphics image. You would be able to achieve the same effect with a single BLOAD statement. For further information on the BSAVE command and binary data, see Chapter 8.

CATALOG

The CATALOG command under DOS 3.3 showed you the type, size, and name of all the files in a volume. Under ProDOS, CATA-LOG shows you a full 80 columns of information on the files in a volume directory or subdirectory file. If you do not have an 80-column card, you should use the CAT command (a command new to ProDOS) instead of CATALOG. This is because the 80-character lines of ProDOS's CATALOG display wrap around to form a second line on a 40-column screen and are very hard to read.

The CATALOG command gives you the same information about a directory as the CAT command. This includes the file name, type, length, and date of the last modification for each file. In addition to this, the CATALOG command will show you the date the file was created, the logical end of the file, and either the length of the file in records (if the file is a random-access text file) or the last loading address (if the file is a binary file).

Both the CAT and CATALOG commands show you the contents of a single directory file. If you do not specify a volume name, you will be shown the contents of the directory specified by the prefix.

If you want to see the contents of a different directory, you must specify its path name after the CATALOG or CAT command.

CLOSE

The CLOSE command must be used to close files that have been opened by the OPEN command (which is discussed shortly). Closing the file ensures that everything that was written to the file buffers has been transferred to the disk. ProDOS places data in the file buffer before it writes it to the disk to improve the speed of execution of a program. If a program ends without closing the files it has opened, the information in the file buffers may be lost.

If a program ends prematurely because of an error and has not had the opportunity to close the files, you can issue the CLOSE command directly from the keyboard in the immediate mode of BASIC. As long as you have not run some other program or cleared memory, the data in your file buffers will be written to the disk. This will also ensure that the file buffers ProDOS has allocated in memory are properly released. If you do not use a path name or file name with the CLOSE command, all open files will be closed.

When using ProDOS, you must use the CLOSE command on open files or risk the possibility of losing data. This is an important difference between DOS and ProDOS, one that you should remain constantly aware of when converting programs from DOS to ProDOS.

DELETE

The DELETE command erases the file or files you specify from the disk. Once you delete a file there is no way to get it back. A file must be unlocked before it can be deleted. If it is a directory file, it must be empty or ProDOS will not allow you to delete it. This is the only difference between this command under ProDOS and under DOS. If you want to delete a directory file, you must first delete all the files within the directory individually and then delete the directory. You can delete a file that is several layers down from the current directory by specifying a path name that ends in the file you want deleted.

EXEC

The EXEC command causes your Apple to take input from a disk file rather than from the keyboard. This disk file may contain a series of statements, such as RUN PROGRAM 1 or DELETE MYFILE, or it may contain a collection of data. It can also contain a combination of statements and data. This command is unchanged from DOS 3.3, except for the requirement to use ProDOS path name syntax to specify a file.

IN#

The IN# command changes the source of input characters for your Apple II. Normally, the Apple expects input from the keyboard. You can use the IN# command to change the source from the keyboard to any device connected to one of the Apple II's eight expansion slots, numbered 0 through 7. If you use any value other than 0–7 with this command, you will see a range error message.

This command can be useful if you wish to control the Apple from an external device, such as a second terminal or a disk drive. In the case of a disk drive, the IN# command activates a machine-language program on the card, which begins the process of booting from whatever disk is available in the drive. The program on the card always looks at the drive attached to the drive 1 connection first.

On an Apple IIc, there are no expansion slots. There are only the ports on the back of the machine and the internal circuitry of the machine. ProDOS recognizes the two serial ports as slots 1 and 2. The built-in 80-column card of a IIc is treated as slot 3, and slot 4 is the joystick controller port on the back of the machine. The internal disk drive is slot 6 and the external drive port is slot 7. This interpretation of the external drive port is an exception to the relationship between slots and ports described in Chapter 3. Normally the IIc considers the external drive port as slot 6, drive 2. Apple has included this interpretation to give you a way to boot your machine if there is a problem with your internal disk drive.

You can restart your system by entering the IN# command with the slot number associated with a disk drive. This will cause a reboot of your system as your Apple attempts to load whatever operating system is on the disk in the drive. Any program you have in memory will be wiped out when the system reboots. Entering the command

IN# 0

will cause the Apple to look once again to the keyboard for input.

The IN# command can also be used to call a machine-language program. By using the address option to designate the starting address with the IN# command, you can force your Apple to execute the routine beginning at that location. Your replacement routine would have to be written in machine or assembly language and placed at the address you specify in the address option. This would be of use only to very advanced programmers—for example, you can use this option to test a device driver. The topic of address options will be treated in detail in Chapter 8.

LOAD

The LOAD command transfers a BASIC program file from disk to memory. This command is commonly used if you want to examine or change a program without running it. If you are interested only in running the program, the RUN command will load your program automatically if you specify a file name. When a program is loaded into memory, anything previously held in memory is erased. You can preserve the values of the variables in the current program in memory by using either the STORE command to place them in a file or by using the CHAIN command.

The BASIC program file on the disk is not changed in any way by the LOAD command. Only a copy of that file is placed in memory. If you make changes to the program in memory, you must use the SAVE command to store those changes on disk.

This command is unchanged from DOS 3.3, except for the requirement to use ProDOS path name syntax to specify a file.

LOCK

The LOCK command allows you to protect a file. When a file is locked you cannot rename it, delete it, or change the information inside the file. All locked files are identified by an asterisk to the left of their file name in a CATALOG display. You cannot lock the volume directory on a disk with a LOCK command, but you can cover the write-protect notch on the disk with a tab to accomplish the same thing. You can lock subdirectory files. This command is unchanged from DOS 3.3, except for the need to follow ProDOS path name conventions when using it.

OPEN

The OPEN command allocates the file buffer for reading and writing to a file. It also prepares to read or write the file beginning at the first byte in the file. A maximum of eight files can be open at one time. (Under DOS, the maximum number of files that could be open at one time was determined by the MAXFILES command. This was normally three files, but it could be raised to as many as 16.) Each open file is assigned a file buffer of 1024 bytes (512 bytes for a directory file). Any file that is opened must later be closed. The OPEN command cannot be used from immediate mode.

This command has no added features under ProDOS, but allocation of buffer space for a file now takes place when the OPEN command is executed. Under DOS, a file was allocated a standard amount of buffer space, which you could modify with the MAX-FILES command. The MAXFILES command is not used under Pro-DOS. The OPEN command will be discussed in much more detail in Chapter 7.

POSITION

The POSITION command is not required by ProDOS; it was retained to maintain compatibility with DOS 3.3. Since it was being retained, the designers decided to update it with a new option to make it consistent with the way ProDOS treats files. This command can be used to look at the data in any field or at any byte within a file. The POSITION command cannot be used from immediate mode. For more information on when and why you would use this command, see Chapter 7.

PR#

The PR# command operates similarly to the IN# command except that it controls the destination of your output rather than the origin of your input. Normally, output from your Apple II is sent to the monitor screen. You can use the PR# command to change the output to a device connected to one of the peripheral expansion slots in the back of your Apple II. For example, after you enter

PR# 1

all characters output by your Apple will be sent to the printer (assuming you have a printer connected to an interface card in slot 1). Entering PR# 0 will return the output to the monitor screen.

You can use the PR# command to restart your system. For example, if you have a disk controller card in slot 6, entering PR# 6 activates the machine-language program on the card in that slot, just as the IN# command does. This causes the system to reboot and load whichever operating system is in the drive. This will wipe out any program that is currently in memory, so be very careful when using this command.

As we discussed earlier, your Apple has only eight available slots, numbered 0 through 7. These are the only numbers that can be used with the PR# command. Any other value will cause a range error. On an Apple IIc, ProDOS recognizes the two serial ports as slots 1 and 2. The built-in 80-column card is treated as slot 3, and slot 4 is the joystick controller port on the back of the machine. The internal disk drive is slot 6 and the external drive port is slot 7.

If your IIe system has an 80-column card and you are using it, you must turn the card off before issuing another PR# command. The normal way to do this is to press the Escape key followed by pressing the Control and Q keys simultaneously. The Apple IIc has a built-in 80-column card that is accessed by PR# 3.

The PR# command can also be used to call a machine-language program. This can be done using the address option, which is the only new feature PR# has under ProDOS. By using the address option to designate the starting address with the PR# command, you can force your Apple to execute the program beginning at that location. Your replacement routine would have to be written in machine or assembly language and placed at the address you specified in the address option. This would be of use only to very advanced programmers—for example, you can use this option to test a device driver. The topic of address options will be treated in detail in Chapter 8.

READ

The READ command tells ProDOS which file to use for the next INPUT or GET statement. You must issue a READ command before you can get any information out of a file, and that file must have already been opened. Once it is issued, the READ command stays in effect until another ProDOS command is issued. The READ command will not work in immediate mode.

This command is used primarily to deal with text files and will be discussed in greater detail in Chapter 7. The READ command has a new parameter that allows you to position yourself within the file by field as well as by byte. This makes the DOS POSITION command unnecessary.

RENAME

The RENAME command allows you to change the name of a file. To use this command, type RENAME followed by a path name ending in the file you want changed and then the same path name ending in the new name of the file. The two path names must be separated by a comma. You cannot rename a file that is locked, and you cannot use this command to move a file from one directory to another. This command differs in usage from the DOS version only because of the ProDOS requirement of a path name to locate a particular file.

RUN

The RUN command causes ProDOS to execute an Applesoft program. If you do not specify a file name with this command, ProDOS will attempt to run the Applesoft program in memory. If there is no Applesoft program in memory, nothing will happen. If you do specify a name with the RUN command, ProDOS will search to find the file indicated, load it into memory, and begin to execute it. Once you have loaded a program in this way, you can execute it again simply by typing RUN and pressing Return (as long as no other program is loaded in its place).

There are two differences between the RUN command under DOS and under ProDOS. The first, naturally enough, is that you can specify a path name after the RUN command. The second is that you can also specify the line number at which you want to begin executing the Applesoft program. This is done by following the path name with a comma, an @ symbol, and the line number. For example, the statement

RUN TEST.PROGRAM,@1000

would execute the program TEST.PROGRAM beginning at line 1000. If you do not specify a line number with this option, the program begins executing at the lowest line number.

SAVE

The SAVE command writes the BASIC program that is currently in memory to the disk file you specify. If you do not specify a file name you will get a syntax error. If the file does not already exist, it will automatically be allocated as a BASIC file. If the file does exist on disk, it cannot be locked. You cannot save a BASIC program as any other type of file with this command. Any attempt to do so will cause an error message to appear. You can use the SAVE command to create backup copies of a program by specifying a different file name than the one that already exists.

You should be very careful when using the SAVE command with existing files. When you save a program to disk, it automatically wipes out the existing file as it replaces it. If you are working with several different program files, be very careful not to SAVE a program under the wrong name. Once a file is changed or deleted, it cannot be recovered unless you have a backup copy. This command is the same under both DOS and ProDOS, although you must follow the ProDOS path name conventions to use it.

UNLOCK

The UNLOCK command allows you to reverse the effects of the LOCK command. Once you use this command, you will be able to delete, rename, or change files that have been locked. You cannot unlock a volume directory, because it cannot be locked in the first place. If you've covered the write-protect notch on your disk with a tab to accomplish this purpose, you can remove the tab to "unlock" the directory. You can use this command on any file that is locked, including subdirectory files. This command is unchanged from DOS 3.3, except for the requirements of the ProDOS path name syntax.

WRITE

The WRITE command must be issued before you can use the PRINT statement to send data to a disk file. The WRITE command tells ProDOS which file you want to send the characters to. The file you are writing to must be open before you issue the WRITE command. WRITE remains in effect until the next ProDOS command is issued. The WRITE command cannot be used from immediate mode.

This command is commonly associated with text files, and we will discuss it in detail in Chapter 7. The WRITE command has been given the same added parameter as the READ command to make the POSITION command obsolete.

NEW COMMANDS

The following commands did not exist under DOS 3.3. They are primarily intended to add new features to the operating system.

CAT

The CAT command is an abbreviated form of the CATALOG command described earlier in this chapter. The CAT command displays only 40 columns of directory information, while CATALOG displays 80 columns. This command displays file names, types, lengths, and the date last modified for each file. This is the same information you can get by listing a directory in the Filer program. ProDOS provides the CAT and CATALOG commands so that you can get a directory listing while you are working in BASIC.

CHAIN

The CHAIN command causes one program to run another. There are several advantages to using the CHAIN command instead of the RUN command. The biggest advantage is that the CHAIN command does not clear the values of all variables before it loads and executes the next program. By using this command within your program, you can divide a very large program into small units while you are creating it and then chain the small programs together to perform complex functions. Since all the variables are available from one program to the next, you save time by not having to reinput the data or write data to a disk file in one program and read it back in another.

CREATE

The CREATE command allows you to create a file of any type, but it is mainly used to create directory files, which is why it is new to ProDOS. BASIC, text, and binary files are created automatically by the SAVE, OPEN, and BSAVE commands. Text files can also be created by the APPEND command, and variable files can be created by the STORE command. When a file is created, an entry is placed in the proper directory file so that ProDOS can keep track of it and locate it. You can use the Filer program to copy these files from one directory to another.

FLUSH

The FLUSH command forces ProDOS to write the contents of the file buffer specified to the disk. Using this command frequently will help ensure that you will not lose data to a system failure or an accidental stopping of the program. However, it does slow down the execution of your program considerably.

One of the reasons ProDOS is so much faster than DOS at writing to the disk drive is that ProDOS waits until the contents of a file buffer are full or nearly full before writing the data to the disk drive. This means that ProDOS will store the same amount of data as DOS will in fewer operations, thus speeding up program execution. The catch to this method is that if you have not already saved the information to the disk when a system failure occurs, the information is lost and has to be reentered. The FLUSH command forces ProDOS to save the file buffer earlier, but it also causes ProDOS to generate more commands and thus slows down execution.

FRE

The FRE command is used to perform garbage collection on old and unused strings in memory. It works exactly the same way as the Applesoft BASIC FRE command, but the ProDOS version is faster. What it amounts to is a small correction to Applesoft BASIC that's been inserted in ProDOS out of convenience.

PREFIX

The PREFIX command works exactly the same way as the Set ProDOS Prefix option in the Filer program. Typing PREFIX and pressing the Return key will show you the current prefix being used by ProDOS. If you type PREFIX followed by a path name, ProDOS will set that new path name as the prefix to be used. If the path name you specify is not valid, you will get the error message PATH NOT FOUND and you will have to try again.

RESTORE

The RESTORE command loads the contents of a variable file into memory. The values in the variable file are those previously placed there by a STORE command. These values are in addition to any variables that have been created by the current program. In the case of duplication of variable names between those in the variable file and those already existing in memory, the values from the variable file will replace those in memory.

STORE

The STORE command writes the names and values of all variables currently defined in memory by a BASIC program into a variable file (type VAR). These values can be passed to another BASIC program with the RESTORE command.

– (Dash)

The – (Dash) command consists of the single character – and is called the Dash command. The Dash command allows you to run any BASIC, binary, EXEC, or system program. You use it simply by typing a dash and the name of the program. You cannot use it with any of the specific options available to you in the RUN, BRUN, or EXEC commands.

OBSOLETE COMMANDS

The following commands were valid under DOS 3.3 but are no longer functional under ProDOS. Four of these commands (FP, INIT, INT, and MON) will cause a syntax error in a program running under ProDOS. If this happens, you will have to remove the offending command from the program before you will be able to run it.

FP

The FP command was used under DOS to switch from Integer BASIC to Applesoft BASIC. ProDOS supports only Applesoft BASIC in ROM and has no need of this command. ProDOS itself is loaded into the area of memory that RAM-based Applesoft or Integer BASIC would use, so it is not possible to load these programs at all.

INIT

The INIT command formatted disks for DOS 3.3. The formatting functions are now handled from the Filer program. This means that you can no longer format disks from inside a program. So it is very important to have enough blank formatted disks available at all times.

Under INIT a greeting program could have any name; under ProDOS it must be called STARTUP. Under DOS greeting programs could be written only in BASIC; ProDOS will let you use a BASIC, machine-language, or EXEC program as the STARTUP program.

INT

The INT command was used under DOS to switch from Applesoft BASIC to Integer BASIC. Because ProDOS cannot load Integer BASIC, it has no need of this command.

MAXFILES

The MAXFILES command was used under DOS to allocate the maximum number of files that could be opened at once. This number was set to 3 by default and could be raised as high as 16 by the MAXFILES command. Under ProDOS a program can have up to eight files open at the same time. ProDOS does not allow any changes to this number and therefore ignores the MAXFILES command. When it finds it, no error will occur.

ProDOS automatically assigns a 1024-byte buffer to each standard file when it is opened. If the file is a directory file, the buffer assigned is only 512 bytes. This affects the maximum size of a BASIC program. On a 64K Apple II, the maximum size of a BASIC program is calculated by the formula

$$\text{maximum size} = 40{,}960 - (1024 \times \text{maximum number of open files})$$

MON

The MON command in DOS allowed you to display all disk input, output, and commands without printing them. This command is not supported by ProDOS in any way.

NOMON

The NOMON command turned off the switch set by the MON command. ProDOS will ignore this command if it encounters it; no error will occur.

CHANGES TO APPLESOFT

As we mentioned in Chapter 1, Applesoft BASIC runs slightly slower under ProDOS than it did under DOS 3.3. This is because ProDOS monitors every line of a BASIC program to see if it contains a PRINT instruction including a Control-D character as the first character to be printed. ProDOS uses this character to recognize the commands intended for it. DOS 3.3 also looked for Control-D, but DOS didn't examine every Applesoft command as it executed. DOS looked only at characters output by the program. This was a faster technique, but it meant that every Control-D character had to be preceded by a carriage-return character (ASCII 13) to be recognized by DOS. Apple opted to make it a little easier to use ProDOS commands in BASIC programs and in the process sacrifice a small amount of execution speed. Because disk operations are faster under ProDOS than under DOS, your programs will probably still operate faster under ProDOS.

In the evolution from DOS to ProDOS, Apple found it necessary to make some changes in commands normally executed by Applesoft. There are ten commands that are affected. Following is a brief discussion of the changes and restrictions imposed on these commands.

The HIMEM command has been affected because ProDOS uses the value of HIMEM to determine where it should place the I/O buffer for a newly opened file. ProDOS manages memory in 256-

byte segments. For this reason, the value of HIMEM must always be a multiple of 256. If you are working with hexadecimal values, this means that HIMEM must always be a multiple of $100.

The HGR, HGR2, and TEXT commands all relate to the graphics portion of your Apple II's memory. Since ProDOS takes up more memory than DOS did, Apple took the compromise route of using this portion of memory for the normal storage of Applesoft programs. If you use the Applesoft HGR or HGR2 commands within a program, the contents of this area of memory will be wiped out. This area will then remain a graphics area until the TEXT command is issued or the system is reset.

The Applesoft INPUT command has been changed. Under DOS, the INPUT statement would ignore any characters typed following a comma or a colon. For example, if you typed the string "ABC-D,EFGH" in response to an INPUT statement, you would get the message EXTRA IGNORED, and only the first four characters would be stored in the variable. Under ProDOS, the last variable in the INPUT list (the statement can be used with more than one) will get all the remaining characters in the line, including commas and colons.

According to the Apple manual, the IN# and PR# commands are no longer Applesoft commands but are intercepted and executed by ProDOS. The manual says that if you try to use IN# or PR# from within a program without a leading Control-D character, they will not work. This is because they would disconnect ProDOS if they were executed from Applesoft. To prevent this, the manual says, ProDOS intercepts and ignores them. The manual is wrong in this regard because the IN# and PR# commands *will* work from within a BASIC program without a leading Control-D character. This can cause a variety of effects, depending on the slot you select. For example, if you select a slot that contains a disk drive, the system will try to boot from that disk drive. If you specify a slot that does not contain any device, your system will lock up and will have to be reset.

The TRACE and NOTRACE commands had no effect on DOS commands. These commands, which cause the line numbers of Applesoft statements to be displayed as they are executed, will work with ProDOS statements.

The FRE statement now belongs to both Applesoft and ProDOS. The Applesoft version is slower and less efficient than the ProDOS version. You use the FRE statement to perform garbage collection on old and unused strings in memory. You have a choice of which version you want to use—if you precede the command with the Control-D character, it is a ProDOS command and the faster routines will be used. If you do not, it is an Applesoft command and the slower routine will be used.

ProDOS, Memory, and Peripheral Devices

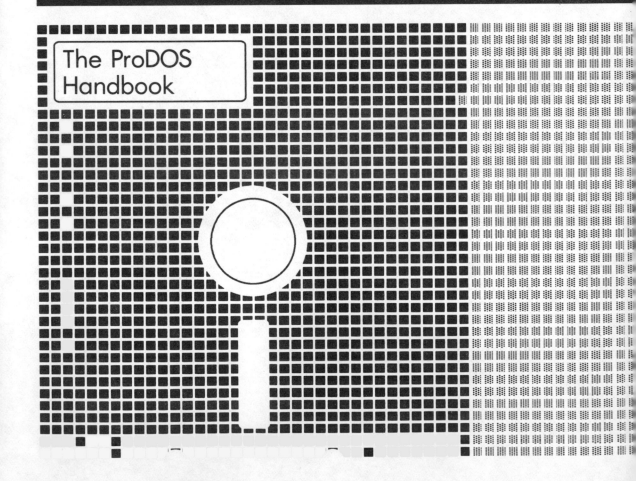

The ProDOS
Handbook

In this chapter we will discuss the relationship between ProDOS and the memory of your Apple II computer. This will include a discussion of which areas of memory ProDOS uses and what it uses them for. We examine the commands that allow the BASIC programmer to access memory directly, as well as the way in which Applesoft shares memory with ProDOS. Finally, we will discuss the relationship between ProDOS and peripheral devices, such as disk drives and clock cards.

This chapter can be used in two ways. It can be skimmed to provide a general background on how ProDOS relates to the memory and devices of your computer system. For the more technically minded, this chapter can provide the detailed information needed to explore ProDOS in depth.

PRODOS AND MEMORY USAGE

Before you can use ProDOS, you must load it into memory from your disk drive. It takes a number of steps, called the loading sequence, to get ProDOS loaded into the right place in memory. Once ProDOS is operating, it uses specific areas of memory, such as the zero page and the system global page, to hold certain kinds of information. We will discuss this information and these areas of memory, but first we should review the addressing information needed to find a particular location within the Apple's memory.

Addressing

The Apple II can use or address 65,536 individual memory locations, each of which can store one byte of data. Each location has a specific address, much like the number of a post office box. This address can be expressed as either a positive or negative value. If you supply a positive value for the address, the negative value can be calculated by subtracting 65,536 from the value you have given. For example, the addresses 100 and −65436 represent the same location. Because 0 is a valid address, the largest possible address you can use is 65535.

In this book, we will be referring to memory addresses in decimal notation whenever they are used by BASIC statements. If we refer to a memory location without using it in a BASIC statement, we may use hexadecimal notation for the address. Hexadecimal is often used because it is easier to translate into binary numbers than decimal notation is. In hexadecimal, counting is done in base 16 instead of base 10. This means that a single character can represent a value from 0 to 15. The letters A, B, C, D, E, and F have been drafted to represent the numbers from 10 to 15. Hexadecimal numbers are usually identified by the use of a $ character before the actual number to avoid confusion. Here are a few examples of hexadecimal values and their decimal equivalents:

Hexadecimal	Conversion	Decimal
$10	$(1 \times 16) + 0 = 16$	16
$0A	$10 \times 1 = 10$	10

$AC	(10 × 16) + (12 × 1) = 172	172
$D3	(13 × 16) + (3 × 1) = 211	211

Hexadecimal numbers are commonly represented in multiples of two digits. This is because the maximum value that can be stored in a single byte is $FF (255 in decimal). A value of 258 requires two bytes of space for storage and is represented by the hexadecimal value $0102. To convert this from hexadecimal notation back to decimal, multiply 1 × 256 and add 2 × 1. Just as with decimal notation, the larger values are on the left side of the number. Because the value is so closely connected to the storage capacity of a single byte, you will not normally see a value expressed by a single character such as $A. Instead, it would be represented as $0A.

Memory Usage and the ProDOS Loading Sequence

Every time you boot your system, a particular sequence of events, called the loading sequence, occurs. Its purpose is to load your operating system from disk into memory where you can use it.

A very small and preliminary loading program is stored on the disk drive controller card. When you turn on the system, you activate this program. The real loader program for ProDOS is stored in blocks 0 and 1 of your disk, which the preliminary program accesses.

The loading sequence is as follows:

1. The program on the controller card reads the loader program from the disk and places it into memory at $0800; then the loader program is executed.

2. The loader program searches for and loads the PRODOS program (which is always a type $FF or system file in the ProDOS directory) at location $2000. This program contains the machine-language interface (MLI). Once it has loaded the ProDOS program, the loader begins to execute it.

3. The MLI determines your computer's memory size, checks to see what devices are available, and sets up the system

global page variables and routines. (The system global page is used primarily for communication between the BASIC-.SYSTEM program and the MLI.) The MLI then moves itself to its appropriate location above $D000.

4. At that point the MLI searches through the volume directory of the startup disk for the first file including in its name the characters .SYSTEM (this file is also a type $FF file). The MLI then loads that file at location $2000 and begins to execute it.

5. The BASIC.SYSTEM program then looks for a program called STARTUP. If it finds it, it loads and executes it. If it doesn't find it, ProDOS takes you immediately to the BASIC prompt. The STARTUP program may be a BASIC program, a system (type $FF) file, or a machine-language program.

If either the PRODOS file or a type $FF file containing .SYSTEM in its name is not found, the system will tell you that it is unable to load ProDOS. Both of these files must be present for ProDOS to boot and operate; they *are* ProDOS. The STARTUP file is simply the first program ProDOS will try to execute.

Zero Page

Each page in memory represents 256 bytes of space, so the zero page of memory represents bytes $0000 through $00FF. Both Applesoft and ProDOS use the zero page for certain tasks.

Most of the zero page is used only by Applesoft. This area is composed of pointers to memory locations needed to execute BASIC programs and storage areas for data. The contents of these areas change constantly as Applesoft executes a program. With them, Applesoft keeps track of such things as which line number is being executed, where the variable arrays begin, and the result of the last multiplication or division. There is no reason to change any of these values in general BASIC programming and many reasons why you should not. If you change these pointers and flags haphazardly, the results will be unpredictable and almost certainly disastrous to your program. Applesoft's zero page usage is given in Appendix I at the end of this book.

The ProDOS MLI uses locations $40 through $4E. The contents of these locations are saved before the MLI uses them and restored when an MLI call is completed. This means that you can store data and instructions in these locations without losing them when the MLI is in use.

The ProDOS disk driver routines that the MLI calls to read or write the disk drives use the locations $3A through $3F. The contents of these locations are not saved when the disk driver routines are used. Any data stored in locations $3A through $3F are replaced by data from the disk driver routines.

The System Global Page

The system global page is a special area of memory located between $BF00 and $BFFF (inclusive). This area contains the system's global variables. The global page is used extensively for communications between the operating system and system programs. Among other information, the system global page contains the system bit map and the version numbers of your system program, the MLI, and ProDOS. The contents of the rest of the system global page are dependent upon the system program being executed.

The following is a discussion of the locations you are most likely to be interested in. For a complete listing of the contents of the system global page, consult Appendix K of this book.

The first location in the global page, and the only one you should call directly, is $BF00. This is the MLI call entry point. All calls to the MLI should be executed by the use of an assembly-language JSR instruction (jump to subroutine) to this address. The use of this entry point is described in Chapter 10.

The location $BF0F is used to return an error code from the system. If the value of this byte is zero, there is no error.

The locations starting at byte $BF10 and continuing through $BF2F are used to maintain a list of vectors to device drivers. This information is recorded in the form of two-byte addresses; $BF10 and $BF11 represent the first address, $BF12 and $BF13 represent the second one, and so on. There are exactly enough bytes to provide for eight slots with two drives each. If one of these addresses contains the value $D0A2, that slot is currently empty. ProDOS uses the list to determine where to begin executing the routine that controls a particular drive.

The bit map of memory is stored in the area from $BF58 to $BF69. Each bit of each byte in this area represents one page (256 bytes) of memory. If the value of a particular bit is set to one, the page it represents is in use. If the bit is set to zero, the page it represents is unprotected and available for use. For a more complete description of the operation and use of the system bit map, see the next section of this chapter.

ProDOS will prevent you from writing file buffer information into protected areas by reading this bit map before it allocates buffers. Each byte of the system bit map represents eight pages of memory. The left-most bit represents the first page for that byte, and the right-most bit represents the last page.

The next eight bytes, from $BF70 to $BF7F, are used to store the buffer addresses for open files. If you make any changes to these values while they are active, ProDOS will lose track of where the file buffer is.

The area of memory from $BF80 to $BF8F is used to store the addresses for ProDOS's four interrupt vectors. (Interrupts are signals, usually generated by an external device such as a modem, that tell your Apple that a response is required.) Changes made to these values while interrupts are active will probably cause a system failure and require rebooting when the next interrupt is received. They should not be changed.

Bytes $BF90 to $BF92 are used to store the date and time. These locations are used by the ProDOS clock/calendar routines and can also be affected by changing the date from the Filer utility on the ProDOS User's Disk. The IIc System Utilities disk does not contain any option affecting these locations.

The byte at $BF98 is used by ProDOS to identify the type of machine you have. A tremendous amount of information is packed into this byte. Bits 7 and 6 contain information on which model of the Apple II you are using. Their interpretation depends on the value of bit 3. If bit 3 equals 0, a value of 00 in bits 7 and 6 means that you are using an Apple II, 01 identifies a II+, 10 indicates IIe, and 11 means that your Apple is emulating an Apple III. If bit 3 equals 1, values of 00, 01, and 11 in bits 7 and 6 are reserved for future definition; a value of 10 means that you are using a IIc.

Bits 5 and 4 contain information on how much memory your machine has. A value of 00 is reserved, 01 means that you have 48K, 10 means that you have 64K, and 11 means that your machine has 128K.

The value contained in bit 2 has been reserved for future definition.

Bit 1 identifies whether you have an 80-column card installed in your machine. If the bit is set to 0 you don't have an 80-column card installed; if it is set to 1 you do.

Similarly, bit 0 identifies whether you have a ThunderClock or other clock/calendar device installed. If it is set to 0 you have no such device; if it is set to 1 you do.

The byte at $BF99 is used to keep track of which slots have cards installed. This is done on a one-for-one basis, with bit 0 representing slot 0 and bit 7 representing slot 7.

The four bytes from $BFFC to $BFFF are used to record information about the version numbers of your system program and ProDOS. These are used by system programs (PRODOS and BASIC.SYSTEM) to check for compatibility between the system program in use, the MLI version, and ProDOS.

The contents of this area of memory should remain inviolate. The continuing operation of ProDOS depends on them, and changes to the values stored in these locations can cause severe disruption in the operating system's activity.

USING THE SYSTEM BIT MAP

As you learned in the last section, the system bit map keeps track of which areas of memory are currently in use in the system. ProDOS uses 24 bytes (from $BF58 to $BF69) in the system global page to record the usage of the lower 48K of the Apple II's RAM. One bit of each byte corresponds to a single 256-byte page of RAM. It takes four bits to record the usage of 1K of RAM. If the value of a bit is 0, the page of memory it corresponds to is not in use; if the bit is set to 1, that page of RAM is unavailable.

Within each byte of the system bit map the bits are used in inverse order. This means that bit 7 of the first byte ($BF58) represents the first 256 bytes of memory, while bit 0 of that byte represents the eighth page of memory. Figure 6.1 shows the memory pages represented by the first two bytes of the bit map.

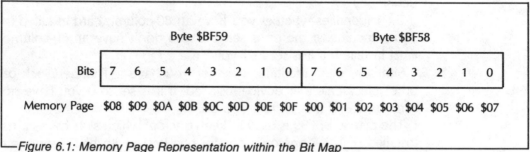

Figure 6.1: Memory Page Representation within the Bit Map

The bit map does not represent the extended memory available on an Apple IIe and IIc and on the language card area on an Apple II+. This area above 48K is always in use. This is because the bit map is intended for use with the machine-language interface (MLI), which is located in those regions (i.e., above 48K) of memory.

Suppose you want to determine whether a particular page in memory is available for use by your program. You can use the bit map to find this out. The high five bits (bits 3–7) of an address provide the number of the byte in the bit map that corresponds to that page of memory. The complement of the low three bits (bits 0–2) of the address tell you the bit within that byte which represents that particular page of memory.

For example, page $00 in memory is represented by the first byte of the bit map, because the high five bits of the address are equal to 0. The low three bits are also equal to 0, and the binary complement of 000 is 111. This is the binary equivalent for the value 7 in decimal, so bit 7 within that byte contains the flag for page $00.

Only very advanced programmers will need to know about and use the system bit map. Its main purpose is to keep track of the areas of memory that are in use and to prevent them from being reused by the operating system. If you wish to use an area of memory, you can use the bit map in the same way as the operating system uses it.

For example, you might want to choose a certain area of memory to store values with the POKE command. By first using the PEEK command to look at the bit map, then analyzing the value you find, you can determine whether that page of memory is in use. Because BASIC does not have the ability to look at individual bits of data, you have to examine the value in terms of its relationship to the powers of two. If the value is greater than 127, bit 7 must be set to 1. If the value is between 64 and 127 or between 192 and 255, bit 6 must be a 1. Some knowledge of binary arithmetic and an understanding of the material in this section are necessary to use the bit map in this way.

Since this technique can lead to chaos for the operating system if it is misused, it should not be attempted without careful consideration of the consequences. Do not attempt to change the contents of the system bit map or the system global page without first being sure that any program you have in memory has already been saved on disk. It is usually wiser to find some other way to accomplish your purpose than to alter these areas. In the normal course of BASIC programming, the system bit map can and should be ignored. Changes in the values of the bit map (such as poking a new value into a byte of the bit map) may allow areas of memory to be reused even though they are currently in use, which can lead to the destruction of data and the lockup of your system.

The system bit map does not protect areas of memory from the BASIC POKE command. It is used only to determine what areas of memory are available or in use when a ProDOS command is executed.

USING BASIC TO ACCESS MEMORY

Now that you know where ProDOS places itself in memory, you will need to know how to access and protect memory locations. The following section discusses BASIC statements that refer directly to memory locations.

There are six BASIC statements that have direct access to memory locations in Applesoft. These are the PEEK, POKE, HIMEM:, LOMEM:, USR, and CALL statements.

The PEEK statement returns the contents of a memory location supplied as the argument. The value returned is the decimal equivalent of the byte found at that location. For example, the statement A = PEEK(222) would set A equal to the value found at memory location 222, which is where the error code is kept.

The POKE statement allows you to change the contents of a memory location. This function requires two arguments. The first is the address of the memory location you want to change; the second is the value you wish to put there. The value of the second argument must be an integer no less than 0 and no greater than 255. For example, the statement POKE 9000,18 places the value 18 ($12) at memory location 9000.

The combination of the PEEK and POKE commands allows you to read from and write to any location within the memory of the Apple. These commands allow you to store and recover bytes of information at will. You can use them to store your own machine-language subroutines. You can control the operation of these machine-language routines by passing values with the POKE command. These two commands are therefore the basis of all direct access of memory from BASIC.

The CALL statement allows you to activate a machine-language or assembly-language routine beginning at the location you specify. The beginning address of the subroutine is passed as the argument of the CALL. For example, the statement CALL −868 will activate the intrinsic Apple monitor routine to clear text from the current cursor position to the end of the line. The CALL statement operates similarly to a BASIC GOSUB statement—the execution of your program resumes with the next line after the CALL statement, once the routine you have called is executed. The CALL statement can be used either with the existing routines in the memory of your Apple or with routines you write yourself.

The USR statement also activates a machine-language routine, with two important differences from the way the CALL statement operates. First, the USR statement passes control to only one location—address $0A. For USR to work correctly, locations $0A through $0C must contain an assembly-language JMP instruction to the beginning address of the machine-language subroutine you wish to execute. The second difference is that the USR function passes a value supplied as an argument to the routine it calls. For example, suppose you write a machine-language routine to calculate the square of a number. You store this routine beginning at address $0300. Then you put a JMP instruction at address $0A, with bytes $0B and $0C containing the address $0300. If you then include in a BASIC program the statement

PRINT USR(3) + 2

you will see the number 11 on your screen. This statement tells your computer to print the result of the machine-language calculation performed on the argument of your USR statement, plus 2, on the screen. Because the machine-language routine you have used calculates the square, and the square of 3 is 9, the statement prints the result 11 (9 + 2) on the screen.

The importance of the CALL and USR statements lies in their ability to add the power of the ProDOS MLI to your BASIC programs. However, if you're going to use the MLI more than once or twice in a program, you'll find it much easier to do from a machine- or assembly-language program. Chapter 10 discusses the MLI and how to use it.

The LOMEM: statement allows you to set the address of the lower limit in memory available for use by a BASIC program. This is done by a statement such as

LOMEM: 3055

which sets the lower limit of memory you can use to location 3055. If you wish to determine the current value of LOMEM, you need to use the PEEK statement to look at locations 106 and 105, which is where the value is stored. The program statement

A = PEEK(106)*256 + PEEK(105)

stores the value of LOMEM in the variable A. Note that the value of the higher byte must be multiplied by 256 to obtain a correct answer.

The HIMEM: statement allows you to set the address of the higher limit in memory available for use by a BASIC program. This is done by a statement such as

HIMEM:44000

which sets HIMEM to location 44000 within memory. The current value of HIMEM is stored in locations 116 and 115. The program statement

A = PEEK(116)*256 + PEEK(115)

stores the value of HIMEM in the variable A.

The LOMEM: and HIMEM: statements can be used to set upper and lower boundaries on the space used by a BASIC program. This is often used to protect the high-resolution graphics area and is discussed in greater detail in Chapter 9.

PRODOS AND PERIPHERAL DEVICES

ProDOS is a disk operating system and is naturally most concerned with the operation of disk drives. However, ProDOS does offer support for the use of the ThunderClock card, and it provides the ability to handle as many as four interrupt-driven devices. The relationship between ProDOS and these devices is discussed in this section.

Disk Drives

ProDOS is a disk operating system, and as such it protects you from most of the details of accessing disk drives. You don't have to know what is necessary to compose a startup volume, or the order in which the volumes will be searched to find a given file, but knowing how ProDOS determines these things will give you a better understanding of how the system operates.

Startup Volume

When you boot your system, you must have a valid ProDOS startup disk in a disk drive connected to your system, or ProDOS will not be able to boot successfully. Apple defines a startup volume as a disk from which ProDOS can be booted. It must contain all of the files needed to bring ProDOS from the disk into memory and begin executing it. This disk must have the following characteristics:

- It must have been formatted using ProDOS.
- It must have the PRODOS program in its volume directory.
- It must have BASIC.SYSTEM or some other program in its volume directory containing the string .SYSTEM in its file name. The .SYSTEM program must have the file type $FF and perform the same functions as BASIC.SYSTEM.

If you want ProDOS to begin executing another program immediately, a program called STARTUP must be in that disk's volume directory. If STARTUP is not found, ProDOS takes you directly to the BASIC prompt.

It is possible to write a replacement program for BASIC.SYSTEM as long as all the conventions and functions of that program are met. We will discuss the requirements of such a program in Chapter 11.

Volume Search Order

When you ask ProDOS for access to a volume that it has not already accessed, ProDOS must search to see if it can find it. ProDOS always checks for volumes in a particular order. It begins by checking the volume that was used to boot the system. For example, if you have booted your system from slot 6 (the normal configuration), ProDOS will look there first. ProDOS will also always look at drive 1 in a given slot before it will look at drive 2.

If ProDOS does not find the requested volume in the slot of the startup volume, it begins to search in descending order all the slots that have disk drive cards in them, beginning with slot 7. For example, suppose you had four disk drives connected to cards in slots 5 and 6. If the startup volume was in slot 5, ProDOS would search for a new volume in the following sequence:

Slot 5, drive 1
Slot 5, drive 2

Slot 6, drive 1
Slot 6, drive 2

If the startup disk is located in slot 6 and a ProFile has been added in slot 7, the search order is as follows:

Slot 6, drive 1
Slot 6, drive 2
Slot 7
Slot 5, drive 1
Slot 5, drive 2

The startup volume is always the volume in the lowest-numbered drive that ProDOS can identify as a startup volume. This means that if you had two different startup volumes mounted in the two drives connected to slot 6 when the system was booted from slot 6, the disk in drive 1 would be considered the startup disk.

Clock/Calendar Cards

If your system has a ThunderClock card from ThunderWare, Inc., ProDOS automatically accesses it to get the correct date and time. If you have some other clock/calendar card, you will have to install a device driver for the card. The manufacturer of such a card can probably supply you with a short program that acts as the device driver. If no driver is available you can write your own, but we do not recommend this unless you have a considerable amount of technical experience and a copy of the ProDOS Technical Reference Manual.

Interrupt-Driven Devices

Some devices generate interrupts, which are signals that tell the computer that the device should be looked at. This is especially common with a device such as a modem, which has to let the Apple know when a message has been received.

ProDOS has the ability to handle as many as four interrupting devices at one time. Each interrupt-driven device needs an interrupt-handling routine stored in memory to operate properly. For ProDOS to be able to access the routine, you have to use an MLI call to add the routine to the system. You must also indicate in the system bit map that that area of memory is used. When this is done, the routine will be called each time an interrupt occurs. When you have more than one routine installed in the system, they will be called to service their devices in the order they were installed. If you turn your computer off, these routines must be reinstalled before they can be used again.

If you wish to remove an interrupt-handling routine, you must first turn off or disable the device it is servicing. Once this is done, you must free the area of memory it is occupying in the bit map and use the MLI call to remove the interrupt routine.

An interrupt handling routine can do anything at all or nothing at all. It must exist so that control can be passed to it when the interrupt is received from the device. However, once control is passed, ProDOS exercises no further requirements on the interrupt-handling routine.

For example, when a modem receives a phone call, it generates an interrupt signal and sends it to the Apple. When the interrupt is received by the computer, it could branch to a communications routine, which performs the work needed in response to an incoming message.

The MLI calls necessary to set up and remove interrupt-handling routines are described in Chapter 10. The system bit map may be changed by poking a modified value into the byte that corresponds to that page of memory.

Other Devices

At the time of this writing, ProDOS does not support any devices other than disk drives and the ThunderClock. If you choose to add devices other than these to your system, you will have to either write your own device drivers or contact the manufacturer in the hope that he will supply you with one. Because of the close relationship of a device driver to the hardware it is controlling, device drivers are usually written in assembly or machine language and are extremely specific to the particular type of hardware they control. This means that you can usually obtain the driver for the device from the manufacturer if he claims that his device can run on your machine.

ProDOS does nothing to help or hinder the use of other devices. You will have to work out your own means of controlling them, providing all communication between your program and the device driver within your own code.

If you are using a IIc, your System Utilities disk will enable you to configure the serial ports on the back of your machine. This is a feature of your IIc computer and is not, strictly speaking, a part of ProDOS. ProDOS is independent of the differences between IIc's and IIe's.

Text Files and BASIC
Programming with ProDOS

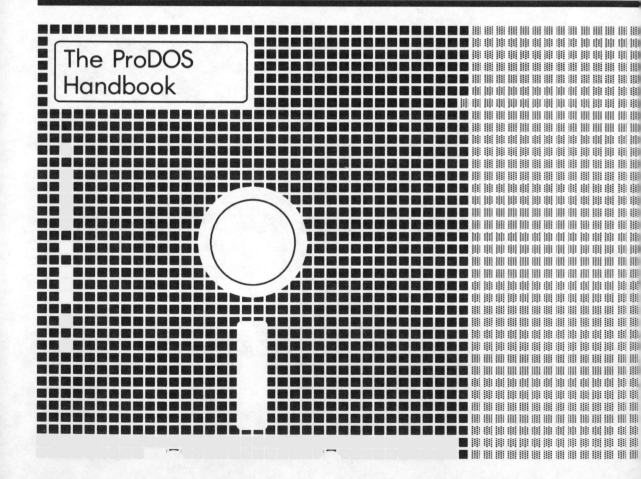

The ProDOS
Handbook

SEVEN

This chapter discusses how ProDOS handles text files. It will be of great interest to anyone who wishes to program in BASIC. We will look at the ProDOS commands that allow you to read, write, and use text files, as well as at the BASIC statements that deal with the different types of text files. The sections on programming sequential and random access files will show you how to unlock the power of ProDOS within your BASIC programs. In addition to this, both the beginner and the experienced programmer can benefit greatly from learning to use the EXEC command with BASIC programs and text files. This command allows you to perform a series of tasks with a single command or to provide a predetermined series of inputs from a text file to a program.

TEXT FILES

A text file is an ordered collection of data records (also called fields). Each record can contain any kind of character data except the carriage-return character (ASCII 13), which marks the end of each record and cannot be included as part of the record. There are two kinds of text files used by ProDOS: sequential files and random access files.

Sequential Text Files

A sequential text file can be accessed in only one way. The records in a sequential text file are stored in exactly the same order as they were written to the file. The first record written is the first record in the file, and the last record written is the last record in the file. When you open the file, the current postion pointer is automatically set to the first record in the file.

When you read or write records to a sequential file, you can move only forward. You can never move the pointer backward while the file is open. If you need to back up, you have to close the file, open it again, and read forward to the record you want. This limitation means that sequential files are best used by programs that have to read them only once.

Random Access Text Files

A random access text file differs from a sequential text file in two ways. The first of these is that each record in a random file has a fixed length, while records in sequential files have variable lengths. The second difference is that any record in a random file can be accessed directly if you know which record you wish to use.

When you create a random file with an OPEN statement, you must specify the record length that will be used for each record in the file. Whenever you wish to open this file again, you must specify exactly the same record length or you will be unable to read the file correctly.

The chief advantage of a random file over a sequential file is its ability to access directly any single record within the file. This naturally makes it much faster to access a record in a random file than in a sequential file. This ability is a result of the fixed record length of a random file.

The disadvantages of a random file are that it uses more space on the disk and it requires slightly more care in operation to prevent errors. Because of this, random files and sequential files both have places in operating systems.

Directory Entries

In the directory, both sequential and random access files are stored as type TXT. The difference between the two entries is apparent only if you use the CATALOG statement to display the full 80-column directory listing. When you do this, the record length is also displayed. The random files will show the record length you specified when you opened them. This information will appear in the form R — record length (for example, R — 50). Sequential text files always display a record length of zero.

Records

A record or field in a text file is always terminated by a carriage-return character (ASCII 13). The first record in a file is everything from the beginning of the file to the first carriage return. The second record or field in a file is everything after the first carriage return and before the second. The carriage return is created automatically when you use a PRINT statement to store data in a file. For example, PRINT A$ will automatically generate a carriage return after A$ is printed.

The Apple manuals refer to this concept as a field, but it is also commonly called a record. In this book we will use the term record.

Data Elements

Each record in a file is composed of one or more data elements. Each data element stored by Applesoft under ProDOS is separated from the other data elements in that record by a comma. The user is responsible for inserting the comma into the data to mark the dividing point between data elements. This can be done with the PRINT statement (we discuss how to do it in the section "BASIC Statements").

The parts of a record are frequently called fields, but because records are also often called fields, this is a confusing term and we will avoid using it. Like the Apple manuals, we will be using the term data elements for this concept throughout the book.

Current Position Pointer

For each file that is open, ProDOS maintains a pointer that indicates your current position in the file. When you read a file or write information to a file, the current position is the character after the last character read or written. The value of this pointer can also be changed by using the F and B parameters with the READ, WRITE, and POSITION statements.

There is no BASIC statement or ProDOS command that will show you the value of the current position pointer. The value can be calculated by keeping a count of every byte read from or written to the file in a program.

The L, F, B, and R Parameters

We mentioned earlier that when you create a random file, you have to specify the record length that will be used for each record in the file. This is done with the L parameter in the OPEN statement. When you open the file again, the L parameter should be exactly the same as it was when the file was originally created. If the length is different, you will be unable to read the file correctly.

For example, suppose you had a file called TESTFILE on disk, which you had originally created and written records to with a length of 50. If at a later time you tried to open this file with the statement

    OPEN TESTFILE, L30

your data would become hopelessly confused. When data is written to a random file, all records are stored at exactly the length given in the OPEN statement. When you try to read them back with a different length, ProDOS will not correct the length for you. You will get truncated records as ProDOS tries to read, for example, ten records of 30 bytes each from a file in which ten records of 50 bytes each are stored.

As we mentioned in the section on the current position pointer, the F and B parameters can be used with several ProDOS commands to advance the current position pointer of a file. They cannot be used to decrease the value of the pointer or backtrack within the file, however.

The F parameter advances the current position pointer by records. This means that a statement such as

   READ MYFILE, F5

would read and ignore the contents of five complete records before returning the contents of a record to your program. ProDOS recognizes the end of a record when it reads the ASCII character 13, which is a carriage return.

The B parameter advances the current position pointer by individual bytes. This means that a statement such as

   READ MYFILE, B10

would read and ignore ten bytes of data from the disk before returning the contents of the next record to your program. If one or more short records were among the ten bytes that were skipped, ProDOS will continue to the next record. You might use the B parameter if you were searching for or creating a particular pattern within a file.

The F and B parameters can be used in combination. When this is the case, the F parameter is always executed first. The statement

   READ MYFILE, F5, B10

would cause ProDOS to read and ignore five complete records from MYFILE and to read and ignore the next ten bytes of data before returning a record to your program.

With random files you can also use the R parameter to set the current position pointer to a specific record. For example, the statement

   READ MYFILE, R10

would read record 10 in MYFILE. ProDOS calculates the location of the record by multiplying the record number you want (10, in this case) by the record length.

   Although the F and R parameters accomplish the same thing, it is much faster to use the R parameter (which can be used only with random files) to access a particular record. This is because with the R parameter ProDOS does not have to read (and ignore) all the records from the current position pointer to the desired record. The other advantage of the R parameter is that it can be used to move both forward and backward in a file.

PRODOS STATEMENTS

   The OPEN, CLOSE, WRITE, FLUSH, READ, POSITION, and APPEND statements are ProDOS commands. In order to use them from a BASIC program, these commands must be used as strings embedded in a PRINT statement. When these commands are issued inside a BASIC program, you must print a Control-D (ASCII 4) before the string containing the command so that ProDOS can recognize them. This character can be generated by the statement CHR$(4). This statement is used so frequently that it is often assigned to a variable (usually D$) at the beginning of a program. For example, look at the following short program:

   ```
   10   D$ = CHR$(4)
   20   PRINT D$; "OPEN SAMPLE"
   30   PRINT D$; "WRITE SAMPLE"
   40   PRINT "TEST DATA"
   50   PRINT D$; "CLOSE SAMPLE"
   ```

ProDOS will recognize that the statements in lines 20, 30, and 50 are intended for it, and ProDOS will ignore the PRINT statement in line 40. This is because the strings being printed in lines 20, 30, and 50 begin with an ASCII character 4 (represented by the variable D$).

The CLOSE and FLUSH commands can be used from the immediate mode of BASIC. To do so, simply type in the command and press Return. None of the other commands can be used from the immediate mode.

OPEN

The OPEN statement must be used before any other command can be issued to a file. The OPEN statement must include the path name of the file you wish to open. When you open a random file you must also specify the length of the record. You may also specify the slot and drive number.

If you have identical volumes in your disk drives and do not wish to use the one ProDOS would find according to the rules of volume search, you can specify the slot and the drive in which the volume is located. For example, the statement

    OPEN MYFILE, S5, D1

would ensure that ProDOS would use the volume located in the drive connected to slot 5 and drive 1. You can use the S and D parameters in combination or separately.

The OPEN statement allocates a 1024-byte buffer in memory for each file that you open within a program. If you have not opened a file, you will not be able to either read from or write to it because there will be no buffer to put the data into.

CLOSE

The CLOSE statement must be issued by your program to ensure that any data in the file buffer have been written to disk and that the file buffer itself has been deallocated. Until this is done, the memory occupied by the file buffer will be unavailable for use. If your program ends without closing all the open files, you will see the error message

    FILES STILL OPEN

If this happens, type CLOSE in response to the BASIC prompt and press Return to close all the open files.

If you use the CLOSE statement by itself, *all* open files will be closed. If you wish to close a particular file, you must specify the path name to that file in the CLOSE statement. For example, placing the statement CLOSE MYFILE at the end of your program would close only that file, leaving any other open files unaffected.

Sequential files can be read in only one direction. This means that if you wish to read the second record in a file and you are currently positioned on the third record in a file, you will have to close that file and then open it again to get back to the beginning. In this case you would want to close only that particular file, leaving any other open files unaffected. Once you have reopened the file, you can read forward to the record you wish to see.

WRITE

You must issue the ProDOS WRITE statement before you can use the PRINT statement to store data in a file. This data is always stored starting at the current position pointer. You can use the F parameter with this statement to advance ProDOS's position in the file. The value supplied in this parameter is the number of records you want ProDOS to read and discard. ProDOS does this by counting the number of carriage returns after the current position in the file and matching this to the value in the F parameter. You can also use the B parameter with this statement to move to a specific position within a file. This specific position is defined in terms of how many bytes farther along it is from the current position in the file.

For example, the statement

WRITE SAMPLE, F5, B5

tells ProDOS to read and discard five records after the current position in the file and update the current position pointer. After it does that, ProDOS moves five bytes past the current position and again updates the current position pointer. This is the position at which ProDOS begins writing any subsequent data sent to it by PRINT statements. Once a WRITE command has been issued, it remains in force until any other ProDOS command is executed. You can use the R parameter with this statement to specify an individual record within a random file. This will work only within a random file because all records within a random file have exactly the same length. For example, the statement

WRITE RANDOM.DATA, R50

would cause ProDOS to change the current position pointer to point to the beginning of record 50. It does this by multiplying the number of records to be skipped (from the beginning of the file) by the record length. With this parameter you can also move to a position previous to the current position pointer.

FLUSH

The FLUSH statement ensures that all data in the file buffers have been written to the disk. If you issue the FLUSH statement with a path name for a file, only that file's buffer will be written to the disk. If you use the FLUSH statement by itself, the contents of all open file buffers will be written to the disk. FLUSH does not deallocate the file buffer as the CLOSE statement does, and there is no need to reopen the file before reading or writing to that file again. As we mentioned earlier in this book, ProDOS derives much of its speed from waiting until a 512-byte file buffer is full before writing it to the disk. Frequent use of the FLUSH command within your program will prevent you from losing the file buffers to an accident, but it will also slow down the execution of your program.

READ

The READ statement must be issued before you can retrieve data from a file. The file must be opened before you issue the READ command for it, or you will cause an error. When this happens, the message

FILE NOT OPEN

appears.

You can use the F, B, and R parameters with this statement in exactly the same way as you do with the WRITE statement.

As with the WRITE statement, once a READ command has been issued, it remains in effect until another ProDOS command has been issued. This means that once you have set a file to READ, your program will look to that file for the data requested by all INPUT or GET statements. You will not be able to enter data from the keyboard while this command is in effect. When you need keyboard input, you will have to use a ProDOS command such as FRE to negate the effects of the READ statement.

POSITION

The POSITION statement can also be used to change the current position in a file, but that is the only thing this statement accomplishes. This statement was included in ProDOS for continuity from DOS 3.3; the ability to use the F and B parameters with the READ and WRITE statements make the POSITION statement superfluous.

The form of the POSITION statement is the same as with the WRITE and READ statements. That is, the statement

POSITION SAMPLE, F5, B5

tells ProDOS to read and discard five records after the current position in the file and update the current position pointer. Then ProDOS moves five bytes past the current position and again updates the current position pointer.

APPEND

The APPEND statement can be used to write records at the end of a file. APPEND acts as a shorthand for three other commands: OPEN, POSITION, and WRITE. When you issue an APPEND command under ProDOS, the file is opened, the current position is changed to the end of the file, and the system acts as if a WRITE command had already been issued. The APPEND command also saves execution time and code space in your programs. This is because you will not have to write code that will read through and find the end-of-file marker in a disk file. When you use the APPEND command on a random file, you must specify the record length by using the L parameter. You may also use the slot and drive parameters with this command.

BASIC STATEMENTS

The following statements are normal Applesoft commands. However, when you use them in a program after a ProDOS READ or WRITE statement, they perform differently. If another ProDOS command is issued after the READ or WRITE statement, they behave as they normally would.

PRINT

When used while a WRITE command is in effect, the PRINT statement will send data to the disk file specified in the most recent WRITE command. The data that are sent are whatever is specified after the PRINT command, whether it be a variable, a literal string indicated by quotes, or a numeric value. All PRINT statements issued under a ProDOS WRITE command always send data to the disk file, not to the screen. Once a different ProDOS command is executed, the PRINT statement no longer sends data to the disk and returns to its normal function.

The PRINT statement normally follows data with the carriage return character (ASCII 13). This character is also used to mark the end of a record in ProDOS. You can avoid marking the end of a record by ending your PRINT statement with a semicolon (;). When the PRINT statement encounters this character, it does not send the carriage return to the disk. This is important because it allows you to use more than one PRINT statement to write data to the same record of a file.

For example, suppose the variable A$ contained the string "PIANO" and the variable B$ contained the string "GUITAR". The following examples show you the effects of the semicolon on the output of the PRINT statement:

Statement	Output
PRINT A$	PIANO<CR>
PRINT A$;	PIANO
PRINT A$;B$;	PIANOGUITAR
PRINT A$;"VIOLIN"	PIANOVIOLIN<CR>

The above represents the output of individual statements. The effect will carry over from one statement to the next, however. For example,

Statement	Output
PRINT A$;	
PRINT B$	PIANOGUITAR<CR>

Notice that the last two statements create a single record ended by a carriage return (designated here by the symbol <CR>). The semicolon at the end of the first statement avoids the carriage return and thus the end of the record. The second statement does not end in a semicolon, so the carriage-return character is generated and the end of the record is marked. If the ProDOS WRITE command is in effect, the output will be sent to a disk file.

The comma (,) character can also be used as an editing character with the PRINT statement. When you use the comma as a continuation marker in your PRINT statement, no spaces are inserted into the data sent to the disk. Instead, the data before and after the comma are combined as though you were performing a string concatenation using the + operator. The combined data are written to the same record of the file.

For example, let us once again suppose that the variable A$ contains the string "PIANO" and the variable B$ contains the string "GUITAR". The following shows you the effect of using the comma with the PRINT statement:

Statement	Output
PRINT A$,"TEST"	PIANOTEST<CR>
PRINT A$,B$	PIANOGUITAR<CR>

```
PRINT A$,                    PIANO<CR>
PRINT A$,",",B$              PIANO,GUITAR<CR>
PRINT A$,B$;                 PIANOGUITAR
```

Note that you can use the semicolon character in the same statement as a comma, and that ending a statement with a comma does not suppress the carriage-return character. In the fourth example, the comma character is actually output to the disk because it is contained inside a literal string. The inclusion of this comma inside a string or a variable is the only way you can use the PRINT statement to create data elements inside a record.

INPUT

The INPUT statement fetches data from the disk drive rather than the keyboard when used after a READ statement in a program. The INPUT statement can be used with the comma to read two or more data elements from the record. If the INPUT statement contains two variables separated by a comma, ProDOS will read two data elements from the record. If there are more than two elements in that record, the rest of the record will be discarded. If there is only one element in that record, the second element is automatically taken from the next record.

GET

The GET statement fetches one character of data from the disk drive rather than from the keyboard when used after a ProDOS READ statement. The GET statement is different than the INPUT statement because it reads only one character at a time and because it reads *every* character. This means that the GET statement will return a comma or a carriage return when it finds one. You will have to interpret this byte correctly if you wish to use this statement. The GET statement can be valuable when you are reading files that have an unknown number of elements per record, a varying number of elements per record, or text that contains punctuation marks.

For example, if you are using the GET statement to read data from a text file, ProDOS will not know when the end of a record occurs. This is because only a single character is being returned at a time. This means that if you are interested in viewing the data in the file as a series of records, you will have to check to see if the character returned from the file is an ASCII character 13. Your code would have to contain a test such as the following:

```
1000   GET A$
1010   IF A$ = ASC(13)THEN GOSUB 2000
```

In this example, GOSUB 2000 takes you to the routine that does whatever it is you want done when the end of a record is encountered. The same would be true for any other character you wish to detect. Your program would have to test each character returned from the file individually to see if it was the character you wanted, and the program would have to make a decision based on that result.

The advantage of using the GET command to read data back from the disk is that you can read every single character on the disk and make your decisions based on what each character means.

PROGRAMMING AND SEQUENTIAL FILES

Sequential files are characterized by a single trait—they can be read in only one direction, from beginning to end. This section will show you how to create, read, and write sequential text files under ProDOS.

Creating a Sequential File

Creating a sequential text file is very simple; it requires only an OPEN statement and the path name for the file you wish to open. When you issue an OPEN statement to ProDOS, it creates a new file on the disk if one does not already exist for that path name. This new file consists of an entry in the directory and an empty seedling file of 512 bytes. If you try to read data from an empty file, an END OF DATA error message will appear. Once the file has been created and opened, you have to use the PRINT statement to write data to the file before you can read any data out of it. As you write more data to the file, ProDOS will expand the file as necessary to a sapling and then to a tree file.

The following program creates a sequential file and writes a number of records to it. When you enter and test this and the other programs in this section, you should use the SAVE command to store them on disk. The programs in this section are all interrelated, and you may wish to recall them later.

```
10    REM CREATE SEQUENTIAL FILE
20    D$ = CHR$(4)
100   HOME
110   VTAB 2: PRINT "CREATING A FILE"
120   GOSUB 1000
199   END
1000  PRINT D$; "OPEN SEQ.DATA"
1010  PRINT D$; "WRITE SEQ.DATA"
1020  PRINT "DESK"
1021  PRINT "PEN"
1022  PRINT "PAPER"
1025  PRINT "CHAIR"
1026  PRINT "TABLE"
1027  PRINT "STOOL"
1030  PRINT "LAMP"
1031  PRINT "BOOKS"
1032  PRINT "BOOKCASE"
1040  PRINT D$; "CLOSE SEQ.DATA"
1099  RETURN
```

The above program simply writes a number of strings out to the file on disk. There is no reason that the strings given in lines 1020 through 1032 have to be used. If you wish to enter your own data, you can modify this program by deleting lines 1020 through 1032 and replacing them with the following:

```
1020   INPUT A$
1022   IF A$ = "END" THEN GOTO 1040
```

```
1024   PRINT A$
1026   GOTO 1020
```

This change will allow you to enter your own data at will. If you enter the string "END" in response to line 1020, A$ will not be written to the disk and the program will close the file before ending.

Reading a Sequential File

Once you have used the previous program to create a sequential file, you need to know how to read that data back from the file. The following short program opens the file SEQ.DATA, reads it, and displays the data on the screen. If you try to run this program without first creating the SEQ.DATA file, you will get an END OF DATA error message when you try to use the READ statement. This is because the OPEN statement in this program will create the file when it finds it is not there, and the file will be empty.

```
10     REM READ SEQUENTIAL FILE
20     D$ = CHR$(4)
30     A = 1
100    HOME
110    VTAB 2: PRINT "READING A FILE"
1000   ONERR GOTO 1040
1005   PRINT D$; "OPEN SEQ.DATA"
1010   PRINT D$; "READ SEQ.DATA"
1020   INPUT B$(A)
1025   A = A + 1
1030   GOTO 1020
1040   PRINT D$; "CLOSE SEQ.DATA"
1050   POKE 216,0
2000   FOR A = 1 TO 9
2010   PRINT "RECORD ";A;" = ";B$(A)
2020   NEXT A
```

This program uses a very common procedure for reading records in a sequential file. Simply put, the program will continue looping between lines 1020 and 1030 until the ONERR statement in line 1000 is activated by an end-of-file condition. When this occurs, the program branches to line 1040 and closes the file. The POKE in line 1050 resets the error flag to zero. This flag was set as a result of this program's trying to read more records from the file than existed on the disk. This is a very handy technique; it is especially useful when you do not know how many records exist in a file.

Once the file is closed, the FOR/NEXT loop in lines 2000 through 2020 will print the contents of the records on the screen for you before ending the program.

Adding to a Sequential File

As we mentioned earlier in this chapter, you can use the APPEND command to open a file, place the current position pointer at the end of the file, and issue a WRITE statement. The following program is an example of how to use the APPEND statement with a sequential file:

```
  10   REM APPEND TO A SEQUENTIAL FILE
  20   D$ = CHR$(4)
 100   HOME
 110   VTAB 2: PRINT "APPENDING A FILE"
 120   GOSUB 1000
 199   END
1000   PRINT D$; "APPEND SEQ.DATA"
1020   PRINT "BOX"
1021   PRINT "CASE"
1022   PRINT "BAG"
1025   PRINT "TELEVISION"
1026   PRINT "CLOSET"
1027   PRINT "PICTURE"
1030   PRINT "MAP"
1031   PRINT "MONITOR"
1032   PRINT "COMPUTER"
1040   PRINT D$; "CLOSE SEQ.DATA"
1099   RETURN
```

As with the program used to create a sequential file, this program simply writes a number of strings out to the file on disk. There is no reason that the strings given in lines 1020 through 1032 have to be used. If you wish to enter your own data, you can modify this program by deleting lines 1020 through 1032 and replacing them with the following:

```
1020   INPUT A$
1022   IF A$ = "END" THEN GOTO 1040
1024   PRINT A$
1026   GOTO 1020
```

This change will allow you to enter your own data at will. If you enter the string "END" in response to line 1020, A$ will not be written to the disk and the program will close the file before ending. Since this program uses the APPEND command to replace both the OPEN and WRITE commands, any data you enter will be added to the end of the file.

PROGRAMMING AND RANDOM ACCESS FILES

Random access files are characterized by two traits. First, each record in the file has exactly the same length as every other record. Second, any individual record within the file can be read at any time. This means that you can move both forward and backward within the file when you read or write a record. The following section will show you how to use ProDOS random access files from BASIC.

Creating a Random Access File

As we mentioned above, when you create a random file, the L parameter of the OPEN statement tells ProDOS the length of each record in the file. This length is expressed as a number of bytes. It must be large enough to contain all the data in the largest record in the file plus one extra byte to store a carriage return.

If you use the WRITE statement to store more data than you have specified room for in the record, the excess data will be written into the next record. The results of this are normally disastrous. If there are already data in the following record, these data may become unreadable. It is usually a good idea to insert a test into your programs to prevent this if you are not sure that the record length is long enough.

For example, if you have opened a file with a record length of 10 and you wish to write the string "THIS IS A TEST" to record 1, the last four characters would be written to record 2. Record 1 would contain "THIS IS A ", and record 2 would contain "TEST" plus whatever was stored in the last six characters of record 2 before your PRINT statement was issued. To prevent this, you could compare the length of the string you are going to write to disk to the length of the record in the file. If the string is too long, your program could allow the operator to reenter the data. Another method for dealing with this problem would be to simply truncate all data being sent to the disk to fit the record length. This runs the risk of losing valuable data at the end of a string, but it does prevent the destruction of the following record.

When you write data to a random file, you must specify the number of the record you wish to use, or ProDOS will automatically write the data to record 0. Any data already stored in record 0 will be lost. Use the R parameter of the WRITE statement to specify the record number.

The following program creates a random file and stores a list of data in the records of the file. Note the use of the OPEN statement's L parameter and the WRITE statement's R parameter.

```
10    REM CREATE RANDOM FILE
20    D$ = CHR$(4)
30    DATA AXE,HAMMER,SAW,SCREWDRIVER
31    DATA PLIERS,WRENCH,PLANE,VISE,NAILS
100   HOME
110   VTAB 2: PRINT "CREATING A FILE"
120   GOSUB 1000
199   END
1000  PRINT D$; "OPEN RANDOM.DATA,L50"
```

```
1010   FOR A = 1 TO 9
1020   PRINT D$; "WRITE RANDOM.DATA,R";A
1030   READ B$
1040   PRINT B$
1050   NEXT A
1090   PRINT D$; "CLOSE RANDOM.DATA"
1099   RETURN
```

This program is very simple in execution. Once the file has been opened with a length of 50 by the statement in line 1000, it performs a FOR/NEXT loop between lines 1010 and 1050 nine times. On each execution of this loop, line 1020 sets the current position pointer to a different record within the file. ProDOS automatically handles all calculations involved in translating the record number to the correct number of bytes from the beginning of the file when setting the current position pointer. Every time line 1030 is executed, a new string is read into B$ from the data in lines 30 and 31. Line 1040 then prints the contents of B$ out to the disk. Once the loop is finished, the program closes the file and ends.

You can modify this program to accept any data you wish by replacing line 1030 with the statement INPUT B$. When this is done, the program ignores the DATA statements in lines 30 and 31 and looks to the keyboard for input data. The program will still perform the loop between lines 1010 and 1050 nine times, but there is no reason these values have to remain. If you wish to write the records 45 through 50 instead of 1 through 9, you could do so by changing line 1010 to read

```
1010   FOR A = 45 TO 50
```

Reading a Random Access File

When reading a random access file, you also have to use the L parameter in the OPEN statement to tell ProDOS the length of each record in the file. Again, this length is expressed as a number of bytes and must be exactly the same as the length that you used when creating the file. If you specify a different length, the data from the file will probably be unintelligible. (In ProDOS you can find the record length of a random file by using the CATALOG command to get a directory listing.)

When you read data from a random file, you must specify the number of the record you wish to use, or ProDOS will automatically read the data from record 0. Again, use the R parameter of the READ statement to specify the record number.

The following program opens a random file and reads a record from the file. The record number you input is the record that will be read from the file. Enter the number 10 when you want to stop the program. Note the use of the OPEN statement's L parameter and the READ statement's R parameter.

```
10    REM READ A RANDOM FILE
20    D$ = CHR$(4)
100   HOME
110   VTAB 2: PRINT "READING A FILE"
120   VTAB 20: PRINT "ENTER 10 TO END"
1000  VTAB 5: INPUT "RECORD # = ";A%
1010  IF A% < 1 OR A% > 10 GOTO 1000
1020  IF A% = 10 GOTO 1099
1030  PRINT D$; "OPEN RANDOM.DATA,L50"
1040  PRINT D$; "READ RANDOM.DATA,R";A%
1060  INPUT B$
1065  VTAB 9: CALL -868 : REM CLEARS SCREEN
1070  VTAB 9: PRINT "RECORD # ";A%;" = ";B$
1080  PRINT D$; "CLOSE RANDOM.DATA"
1090  GOTO 1000
1099  END
```

One feature worth noting in this program is the error-checking statement in line 1010. Without this statement it would be possible to enter a value such as 14, for which there is no corresponding record in the file. When ProDOS encounters a request to access a record that does not exist in a random file, it generates the RANGE ERROR message and causes a break in your program. This is why we chose the value 10 to end the program.

If you wish to use this program with more than nine records in the file, you will have to change the values in the IF test in lines

1010 and 1020. For example, if you want to have a file that will allow 99 records, and you want to end the program when you enter a value of 100, you will have to change the program as follows:

```
120   VTAB 20: PRINT "ENTER 100 TO END"
1010  IF A% < 1 OR A% > 100 GOTO 1000
1020  IF A% = 100 GOTO 1099
```

This will allow you to enter the greater values for A%. However, if you try to access a record that does not exist (i.e., the value Pro-DOS computes for the current position pointer based on the record number is beyond the end-of-file pointer in the directory entry), you will cause an error to occur.

Modifying Records in a Random Access File

A major advantage of random access files is the ability to modify existing records within the file. This is very difficult to do with sequential files because of the variable length of the records. But with a random access file you can simply read in the record you want, change the data as necessary, and write it back to the same position in the file.

The following program demonstrates this principle. This program allows you to read any record within the file RANDOM.DATA, modify it, and write it back to the disk.

```
10    REM MODIFY A RANDOM FILE
20    D$ = CHR$(4)
100   HOME
110   VTAB 2: PRINT "MODIFYING A RANDOM FILE"
120   VTAB 4: PRINT "ENTER STOP TO END"
130   GOSUB 1000
999   END
1000  PRINT D$; "OPEN RANDOM.DATA,L50"
1010  VTAB 10: INPUT "RECORD NUMBER = ";A%
1020  PRINT D$; "READ RANDOM.DATA,R";A%
1030  INPUT B$
```

```
1040   VTAB 12: PRINT B$
1050   PRINT D$; "WRITE RANDOM.DATA,R";A%
1060   VTAB 12: INPUT B$
1070   IF B$ = "STOP" THEN GOTO 1200
1080   PRINT B$
1090   GOTO 1010
1200   PRINT D$; "CLOSE RANDOM.DATA"
1299   RETURN
```

By using the arrow key you can move the cursor to where you want to make a change in the data and then just type over the other data. If you do this, make sure to continue to the end of the line before you press Return, or the data written back to the disk will be truncated at the position you press Return.

Adding to a Random Access File

The following program uses the APPEND command to add five records to the end of the file RANDOM.DATA. If you run this program after the create program, there should be a total of 14 records in the file. (If you have saved to disk the read program we provided, you can modify it slightly and use it to see the extra records. Simply change the value 10 in lines 120, 1010, and 1020 to 15. This will allow you to read the records from 10 to 14 and to end the program by entering 15.)

```
10     REM APPEND RANDOM FILE
20     D$ = CHR$(4)
30     DATA SHOES,SHIRT,PANTS,JACKET,TIE
100    HOME
110    VTAB 2: PRINT "APPENDING TO A FILE"
120    GOSUB 1000
199    END
1000   PRINT D$; "APPEND RANDOM.DATA,L50"
1010   FOR A = 1 TO 5
1030   READ B$
1040   PRINT B$
1050   NEXT A
```

```
1090  PRINT D$; "CLOSE RANDOM.DATA"
1099  RETURN
```

The APPEND statement has an advantage when you are adding records to the end of a random file. You will notice in the program above that the loop that writes data to the file does not contain a WRITE statement. When you are in an APPEND mode, there is no need to constantly issue WRITE statements with the record number you wish to use. This is because the current position pointer is constantly being updated as you send data to the disk. You should, however, check to see that this data is of the proper length by using the techniques discussed earlier. If you do not, the data you are sending to the disk may not match up with the record length of the file, and in that case you will be unable to read it back properly in subsequent programs. You would, however, be able to treat this file as a sequential file in order to retrieve the data. To do this you would have to open the file and read it through sequentially from beginning to end.

THE EXEC STATEMENT AND TEXT FILES

ProDOS has one more powerful statement for dealing with text files. This is the EXEC statement, which can be used to control the execution of common tasks or individual programs from a file.

The EXEC statement causes your Apple to take input from a disk file rather than from the keyboard. This disk file may contain a series of statements, such as RUN PROGRAM 1 or DELETE MYFILE, or it may contain a collection of data. It can also contain a combination of statements and data.

Before continuing, a few definitions are in order. An EXEC statement is a command and is used in the same fashion as all other ProDOS commands. An EXEC file is any text file containing data or commands used with the EXEC statement. An EXEC program is an EXEC file that contains commands to Applesoft or to ProDOS, as opposed to one that contains only data for input purposes.

The file used with an EXEC statement can be either a random file or a sequential file, but it is always treated as a sequential file (it's read from beginning to end in order). This is true even though you can refer to these files as EXEC files to designate that they are not standard data files.

When an EXEC command is issued, it remains in effect until the end of the file you specified in the command is reached. This is important to realize, because it means that you cannot interrupt an Applesoft program running under an EXEC command by typing Control-C—the Apple is looking at the EXEC file for input, not the keyboard. For this same reason, you will not be able to interrupt the execution of commands from an EXEC program, even when it is not executing an Applesoft program, by typing Control-C. You have to resort to drastic measures, such as turning off the computer, to stop an EXEC program.

You can use the F parameter with the EXEC command to skip a number of records at the beginning of the file. For example, if you have a file that contains ten commands and you want to execute only the last eight, you could use the statement

    EXEC EXEC1.EXE, F2

to skip the first two records in the file when it begins to execute the commands.

The EXEC command can be used in several different ways. For example, you can use an EXEC command with a file to control all the input into a program. This can be very useful for testing and debugging programs, because it allows you to keep one standard set of data for input as a test case. This eliminates typing mistakes and saves time in repeating the test of a program.

You can also use the EXEC command to issue a series of commands at the BASIC prompt. This allows you to set up standard procedures that require many steps and store them in a file on disk. Once this is done, you can repeat the entire procedure any number of times simply by using the EXEC command with the file that had that procedure stored in it.

Another major use of the EXEC command is to merge programs together. By doing this, you can avoid having to reenter the same lines of code for program after program. Partial programs as well as entire programs can be merged.

Examples of these functions are given in the sections that follow.

Creating an EXEC File

The following program creates a sequential file containing the instructions you type in. When you have typed in all the instructions you want in the file, enter the word STOP at the prompt. Your instructions or data will then be saved in the file for later use.

```
50    DIM B$(50)
100   D$ = CHR$(4)
110   GOSUB 1000
120   GOSUB 2000
999   END
1000  HOME : PRINT "EXEC INPUT PHASE": VTAB 4
1005  A = 0
1010  A = A + 1
1020  PRINT A;
1040  INPUT " ";B$(A)
1050  IF B$(A) = "STOP" GOTO 1090
1060  GOTO 1010
1090  B = A
1095  B$(A) = ""
1099  RETURN
2000  HOME : PRINT "EXEC FILE CREATION PHASE"
2010  PRINT D$; "OPEN EXEC1.EXE"
2020  PRINT D$; "WRITE EXEC1.EXE"
2030  FOR A = 1 TO B
2040  PRINT B$(A)
2050  NEXT A
2060  PRINT D$; "CLOSE EXEC1.EXE"
2099  RETURN
```

The first part of this program allows you to input as many as 50 lines of text into the B$ array. If you need more than this, you will have to change the DIM statement in line 50. If at any time you enter the string "STOP", the first subroutine will end and the second subroutine will write all of the lines you have input out to the file EXEC1.EXE. Line 1095 clears the "STOP" from the array so that it will not be written to the file.

If you had typed the three lines

```
CAT
DELETE RANDOM.DATA
CAT
```

into the file EXEC1.EXE and then used the statement EXEC EXEC1.EXE, each of these statements would be executed individually. First you would see ProDOS execute the CAT command, showing you all the files on the current disk. Then ProDOS would execute the DELETE statement (assuming RANDOM.DATA is on the disk). Finally, ProDOS would execute the second CAT statement showing you once again the files on the disk, from which RANDOM.DATA would be missing.

You can use this technique to run a series of programs simply by typing in a number of RUN commands as lines in the EXEC file and then using the EXEC statement with EXEC1.EXE.

Supplying Input Data with EXEC

One of the interesting things you can do with EXEC is write input data to files and then use that data to control the flow of a program. You can use the program listed above to create a file filled with numeric data rather than instructions and then type in and execute the following short program to see how this works in practice. This technique is widely used for demonstrations and tutorials.

```
 1   REM TEST OF EXEC
 5   D$ = CHR$(4)
10   ONERR GOTO 99
20   PRINT D$; "EXEC EXEC1.EXE"
30   INPUT A
40   INPUT B
50   INPUT C
```

```
55   D = C * (A / B)
60   PRINT "D = ";C;" * (";A;"/";B;")"
70   PRINT "D = ";D
80   GOTO 30
99   PRINT D$; "CLOSE EXEC1.EXE"
```

If you had created the file above with ten lines of text and those lines contained the values 5, 10, 12, 15, 16, 17, 21, 22, 23, and 50, the above program would execute three complete loops. The first time through the values of A, B, and C would be 5, 10, and 12. The second and third times through the loop would each select the next three values. On the fourth time through the loop A would get the value 50. But when the input statement in line 40 for B was executed, the end of the file would be encountered and the ONERR GOTO statement in line 10 would be activated. This would cause the file to be closed and the program to end.

It is important to note that the type of data that the EXEC statement reads from the file must match the variable type of the INPUT statement. If it does not, an error will occur. For example, if the first data item in the file were not 5, as in the above example, but instead "CAT", an error would occur when line 30 was executed. The string "CAT" cannot be put into the numeric variable A.

Using EXEC to Copy Programs

Very often you will find that you have already written a large portion of the code you need for a new program in other programs. This is particularly true if you follow modular programming practices and develop unique subroutines to perform common functions. You can use the EXEC command to copy your old code into your new BASIC program, saving yourself a lot of work.

To do this you first need to create a sequential text file that contains the lines of code you wish to copy. The following subroutine can be inserted in any program and then executed by the statement RUN 63500 to accomplish this. (This begins executing the program at line 63500.) The line numbers used with the LIST command can be changed to include only the lines you wish to copy.

```
63500   D$ = CHR$(4)
63506   INPUT "FILE:";XX$
63508   PRINT D$; "OPEN ";XX$
63510   PRINT D$; "WRITE ";XX$
63512   LIST 1,63499
63514   PRINT D$; "CLOSE ";XX$
63516   END
```

When this subroutine is executed, line 63512 causes all the program lines from 1 to 63499 to be printed out to a sequential text file. The variable XX$ is used to store the file name you input in line 63506. The name you enter is the name of the output file.

The second thing you have to do is use the EXEC command to get those lines of code included in your new program. You can do this by loading your new program into memory and entering EXEC with the file name you saved the code under. Since the contents of the file are commands with line numbers and are consequently executed only in deferred mode, they will simply be placed in memory with the rest of your program.

For example, if you have saved lines 500 through 1000 of your code in a file called CODE500 and your new program is in a file called NEWCODE, you can merge these two files in the following manner. First, enter the command LOAD NEWCODE. This will load your new program into memory. Second, enter the command EXEC CODE500. This will merge the contents of the CODE500 file with the NEWCODE file in memory. Third, save the program you now have in memory under whatever name you wish (for example, SAVE MERGED).

Be aware that any line in the EXEC file containing the same line number as the code in memory will replace that line when the EXEC file is read in.

HELPFUL HINTS

The following ideas are a collection of hints and suggestions that you may find helpful when programming with text files.

The READ and WRITE statements remain in effect until any other ProDOS command is issued. You will often find that you want to go to the keyboard for input immediately after receiving input data from a disk file and displaying it on the screen. Similar situations will arise when using the PRINT command after the WRITE statement. An easy way around this is to perform a GOSUB to a routine such as

    PRINT D$:PRINT:RETURN

What ProDOS actually needs to cancel the effect of a previous READ or WRITE statement is a Control-D character, not a ProDOS command. This subroutine serves to "wake up" ProDOS with the Control-D character without performing any ProDOS commands.

When you are using random files you must keep track of the record length of the file. Handwritten notes with file lengths often disappear when they are needed most. Many programmers include the length of the record in the name of the file to keep from losing it. Others always use record zero of a file to keep header information readily available, including the record length and the number of data elements in a record. Try these methods to see if they work for you.

This technique is no longer as important as it was under DOS 3.3, because you can now get the record length of a random access file from the ProDOS CATALOG command. However, you may still wish to use it to ensure compatibility with earlier versions of your programs or to provide documentation for moving files to an older DOS 3.3 system.

DIFFERENCES FROM DOS 3.3

The major improvement in the way ProDOS deals with text files is its ability to use the F and B parameters with the READ and WRITE commands. Under DOS, if you wanted to get to a particular location within the file, you had to either code a loop to read the file or use the separate POSITION statement. Because of this added ability, the POSITION statement becomes obsolete, although it has been included in ProDOS to maintain continuity with DOS.

The second major difference between DOS and ProDOS involves random files. DOS 3.3 stored all text files in the same way and did not keep track of the record length of each file in the directory. Therefore, you will not be able to transfer DOS random files to ProDOS random files. You can, however, transfer a DOS random file as a sequential file and then write a short program to read the sequential file and write a random file in ProDOS format.

ProDOS and Binary Files

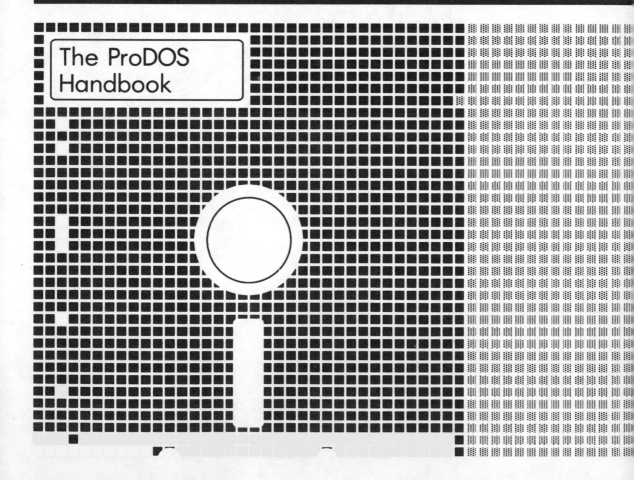

The ProDOS
Handbook

EIGHT

This chapter concentrates on the use of binary files under Pro-DOS. ProDOS treats these files similarly to text files, but because *any* type of data may be contained in a binary file, you must use special commands with binary files. These commands are BRUN, BLOAD, and BSAVE. We will be covering these commands and their use in the pages that follow.

BINARY FILES

Technically, all files are binary files. This includes text files and BASIC programs, as well as files that are listed with a ProDOS type of .BIN when you catalog them. This is because all data used by the computer are stored as binary data. ProDOS file types, such as TXT, BAS, and BIN (see Appendix A), are another level of categorization. Text files (type TXT), for example, are files that are treated according to special rules when accessed through the ProDOS commands. The BASIC statement INPUT will recognize the ASCII character 13 in text files as the end of a record.

For ProDOS, we will define binary files as type BIN files. These can be manipulated only with the BSAVE, BLOAD, and BRUN commands. Binary files can be saved directly from memory to disk or read from disk into memory with these commands. You can even designate exactly which area of memory you wish to save or write to. This can be a powerful tool when dealing with graphics or machine-language programs. It allows you to control the functioning of your computer with an accuracy and precision that the normal operations of the computer might not allow you.

For example, one common use of binary files is to load machine-language subroutines from disk into memory to be called by a BASIC program. The BASIC program must know precisely where to find the subroutine it wants, and that subroutine must be in an area of memory that will not be used by other parts of the program. The ability to load a file directly from disk to a specific area of memory is essential in this case.

Another big difference between binary files and other file types is that the BLOAD, BSAVE, and BRUN commands make no attempt to interpret the contents of the file they are transferring. This means that a character such as ASCII 13 will be treated exactly the same as every other character, not as an end-of-record marker.

This lack of data interpretation allows ProDOS to store machine-language programs in binary files without causing any errors. It also allows you to save graphics images from the graphics area of memory directly to disk and later recover them. These are the two most common uses for binary files.

PRODOS COMMANDS FOR BINARY FILES

ProDOS supplies three statements for dealing with binary files: BSAVE, BLOAD, and BRUN. These statements allow you to save binary data to disk, load binary files into memory from disk, and execute binary files as if they were programs. They are essentially the same as the SAVE, LOAD, and RUN statements used with BASIC programs, but BSAVE and BLOAD will operate with *any* file type. The BRUN command will work properly only with machine-language BIN files. To distinguish these commands from the commands that deal only with BASIC programs, they are all preceded with the letter B to designate them as binary file commands.

BSAVE, BLOAD, and BRUN also existed under DOS 3.3, but several improvements have been made that make them more flexible and powerful. For example, you can now load or run only a portion of a binary file if you wish, you can use two different methods to specify the length of a file, and BSAVE and BLOAD will now work with any type of file, not only with binary files.

You can also use the Dash command to attempt to run a binary file. This command works with binary files in the same way that it works with BAS, SYS, and EXE files. (SYS files are treated as BIN files by the Dash command; they are operating-system programs such as BASIC.SYSTEM.) You cannot, however, use any of the memory address options we will be discussing in this chapter with the Dash command.

ProDOS's improved directory structure records the memory address from which a file is saved (with BSAVE) in a directory entry with the file name. If you issue a BRUN or Dash command without specifying a load address, ProDOS uses the value in the directory entry as a default. This feature can save you much time and trouble when you need to run a program.

A word of caution is needed on the use of the BRUN and Dash commands. The BRUN command checks to see if the file type is BIN, but it cannot check to see if the file contains a valid program. Since a type BIN file can contain anything at all, from a valid machine-language program to graphics data to numeric data or even random data from previous programs, there can be no guarantees that the file you try to run with BRUN will execute successfully. If the file contains a valid program, it will. If it does not, it might or it might not. Graphics data, for example, will be interpreted by the BRUN statement as machine-language commands, and some or all of this data might combine to form a series of instructions the Apple can execute. A series of syntax errors might be generated, your system might lock up and have to be rebooted, or nothing at all might happen. It is even possible, as in the example of a monkey pounding on a typewriter for a million years, producing the works of Shakespeare by pure chance, that a valid, worthwhile program would be found.

This is also true with the Dash command, although this command does not even check the file type. Experiment with this yourself. Use the Dash command to attempt to run a file that should not run, such as a text file. Try it on more than one file, and note the different results you produce.

This is what we mean when we say that you can "attempt" to run a file. The BRUN or Dash commands will load the file and will begin to execute the first instruction (the first byte of the file). If the contents of the file do not represent a valid series of commands, your Apple will not be able to successfully complete the execution of the "program."

BSAVE

The BSAVE statement writes the specified number of bytes directly from the active memory of your Apple to the disk file you specify in the command. If that file does not already exist on the disk, a new file will be created. The contents of any existing file with the path name you specify will be destroyed and replaced with the new information. If you use the T parameter with this statement, you can save any type of file from the disk into memory. If you do not use the T parameter, you can save only binary files. Any attempt to do otherwise will cause a FILE TYPE MISMATCH error.

You must use the A parameter (which specifies the starting memory address) and either the L or the E parameter (which both specify the ending memory address) with this command. This is so that ProDOS can determine the starting point in memory and the number of bytes to write to disk. You can also use the B parameter we discussed in Chapter 7 with the BSAVE command to specify the first byte within the file that is to be written to, so that ProDOS will know where to start within the file itself.

If you do not specify these parameters, two different things can happen. If you use BSAVE to save a file that does not yet exist on the disk, ProDOS reads the directory from the disk and comes back with the message

PATH NOT FOUND

If the file already exists on disk, ProDOS reads the directory to obtain the information about the starting address and length of the file and then saves it from memory. This has advantages. When you are dealing with graphics files, for example, the starting address and length are unlikely to change often. The ability to simply type BSAVE and the file name can save you some fumbling with the manual to find out where the graphics area begins, although you still will need to use the A and L or E parameters when the file is first saved. The disadvantage to this feature is that your program or data must be in exactly the right spot for the command to work correctly. If you have moved your code around in memory, possibly using one area for development and another area for execution, remember that the address on file in the directory will be the one from which it was last saved with the complete BSAVE command—BSAVE plus the path name, the A parameter, and the L or E parameter. If that address and length are different from the area you are now trying to save, your code on disk will be replaced by whatever is now in the memory area from which the file was last saved.

The BSAVE command makes no distinctions about the type of data it is saving. It works with any legitimate range of memory, as long as there is a sufficient amount of disk space available to store the contents. The data being saved do not have to comprise a valid program; indeed, they do not have to consist of coded instructions of any kind. This makes it possible to store images from the Apple's graphics pages, which can then be recalled swiftly and accurately with the BLOAD statement.

BLOAD

The BLOAD statement is used to transfer the contents of a file directly from disk to memory. If you use the T parameter with this statement, you can load any type of file from the disk into memory. If you do not use the T parameter, you can load only binary files. Any attempt to do otherwise will cause a FILE TYPE MISMATCH error.

The BLOAD statement requires the A parameter (the starting memory address) whenever the file to be loaded is not a binary file. This is because the address from which a BIN file was BSAVEd is stored in the directory entry. When no address is specified in the BLOAD statement, the address in the directory is used as a default. But files that were not BSAVEd do not store this address, which is why you need the A parameter when BLOAD is used with non-binary files.

The E or L parameter can be used to specify the number of bytes you wish to read from the file. In this way you can treat a binary file as a library. For instance, you might have a number of different machine-language routines saved in a single binary file. You can make more efficient use of the available space by reading only the ones you need out of the file and into memory. The B parameter we discussed in Chapter 7 can be used in conjunction with this to skip a specified number of bytes in the file.

The BLOAD statement can be a very dangerous command, because the operating system will make no attempt to prevent you from writing over any area of memory. This means that you could cause your system to lock up, or you could write the data from the binary file into locations where important data is stored. If the program or data you have thus wiped out has not previously been saved to disk, it will be gone for all time. You should always be careful to save any new programs or sensitive data you have entered before you use the BLOAD command. You would also be well advised to check your calculations concerning the correct memory locations before executing this command.

BRUN

The BRUN statement can be used to load and execute a binary file. In practice, this is equivalent to first issuing a BLOAD statement and then transferring control to the instructions at the starting address where the program has been loaded. For this reason, the list of parameters that can be used with the BRUN statement is almost exactly the same as that for the BLOAD statement. The exception to this is the T parameter, which is not necessary because the BRUN statement can be used only with binary files (type BIN).

Although the BRUN statement protects you from running non-binary files, it does not protect you from running BIN files that do not contain valid machine-language programs. For example, if you use the BRUN statement on a binary file that contains an image from the Apple's graphics page, anything might happen. There might be an immediate error that would cause execution to halt, or even worse, there might by random chance be a valid series of instructions that would cause your Apple to do something—something quite literally unpredictable and that might be anything at all, including deleting files from the disk.

In order to reduce the risk of running nonprogram BIN files, many programmers use descriptive names on their files. Apple suggests, for example, that files containing images saved from the graphics pages always end with the extension .PIC. You can then determine at a glance whether a file contains a program or data. For example, the statement

BSAVE TEST1.PIC,A8192,E16383

will write a type BIN file to disk with the name TEST1.PIC. You will be able to recognize this easily as a graphics file by the .PIC in the file name when scanning the results of any CAT or CATALOG command.

The Memory Address Options and the T Parameter

In addition to the slot and drive parameters, each of the three binary commands may use any or all of the following memory address options. Each one of these has a particular meaning when attached to one of the binary commands.

The A option is an option only with the BLOAD and BRUN commands; it *must* be used with the BSAVE command. This parameter specifies the starting memory address at which you wish to either save or load a binary file. The value after the letter A may be given in either decimal or hexadecimal form. For example, the following two statements are identical:

```
BSAVE TEST,A8200,E8300
BSAVE TEST,A$2008,E8300
```

Both of these statements will cause the area of memory from address 8200 through address 8300 to be sent to disk by the BSAVE command. Notice that the second statement contains one value in decimal and the other in hexadecimal. They will both be evaluated correctly.

The E parameter is used to give the address of the last byte to be moved. This value must be greater than the value supplied in the A parameter. The value is inclusive, meaning that the byte of data stored in the location given in the E parameter will also be stored. The E and A parameters enable you to read and write blocks of data to and from memory. For example, if you want to write exactly 100 bytes starting in location 8192 to memory, you can use the following statement:

```
BSAVE TEST,A8192,E8291
```

The L parameter is used to specify a length in bytes. This is simply a different way of looking at the E parameter. The L parameter specifies the number of bytes to be saved, while the E parameter specifies the last byte to be saved. The value in the L parameter is always equal to the ending address (E) minus the starting address (A) plus 1. For example, the following statements are equivalent:

```
BSAVE TEST,A8192,E8291
BSAVE TEST,A8192,L100
```

Both of these statements will cause the area of memory from address 8192 through address 8291 to be sent to disk by the BSAVE command.

The T parameter can be specified when you wish to use the BSAVE or BLOAD commands with a nonbinary file. This parameter will not work with the BRUN command. The three characters comprising the file type are included after the letter T to notify Pro-DOS that you wish to use a non-BIN file with this command. For example, the following statement could be used to load the BASIC program SEQ.CREATE at location 3000 of memory:

BLOAD SEQ.CREATE,A3000,TBAS

If you want to use the BSAVE command with a nonbinary file that is not yet on disk, you must first set up that file with the Pro-DOS CREATE command using using the T parameter with the proper file type. For example, the following two statements create and save a type $F1 file on disk:

CREATE TEST,T$F1
BSAVE TEST,A8192,L100,T$F1

Appendix A lists the valid ProDOS file types. The only user-defined file types allowed begin with $F and must end in a number from one to eight.

Why would you want to use the BLOAD or BSAVE commands with a nonbinary file? The answers to that can be as varied as your imagination. The files might contain data that you need in specific locations for a machine-language program or data you wish to display. You might want to create your own file types for some purpose. You might want to use certain files in a way that ProDOS would not ordinarily allow, such as to read and write BASIC programs from within a program, as a text editor must do. The ability of ProDOS to access any file with the BLOAD and BSAVE commands allows you the freedom to do these and many other things.

You can also use the B parameter discussed in the last chapter with the binary commands. For example, the following statement skips the first 50 bytes of a file when loading it into memory at location 8192:

BLOAD TEST,A8192,B50

This parameter can also be used to skip over bytes of a file on disk when writing with the BSAVE command. The ability to skip over sections of a file can be important if you are interested in only a portion of a file. For example, you may wish to use binary search-ing to locate a particular item or string. (Binary searching is a fast method of searching through an ordered list by selecting the mid-point and comparing the data there to the item you are searching for. If the data is less than the item, you search above that point; if the data is greater, you search below that point.) Assuming you knew the file was in order, this might be the fastest method of find-ing a record in a large file. Or if your binary file contains a library of machine-language routines, you may want to load only those routines in the second half of the file, for example. Using a binary file in this way is discussed, with a programming example, at the end of this chapter.

USING BINARY FILES

Now that we have described how the commands work, we will show how they might be used from within a BASIC program. The following sections will give examples of how to use the BSAVE and BLOAD commands with a common graphics application. We will then discuss the advantages of programming in machine language and using the BRUN command to execute a file.

Creating a Binary File

Binary files are created automatically when the BSAVE command is used without the T parameter. These files are always stored as type BIN. You can also use the CREATE command to allocate a type BIN file. The CREATE command will not cause any data to be written to the file. Files created with the CREATE command will be empty until you write something to them.

The following program creates three small binary files that store images from the Apple's high-resolution graphics pages. Once you have created the images and stored them, you can recall them any time you wish.

```
10   REM PRODOS BINARY STATEMENTS
11   REM BSAVE DEMO
```

```
  20   HOME
  30   D$ = CHR$(4)
 100   GOSUB 1000
 110   GOSUB 2000
 120   GOSUB 3000
 150   TEXT
 199   END
1000   REM DRAW SHAPE 1 AND SAVE
1010   HGR : HCOLOR= 3
1020   HPLOT 5,5 TO 274,5 TO 274,136 TO 5,136 TO 5,5
1030   PRINT D$;"BSAVE BINARY1,A8192,E16383"
1999   RETURN
2000   REM DRAW SHAPE 2 AND SAVE
2010   HGR : HCOLOR= 3
2020   HPLOT 10,10 TO 269,10 TO 269,131 TO 10,131 TO 10,10
2025   HPLOT 130,10 TO 130,131
2030   PRINT D$;"SAVE BINARY2,A8192,E16383"
2999   RETURN
3000   REM DRAW SHAPE 3 AND SAVE
3010   HGR : HCOLOR= 3
3020   HPLOT 15,15 TO 264,15 TO 264,126 TO 15,126 TO 15,15
3025   HPLOT 15,60 TO 264,60
3030   PRINT D$;"BSAVE BINARY3,A8192,E16383"
3999   RETURN
```

In each of the subroutines in this program (1000, 2000, and 3000), the same procedure is followed. First, an HGR instruction is executed to clear the high-resolution graphics area and switch your Apple from displaying the text area of memory to displaying the graphics area of memory. Second, a figure is drawn in the high-resolution area of memory. Third, a command is issued to ProDOS to BSAVE a file from memory. The A and E parameters used here specify the contents of the high-resolution area of the Apple's memory. ProDOS will have the correct starting address information stored in the directory and will use it as the default address when loading the file.

Loading a Binary File

Once you have saved the data in a binary file on disk, you will most likely want to recover that information and use it in other programs. You can do this with the BLOAD statement. The program that follows demonstrates a typical use of the BLOAD statement, the loading of binary graphics information directly from disk into the high-resolution graphics pages. We will use the files saved in the previous example to demonstrate this.

```
  10   REM PRODOS BINARY STATEMENTS
  11   REM BLOAD DEMO
  20   HOME
  30   D$ = CHR$(4)
 100   GOSUB 1000
 110   GOSUB 2000
 120   GOSUB 3000
 150   TEXT
 199   END
1000   REM LOAD SHAPE 1 AND DISPLAY
1005   HGR
1010   PRINT D$;"BLOAD BINARY1"
1030   VTAB 22: INPUT "HIT RETURN TO CONTINUE ";W$
1999   RETURN
2000   REM LOAD SHAPE 2 AND DISPLAY
2005   HGR
2010   PRINT D$;"BLOAD BINARY2"
2030   VTAB 22: INPUT "HIT RETURN TO CONTINUE ";W$
2999   RETURN
3000   REM LOAD SHAPE 3 AND DISPLAY
3005   HGR
3010   PRINT D$;"BLOAD BINARY3"
3030   VTAB 22: INPUT "HIT RETURN TO CONTINUE ";W$
3999   RETURN
```

In each of the subroutines in this program (1000, 2000, and 3000), the same procedure is followed. First an HGR instruction is executed to clear the high-resolution graphics area and switch your Apple from displaying the text area of memory to displaying the graphics area of memory. Second, a command is issued to ProDOS to BLOAD a file into memory. Since these are the files we saved from the high-resolution area in the previous program, ProDOS will have the correct starting address information stored in the directory and will use it as the default address. If you want to use a file that was not saved from this area, you would have to specify the starting address with the A option (for example, BLOAD SOME-FILE,A8192). Then the program positions the cursor and waits for an input before continuing, to allow time to view the result.

Note that you do not have to issue any other command to display these files once they are loaded into memory. Your Apple constantly updates the monitor with the contents of the memory area being displayed. Since we have placed the Apple in high-resolution mode, simply changing the contents of high-resolution memory changes the display on the screen.

Running a Binary File

The main reason programs are written in machine language is that they execute much faster. This is because the computer does not have to spend time interpreting instructions; it can simply execute them. It is also true that it generally takes much longer to write a program in machine language or in assembly language (which is then converted into machine language) than it does to write a comparable program in a higher level language such as BASIC. Because of this, compilers have been developed for the higher level languages that gain much of the speed of execution available with machine language without sacrificing the ease of development you have with higher level languages. These compilers translate BASIC statements into machine language and save the results on disk to speed up the execution of your program.

The savings in time is a result of the program being *executed* in a machine-language form. While this produces a program that will run faster, this process of compiling the program adds to the development time because a program must be recompiled every time a change is made. The binary or machine-language program, generated by machine or assembly programming or a high level compiler, is stored on disk as a binary file. Because this program is in the native language of the machine, it does not have to be run through an interpreter before it can be executed. This is why a machine-language program will always execute faster than a BASIC program that does the exact same thing—each instruction of the BASIC program must be interpreted every time it is executed. A compiled BASIC program will run faster because it already has been translated to the machine's native language. (Note: some languages, such as Pascal, compile from the source code to a psuedo-code or p-code, which is not in machine language and must be interpreted when the program is run.)

In any of these cases it is necessary to execute the instructions in the resulting binary file. ProDOS provides the BRUN and Dash commands for this purpose. The Dash command automatically loads the program into the area of memory it was saved from and then attempts to execute it. As mentioned above, the BRUN command allows you to specify where to load the program as one of its parameters.

Binary Files and Machine-Language Routines

If you do much programming, you will find it advantageous to convert certain common functions to machine language and store them on disk, where they can be used to benefit all your BASIC programs. In this way you gain many of the advantages of machine-language programs while still using BASIC as your primary programming language.

The ability to save selected areas of memory to disk files and to use the B parameter to control which area of the file you are writing the data to means that you can construct library files composed of machine-language routines. A library file is a file composed of many different units, each of which is independent of the others. By keeping track of where each routine is in the file, you can use the binary commands to save and load only the portions of the file you need. This means that you could have a library file composed of 100 common machine-language routines used by a program that required only a few of them. Your BASIC program can selectively read into memory the routines it needs while ignoring all the others. This technique is very effective in saving programming time, execution time, and memory space.

For example, suppose you knew that the longest of the 100 routines mentioned above was 50 bytes long. You could space your routines so that a new one started exactly every 50 bytes within the file, with the first one starting at byte 0, the next at byte 50, and so on. Then when you need to read one of these routines in, you simply multiply to get the correct starting position ((routine number − 1) × 50) and use the BLOAD command with the B parameter set to your result. Assuming that R is the variable that contains the routine number, the following statements would accomplish this for you:

```
50000   N = (R − 1) * 50
50010   PRINT D$;"BLOAD LIB.ROUTINE,A8000,L50,B";N
```

The variable D$ is, of course, our old friend CHR$(4). The statement in line 50010 will load exactly 50 bytes from the file to memory location 8000, starting at the position in the file calculated by line 50000.

This method will always waste space in the file, because routines shorter than 50 bytes will still be allotted 50 bytes to maintain a regular interval between routines. The only way to avoid this loss of space is to know the exact length of each routine at all times. If you want to do this, you must either keep the information available in your program (probably by storing it in an array) or keep it on disk in some file that your program can read. The first 100 bytes of your file could be used to store this information as binary data. Your program would have to read this index first so that it would know where to find the other routines. Your program would then have to total the lengths of all the previous routines and add 100 bytes for the index to calculate the starting position of a particular routine. For example, routine 43 would start at the sum total of the lengths of the first 42 routines plus 100 bytes.

This leaves the question of how to get the routines to the disk in the first place. You should add routines to a disk file only at the end of the file, or you will lose any routines that follow the one you are saving to the disk. For example, suppose you want to save a new version of routine 10 to your file. You are spacing the routines 50 bytes apart, so you know that routine 10 begins at byte 450 in the file ((10 − 1) × 50). If you use the BSAVE command with the B parameter set to 450, the file would end at byte 499 and routines 11 through 100 would be lost. This is clearly not what you want to do.

If, however, you use the BLOAD command to place the contents of your file in memory, you can edit the routines as you wish and then save the results back to disk with the BSAVE command. With this method you do not face the possibility of losing your code, and you have the entire file in memory, where you can work on it more easily. If you are working from BASIC, you will have to edit using the BASIC PEEK and POKE commands. You can also use the Apple's Monitor (described in Chapter 11) to change the contents of memory as you wish.

If you use this technique to store machine-language routines, be sure to keep a record of which routine does what and any data requirements the routines might have. ProDOS does not offer any features to help you with this. *You* will have to record the information, either in a file on disk or simply on paper. Once your record is lost, the only thing you can do is read your code to reconstruct the lost information. With machine code, this is a very difficult and unpleasant thing to do.

Graphics and
Sound in ProDOS

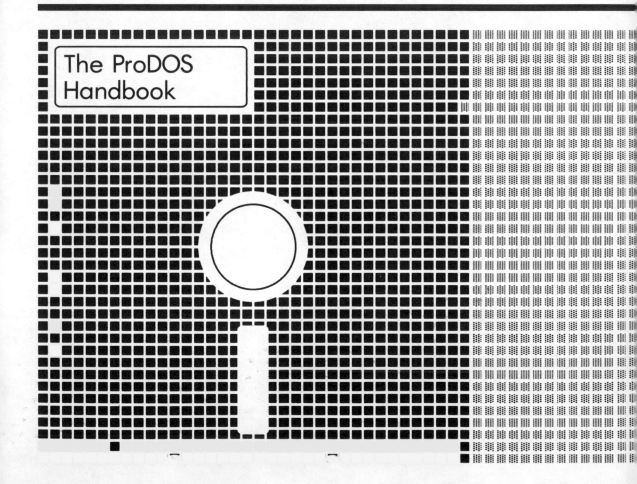

The ProDOS
Handbook

NINE

Your Apple II computer offers a number of special features that allow you to take advantage of its graphics and sound capabilities. You can use these features directly from BASIC with the GR, HGR, and HGR2 commands. They can be manipulated with more precision by a series of PEEKs and POKEs to the appropriate locations. How you use the graphics areas is particularly important under ProDOS because of the large amount of memory ProDOS requires. ProDOS is a larger operating system than the older DOS 3.3 and leaves less memory available for the programmer. To make up for this memory shortage, ProDOS allows Applesoft programs to use the high-resolution graphics area for additional space when necessary. This fact places a premium on the efficient use of the memory that is available. In this chapter we will discuss the ways in which programmers can make the best use of the graphics and sound features under ProDOS.

GRAPHICS AND MEMORY

The text and graphics displays of your Apple II are mapped directly into particular locations in memory. There are three different modes of display used by your Apple: text, low-resolution graphics, and high-resolution graphics. The areas that are displayed on the screen are referred to as pages of memory; each of the three display modes has two separate pages that can be displayed. The text and low-resolution graphics displays share the same area of memory, while the high-resolution graphics display uses an entirely separate area of memory.

When your Apple displays information on the screen, it checks certain memory locations to see which display mode it is in and which screen page it should display. The values in these locations are automatically changed when you use the TEXT, GR, HGR, or HGR2 commands from BASIC. In addition, you can change the values in these locations with the POKE command to allow you greater control over which area and mode your Apple will be using.

During normal operation your Apple uses the text display mode. You can, however, cause it to display data in either the low-resolution or high-resolution graphics mode. In either graphics mode, the Apple controls the display by matching the value in a particular location in memory to a particular location on the screen and turning the display on or off for that one location. In low-resolution graphics mode the Apple displays 40 columns and 48 rows of information. In high-resolution mode the Apple displays 280 columns and 192 rows of information.

The High-Resolution Graphics Area

The high-resolution graphics pages occupy the area between $2000–$5FFF (8192–24575) in memory. The first half of this area represents high-resolution graphics page 1, and the second half represents high-resolution graphics page 2. These areas are independent of the area in memory used for displaying text and low-resolution graphics. The HGR command causes the Apple to use page 1 as the display area, and the HGR2 command causes it to use page 2.

The Text and Low-Resolution Graphics Area

The text and low-resolution graphics pages use the same area of memory. This is possible because the difference between the text and graphics mode is not caused by a difference in data. The same data, stored in exactly the same location, will result in different displays on the screen.

The difference is caused by the way the different modes interpret the data contained in a byte. The text mode looks at the numeric value represented in the binary value of a byte to determine which ASCII character is to be displayed. For example, a byte that contains the value 86 ($56 or 01010110 in binary) will display the character V. The graphics mode, on the other hand, maps each bit of every byte to a particular pixel (one dot) on the screen. A bit can have a value of only zero or one. The graphics mode uses these values to determine whether the pixel in a particular location should be turned on or off. This means that a byte containing the value 86 ($56 or binary 01010110) would have four pixels on and four off.

The text and low-resolution graphics page 1 area of memory extends from $0400–$07FF (1024–2047). Page 2 of text and low-resolution graphics memory occupies the area from $0800–$0BFF (2048–3071). Because this area of memory is shared between the two modes, things that are printed or drawn in memory in either of these modes can sometimes disrupt the display in the other mode when you switch from one to the other.

Page 2 of the text and low-resolution graphics area is rarely used, because no BASIC command directly addresses it—it can be accessed only through a series of POKE commands.

The POKE Command and Display Modes

You can use the POKE command to set a series of switches in the memory of your Apple to tell it which area should be displayed.

The locations that will affect these changes are listed for easy reference in Table 8.1. The commands will be discussed in greater detail in the sections that follow, with the display modes they affect.

LOW-RESOLUTION GRAPHICS

The BASIC GR statement switches the display monitor from text to low-resolution graphics mode. When this statement is executed, the screen clears and the color is set to black. The bottom four lines (eight rows) of the screen remain open as a window into the text area. Your computer remains in low-resolution graphics mode until you issue a TEXT command.

The TEXT command returns the Apple to the normal, full-screen text mode. This command does not clear the screen when it executes, but it does try to interpret as text any graphics information it finds. This means that you will probably see a number of odd characters on the screen. For this reason, when you use the TEXT command in a program you will probably want to follow it with the HOME statement.

You can also switch from text to low-resolution graphics mode by issuing the commands

    POKE – 16304,0
    POKE – 16298,0

The first command sets the display mode to graphics. The second command defines the graphics mode as low resolution.

Location	Effect
– 16297	High-resolution graphics
– 16298	Low-resolution graphics
– 16299	Page 2
– 16300	Page 1
– 16301	Graphics with text window display
– 16302	Full screen graphics (no text window)
– 16303	Text only
– 16304	Graphics (from text)

Table 9.1: POKE Locations Affecting the Display Areas

The POKE statement can also be used to close the text window so that you can replace the bottom four lines (eight rows) of the screen with graphics. The statement

POKE − 16302,0

will make the text window disappear. You can reopen the text window by issuing the GR command, which also clears the screen and resets the color to black. If you do not wish to clear the screen, you can simply issue the command

POKE − 16301,0

which reopens the text window without disturbing the first 40 rows of graphics. The following program demonstrates the use of POKE statements in connection with the low-resolution screen text window:

```
10   REM LOW-RESOLUTION GRAPHICS
11   REM POKES AND THE TEXT WINDOW
20   GR : COLOR= 2
30   HLIN 10,30 AT 5: HLIN 10,30 AT 16
40   VLIN 6,15 AT 10: VLIN 6,15 AT 30
50   INPUT "HIT RETURN TO ERASE THIS WINDOW ";A$
60   HOME : POKE − 16302,0
70   COLOR = 0
72   FOR A = 41 TO 47: HLIN 0,39 AT A: NEXT A
74   COLOR = 2
80   FOR A = 2 TO 38 STEP 2
82   PLOT A,42
84   NEXT A
90   FOR A = 1 TO 5000: NEXT A
95   POKE − 16301,0: HOME
100  INPUT "HIT RETURN TO GO BACK TO TEXT MODE ";A$
110  TEXT : HOME
```

This program begins by clearing the screen and going into graphics mode. Lines 30 and 40 draw a box on the screen. Line 50 simply waits for you to hit Return before continuing. Once you do, the screen is cleared and the text window is closed by the POKE statement in line 60. Lines 70 to 84 draw a figure in the area where the text window used to be. A delay loop in line 90 allows you to see the result before the program brings the text window back. Finally, the program waits for another carriage return before it returns to text mode.

There are two POKE commands that affect the page of memory that is displayed on the screen. Issuing the command

    POKE – 16299,0

always switches the display to page 2 of any mode you are in. The command

    POKE – 16300,0

switches you to page 1 of the text or graphics mode you are currently in. Issuing a POKE to location – 16299 is the only way you can display page 2 of the text or low-resolution graphics area. These same commands also affect the display of the high-resolution graphics pages.

HIGH-RESOLUTION GRAPHICS

The HGR statement sets the high-resolution graphics mode, leaving four lines open for a text window at the bottom of the screen. The screen clears and displays page 1 of high-resolution memory. The drawing color is not changed from that currently in use. Because the text mode and the high-resolution graphics mode occupy two different areas of memory, the actual text area of memory is still 24 lines long, but only four lines are displayed on the screen. If the cursor is located anywhere other than the bottom four lines of the screen, it is not visible.

The HGR2 statement places your Apple in full-screen, high-resolution graphics mode. It sets the graphics mode to high resolution, clears high-resolution page 2, and displays it. This command does not affect the contents of the low-resolution and text pages, nor does it affect the contents of page 1 of high-resolution memory. HGR2 does not reserve the bottom four lines of the screen for a window into the text area. The drawing color remains exactly as it was before the HGR2 statement was executed.

Because the HGR and HGR2 statements address different areas of memory, it is possible to draw different figures in page 1 and page 2 and create the illusion of movement by switching back and forth from one page to the other. You can also keep two totally unrelated figures in the different areas of memory, if you wish, and still make rapid changes from one page to the other. However, if you use HGR and HGR2 to switch back and forth from one page to the other, the very act of switching will destroy the images you have created. This is because these commands automatically clear the area of memory they are going to display when they are issued.

For this reason, you should use the POKE command to switch the display page when you want to avoid destroying the images you have created. If you are currently in high-resolution graphics and you wish to display page 1, issue the commands

POKE -10300,0

The command

POKE -16299,0

switches the display to page 2. Neither of these commands will have an effect if you are already displaying the page specified. The advantage to using these commands is that the contents of the relevant pages of memory will not be changed. (These are the same commands that allow you to switch pages of the text or low-resolution graphics areas.)

If you are not already in high-resolution mode and you wish to display one of the high-resolution pages, you can use the POKE command to set high-resolution mode without erasing either page of high-resolution memory. If you are in low-resolution mode, you can switch to high resolution by issuing the command

POKE -16297,0

If you are in text mode and you want to switch directly into high-resolution graphics, issue the command

POKE – 16304,0
POKE – 16297,0

These commands do not erase the contents of any area of display memory. If you have previously switched to page 2 of the text or low-resolution graphics display with POKE – 16299,0, you will be in page 2 of high-resolution graphics after these commands. Otherwise, you will be in page 1.

If you are in any graphics mode (low resolution or high resolution), the command

POKE – 16303,0

will place you in text mode. The page of memory you are displaying will depend on which page you were in before the command was issued.

SAVING THE GRAPHICS PAGE

As we mentioned in Chapter 8, you can use the ProDOS BSAVE statement to place the contents of any graphics page in a disk file. All you need to make use of this feature is to know the beginning and ending locations of the page you wish to save. For example, high-resolution graphics page 1 starts at location 8192 and ends in location 16383. The command

BSAVE HR1,A8192,E16383

will save the entire 8K of high-resolution graphics page 1 to a binary file named HR1. You can then reload this file using the BLOAD statement to restore the contents of your graphics page. Because with the BLOAD command a file can be reloaded into any area of memory you specify, you can just as easily load it starting at location 16384 and use it in high-resolution graphics page 2.

Remember that both the BLOAD and BSAVE ProDOS statements will work in immediate mode. This means that you can use the BSAVE command to store the contents of your graphics pages even if your program has aborted. Simply use the BSAVE command directly from the BASIC prompt with the appropriate parameters; if you have not done anything to change the contents of the graphics pages since your program stopped, the exact images you left behind will be saved to disk.

You can also use the BLOAD statement to explore the contents of disk files to see if they contain graphics information. To do this, you would first have to execute one of the graphics commands (GR, HGR, HGR2). Then you would use BLOAD to load the file you wish to examine to a graphics area and observe the results. The Apple interprets whatever data you load into the display area according to the mode it is in. You will see an image on the screen corresponding to the data in the file. Even if the file you are examining is not a graphics file, the display will still appear. You can then decide whether the image you see is something you want.

PROTECTING THE GRAPHICS PAGE

If you study the memory map of your Apple given in Appendix J of this book, you will notice that the high-resolution graphics pages lie directly in the middle of the area used by your Apple for Applesoft programs. (This is because ProDOS is a larger operating system than DOS 3.3 and thus leaves less space available to BASIC programs in memory.) As your program grows in memory (either through the addition of program lines or through changes due to variable storage and usage), the area of your high-resolution graphics pages can be disrupted. ProDOS does not protect these areas of memory, and they will be overwritten by your program code if Applesoft needs the space for other purposes.

There is only one way to protect this area, and that is by using the HIMEM: and LOMEM: statements. You can, for example, set LOMEM to 24576, which will keep your Applesoft program above high-resolution page 2 in memory. You can also set HIMEM to 8191 and keep your entire program below high-resolution page 1. These statements protect your graphics areas, but it is at the cost of restricting the size of your program. For this reason, you may find that it is better to use only one page of high-resolution graphics and free the area of the other one for use by your program.

If you are going to use the HIMEM: and LOMEM: statements to control and protect memory, you need to know what they represent. HIMEM sets the value of the highest memory location that is available for use by Applesoft. LOMEM sets the value of the lowest memory location available for use by Applesoft.

When a program is executing, all the lines of code are below LOMEM. All variables are stored in the area between LOMEM and HIMEM. Applesoft stores variables and their constants in a particular way. Integer and real variables are allocated space in the order they are encountered, beginning at LOMEM and ascending towards HIMEM. String variables are allocated differently. The actual contents of string variables are stored beginning at HIMEM and grow down towards LOMEM as space is used up. But the pointers to the contents of the strings are allocated in the same way that integer and real variables are allocated (that is, beginning at LOMEM and continuing towards HIMEM).

If the string variables grow down into the high-resolution area, they will replace the graphics data stored there and change your screen display if you are using high-resolution graphics. The same thing will happen if the integer and real variables grow up into the high-resolution display area.

When your program is first loaded into memory, LOMEM is set to the location one byte above the end of the last program line. HIMEM is set to the location one byte below the BASIC.SYSTEM program ($BF00). If you do not wish to use high-resolution graphics, you can simply leave these values alone and the space will be used when it is needed by the program. However, if you are using the graphics area and need to protect it, you must either set HIMEM below it or LOMEM above it to keep it secure. Since setting HIMEM below the high-resolution graphics area constricts a program greatly, you will normally set LOMEM to a higher value.

The value of HIMEM is affected by the ProDOS OPEN and CLOSE commands. When a file is opened, ProDOS reduces the value of HIMEM by 1K (1024 bytes) and allocates a 1K buffer for file input and output. This buffer will always begin and end exactly on a page boundary in memory (that is, a multiple of 256 bytes). When a file is closed, ProDOS reverses this procedure. The value of HIMEM increases by 1K. This is true even if the file that is closed is not the most recently opened file. ProDOS pushes the contents of the lower buffers up to the higher buffers to accomplish this.

The result of these actions by ProDOS is that HIMEM has become a constantly shifting value. This shifting can be minimized if you open all your files at the beginning of your program and leave them open until the end of your program. It also forms another argument for not reducing the value of HIMEM unnecessarily, because ProDOS will reduce the value whenever it needs to assign a new buffer. When it does, all the strings below it are shifted downward and may be pushed into the graphics area. If you are using the graphics area, this string data will overwrite the graphics data. The string data is then interpreted as graphics data and displayed on the screen.

GENERATING SOUND

Your Apple contains a small speaker located under the keyboard of your machine. You can use this device to generate simple sounds from within your programs. The speaker is extremely easy to use, because there is only one location that affects it. Unfortunately, this also limits what you can do with the speaker device.

You can make the speaker on your Apple click simply by using the PEEK command to look at location −16336. (You can also use the POKE command.) Because every time you PEEK (or POKE) at this location the speaker clicks, you can change the quality of the sound you hear by changing the frequency with which you PEEK at location −16336—the higher the frequency, the higher the sound. The following program demonstrates this:

```
10   REM SOUND DEMO
100  HOME
110  VTAB 5: INPUT "DELAY: ";D
```

```
150  FOR A = 1 TO 100
160  S = PEEK ( – 16336)
170  FOR B = 1 TO D: NEXT B
190  NEXT A
```

Notice that there are two loops in this program. The loop in line 170 serves as a delay to allow you to control the sound you hear when you run the program. The longer you make the delay (represented by D in the program), the slower the sound emanates from the speaker.

Even at its best, the above program will cause your Apple to generate only low-frequency sounds. This is because Applesoft is an interpretive language and cannot execute quickly enough to generate sounds in the higher frequencies. If you wish to generate sounds of higher frequencies, you will have to write a program that executes faster. This means a machine-language program or subroutine that can be called by your BASIC program. This subroutine must accomplish exactly the same task as the BASIC program above. The only reason it will execute faster is that it is already in machine language and does not have to be translated by the BASIC interpreter every time a line of the program is executed.

If you have used an Apple II under DOS 3.3, you have probably noticed that the standard ProDOS warning beep is much softer than the DOS beep. ProDOS accomplishes this with a brief machine-language routine. You can write your own routines to use the speaker as you wish, in BASIC or machine language, simply by changing the timing with which you look at this location ($C030 or – 16336). If you use assembly language, the commands STA or LDA used with this location will cause the speaker to beep.

ProDOS and the Machine-Language Interface

Interface

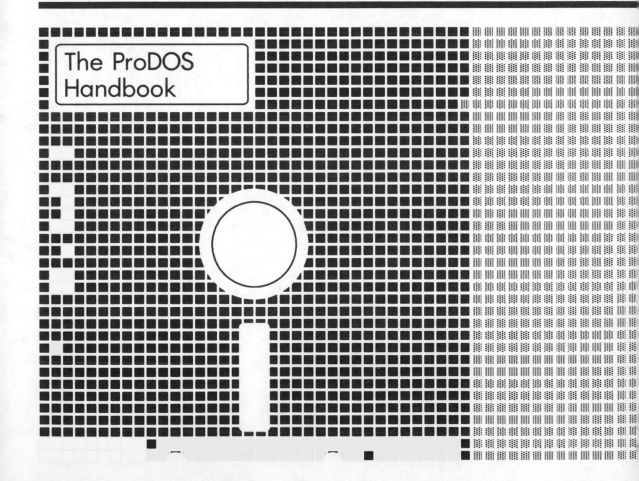

The ProDOS
Handbook

This chapter describes the ProDOS machine-language interface (MLI). The MLI is a set of routines that allows the machine- or assembly-language programmer to use the features ProDOS provides in programs of his own. The ProDOS commands that you use from BASIC or from within the ProDOS utility menus make use of these same routines to perform their operations. Many of the functions you see described in this chapter will be familiar to you from our discussions earlier in this book, so don't be afraid if at first glance they look imposing and technical. Even if you are not interested in using the MLI yourself, reading this chapter may give you a better idea of how ProDOS operates.

THE COMPONENTS OF THE MLI

We'll start with some basic definitions. The ProDOS machine-language interface (MLI) is an independent set of machine-language routines that deal primarily with files on disks. Because it is independent of the ProDOS BASIC.SYSTEM program, it can be used to form the basis of other programs. The MLI is composed of four components, all working together to perform the operations:

- The command dispatcher
- The block file manager
- The disk driver routines
- The interrupt handler

The Command Dispatcher

The command dispatcher within the MLI validates the call number and the parameters of a call, updates the system global page, and transfers execution to the appropriate routine of the block file manager. It validates the parameters by checking to see if the correct number of parameters for the call has been specified as the first byte in the call's parameter list. If the parameters of the call are correct, the command dispatcher updates the system global page (flags and pointers used to keep track of system operations) and passes control to the block file manager. It changes the system global page as required by the machine-language routines in ProDOS that do the actual work of the call. The changes in the data stored in the system global page are used internally by the MLI routines. We will not discuss them here.

The Block File Manager

The block file manager executes all calls to the MLI. All disk access functions are performed by calls to the disk driver routines within the MLI. The block file manager keeps track of which disks are mounted, performs simple memory management functions, and supervises the condition of all open files. The block file manager also dispatches calls to the interrupt handler.

Essentially, the block file manager consists of the housekeeping and filing routines of the MLI. The disk driver routines and the interrupt handler are subservient to the block file manager, because they are called by it to perform tasks. The block file manager itself takes its orders from the command dispatcher. This structure is illustrated in Figure 10.1.

The Disk Driver Routines

The disk driver routines perform the actual reading and writing of data to and from the disk. All MLI calls (and therefore all ProDOS commands) that get information from or place information onto a disk use one of the two disk driver routines (READ_BLOCK and WRITE_BLOCK) to do the work.

The Interrupt Handler

The interrupt handler allows you to install as many as four interrupt-handling routines. When an interrupt is generated, the interrupt handler calls each of these routines in sequence until one of them claims the interrupt. The interrupt handler maintains a table of vectors or pointers to the entry point of each interrupt-handling routine. Positions in this table are assigned by the sequence in which the routines are installed by the MLI.

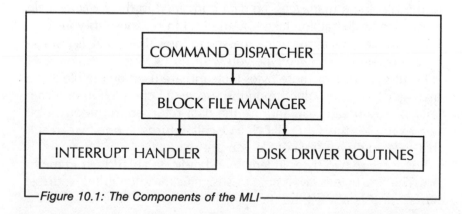

Figure 10.1: The Components of the MLI

PARAMETER LISTS

MLI calls require data to operate on. This data is passed to them through a parameter list, which contains either the data itself, a pointer to the location of the data, or space to store data returned by the call.

All MLI calls require a two-byte pointer to a parameter list. The first element of this parameter list is always the parameter count for that call. This is the number that the command dispatcher uses to verify that the call was issued correctly. For example, a CREATE call requires seven parameters. If you issue this call with a parameter count other than 7, the MLI will be unable to execute the call and will return an error code of $04 (meaning bad system call parameter count) in the accumulator.

The parameter count itself is not considered one of the parameters of a call. In the CREATE example we used above, there are actually eight elements in the parameter list: the parameter count and seven others. To signify this, the parameter count will always be listed as element zero in the parameter lists for each of the calls we discuss in this chapter.

There are three types of elements in a parameter list: values, results, and pointers. These elements are used to provide data to the MLI routine and to return information from the MLI when the call is completed.

Values are one or more bytes in length and are used to pass data to the block file manager. The data contained in these values help to determine the action taken by the MLI in response to your call. For example, one of the values passed to the CREATE call is a single byte representing the file type you wish ProDOS to create.

Results are one or more bytes long and are used by the block file manager to return values upon the successful completion of a call. Your program can read and use the data returned in these results. For example, the GET_FILE_INFO call returns a one-byte result that tells you what type of file you are reading.

Pointers are two bytes in length and indicate an address in memory. The first byte is always the least significant value in the address; the second is always the most significant byte. This means that a human would have to reverse the two bytes to calculate the correct address. (The address can also be calculated by multiplying the contents of the second byte by 256 and adding the results to the contents of the first byte.) Pointers are used to tell the block file manager the location where data are stored or where space in memory exists to store data returned from the call.

MLI PARAMETER TYPES

The MLI calls do not all use the same parameters. The data required for each routine to do its work is different, and the parameters change to reflect this. In this section we will briefly describe these parameters by name to provide a basis for our discussion of the MLI calls themselves.

As previously described, the parameter count is a single byte that stores the number of parameters in the call. The parameter count itself is not included in this number. For example, a call with five parameters will have a parameter count set to 5 and five parameters following the parameter count in the list.

The Pathname parameter is a two-byte pointer to the address of an ASCII string in memory. The first byte of the string must contain a binary number equal to the number of bytes in the string. The string itself cannot be longer than 64 characters. If the first character in the string is not a /, the current ProDOS prefix will be added to the beginning of the path name. For example, the parameter could contain the address $3000. Beginning at $3001 could be the string "/PRODOS/DIRECTORY".

The Access parameter is a single byte that determines how the file can be accessed. Individual bits within this byte act as flags, with a 1 in each position representing an enabled condition and a 0 in each position representing a disabled condition. The layout of the byte is as follows:

Bit	Condition
0	Read enable
1	Write enable

2	Reserved
3	Reserved
4	Reserved
5	Backup needed
6	Rename enable
7	Destroy enable

The Write, Rename, and Destroy bits are set to 0 when a file is locked and to 1 when a file is unlocked. Bits 2 through 4 are reserved for future expansion of ProDOS and should always be set to 0. Bit 5 will be a 1 unless you have modified the access byte of a file entry with a program that does not use an MLI call. ProDOS always sets this bit to 1 after a CREATE, RENAME, or SET_FILE_INFO call and also when a file is closed after a WRITE call. The purpose is to keep track of files that have been changed.

The File Type parameter describes the type of file you are dealing with. This single byte must have a value equal to one of the types listed in Table 10.1.

The Aux Type parameter is a two-byte field used to store the record length of text files and the memory loading address of binary files. The BASIC.SYSTEM program stores this information in the directory as it manipulates files; any program you write in assembly or machine language should do the same to maintain consistency for ProDOS.

The Storage Type parameter is a single byte used to define the way in which a file is stored on disk. A value of $01 in this byte represents a standard file; a value of $D0 represents a linked directory file. All other values are reserved for future use by ProDOS.

The Create Date parameter uses two bytes to record the date on which a file was created. The day is contained in bits 0 through 4 of the first byte. The month is stored in bits 5 to 7 of the first byte and bit 0 of the second byte. The year is contained in bits 1 through 7 of the second byte. This is shown diagrammatically in Figure 10.2.

The Create Time parameter uses two bytes to store the time at which a file was first created. The minute is contained in bits 0 through 5 of the first byte, and the hour is stored in bits 0 through 4 of the second byte. Figure 10.3 illustrates the storage scheme. Bits 6

File Type	Meaning
$00	Typeless file (SOS and ProDOS)
$01	Bad block file
$04	ASCII text file (SOS and ProDOS)
$06	General binary file (SOS and ProDOS)
$0F	Directory file (SOS and ProDOS)
$12–$BF	SOS reserved
$C0–$EF	ProDOS reserved
$F0	ProDOS added command file
$F1–$F8	ProDOS user-defined files 1–8
$F9	ProDOS reserved
$FA	Integer BASIC program file
$FB	Integer BASIC variable file
$FC	Applesoft program file
$FD	Applesoft variable file
$FE	Relocatable code file (EDASM)
$FF	ProDOS system file

Table 10.1. ProDOS File Types

and 7 of the first byte and bits 5 through 7 of the second byte always contain zeros.

The New Pathname parameter is used to point to a second path name. This follows the same rules as the Pathname parameter described above, except that it must point to a different memory location where the second path name is stored.

The Mod Date parameter is used to store the date on which a file was last modified. It has the same format as the Create Date parameter.

The Mod Time parameter is used to store the time of the last modification to a file. The data in this byte use the same format as the Create Time parameter.

The Blocks Used parameter is two bytes long and stores the total number of bytes used by a file. This information is stored in the directory by ProDOS. When this parameter is used to retrieve

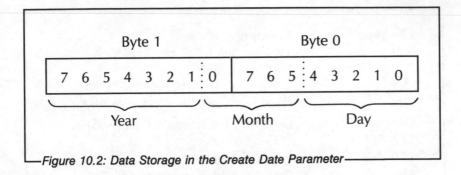

Figure 10.2: Data Storage in the Create Date Parameter

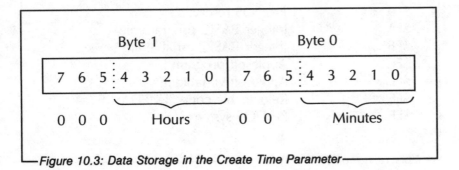

Figure 10.3: Data Storage in the Create Time Parameter

information about a volume directory, it returns the total number of blocks used in the entire volume rather than the space used by the volume directory itself.

The Unit Number parameter is a single byte used to specify the location of a device by slot and drive number. Bit 7 of that byte is used to indicate the drive (0 indicates drive 1; 1 indicates drive 2). Bits 4 through 6 are used to indicate the slot number. Bits 0 through 6 are unused.

The Data Buffer parameter is a two-byte pointer to the beginning of a buffer used for storing data when it is returned from the disk. The minimum size of this buffer will change with different MLI calls and will sometimes be dependent on the value of one of the other parameters of the call. We will discuss this for each individual call that uses this parameter.

The I/O Buffer parameter is a two-byte pointer to a 1024-byte buffer used for input and output operations on a file. This buffer must start on a page boundary (a multiple of $0100) in memory and must be in an area of memory not already used by the system. For a standard file, the first 512 bytes of the buffer contain the current block of data being accessed, and the second 512 bytes contain the current index block (when dealing with sapling and tree files). For a directory file only the first 512 bytes are used to contain the current block of the directory file; the rest of the buffer is not used.

The Reference Number parameter is a one-byte result returned for each file when it is opened by the OPEN call. All subsequent calls affecting that open file must include this number as one of their parameters. Since no more than eight files can be open at one time, this number will always be between 0 and 7, inclusive.

The Enable Mask parameter is a single-byte value used to determine which bits in a character are to be tested. For a detailed discussion of the use of this parameter, see the NEWLINE call later in this chapter.

The Newline Character parameter is a single byte used to represent the character that will cause a read operation to terminate. This parameter is also discussed in more depth in the NEWLINE call section of this chapter.

The Request Count parameter is a two-byte value used to specify the maximum number of bytes to be transferred by a call. This number cannot be greater than the number of bytes between the start of the data buffer and the beginning of the next page of memory that has been marked used in the bit map.

The Transfer Count parameter is a two-byte value used to return the number of bytes actually transferred by a call. For reasons explained with the calls that use it, this value may be different than the Request Count parameter.

The Position parameter is a three-byte value used to represent the next position in the file at which a read or write operation should begin. The value contained here cannot be greater than the file's EOF (end-of-file) value. The first of these three bytes is considered the lowest and the last the highest. This means that the value $123456 would actually be stored with $56 in the first byte, $34 in the second byte, and $12 in the last byte.

The EOF parameter is used to specify the location of the end of the file. This value is three bytes long and is stored in the same fashion as the Position parameter.

The Interrupt Number parameter is a single byte containing a value from 1 to 4. This number is assigned by the interrupt handler when an ALLOC_INTERRUPT call is executed and must be used to remove an interrupt routine with the DEALLOC_INTERRUPT call.

The Interrupt Code parameter is a two-byte pointer to the entry point in the routine that is to be called by the system when an interrupt occurs.

The Block Number parameter is a two-byte pointer that specifies which block of data is to be read from or written to the disk. For example, a disk formatted for the Disk II drive contains blocks from $00 to $117. These are the logical block numbers for the device. Disks are manufactured in tracks and sectors, however. ProDOS converts logical blocks to track and sector locations as it reads the disk. All translation from logical blocks to physical tracks and sectors is done by the disk driver routines.

CALLS TO THE MLI

Calls to the MLI consist of three elements. The first is an instruction, an assembly-language JSR (jump to subroutine), which causes the program to initiate the call. The second and third elements consist of data. The second element is one byte long and contains the number of the call you wish to execute. The third element is two bytes long and contains a pointer to the starting address of the parameter list for this call.

The MLI will check to see that a valid call number has been passed to it. The valid call numbers are listed in Table 10.2.

You must execute a call to the MLI in a specific way. The JSR instruction must direct the program to address $BF00, which is the MLI call entry point. The instruction must be followed first by a single byte of data representing the call number, and then by a two-byte pointer (with the low byte first) to the address of the parameter list.

When the call is completed, the MLI always returns to the address of the JSR instruction plus three bytes. It is good programming practice to place a test for an error condition at this location. The MLI will not display any error message on the screen when an

Call	Call Number
CREATE	$C0
DESTROY	$C1
RENAME	$C2
SET_FILE_INFO	$C3
GET_FILE_INFO	$C4
ON_LINE	$C5
SET_PREFIX	$C6
GET_PREFIX	$C7
OPEN	$C8
NEWLINE	$C9
READ	$CA
WRITE	$CB
CLOSE	$CC
FLUSH	$CD
SET_MARK	$CE
GET_MARK	$CF
SET_EOF	$D0
GET_EOF	$D1
SET_BUF	$D2
GET_BUF	$D3
ALLOC_INTERRUPT	$40
DEALLOC_INTERRUPT	$41
READ_BLOCK	$80
WRITE_BLOCK	$81
GET_TIME	$82

Table 10.2: The MLI Calls

error occurs; you will have to determine what action your program takes when an error is encountered. The next section, "MLI Errors," contains further information on this subject.

The following is an example of an assembly-language subroutine used to execute an MLI call:

```
MCALL   JSR   $BF00     ;call the Command Dispatcher
        DB    CNUMBR    ;MLI call number
```

```
DW    PARLIST      ;point to parameter list
BNE   BOOBOO       ;test for errors
RTS
```

The first instruction causes this subroutine to execute a jump to the subroutine (JSR is similar to the BASIC GOSUB statement) beginning at $BF00. This is followed by an instruction defining a single byte of memory, the variable CNUMBR, as data. The MLI call number should be stored in this variable before MCALL is begun. The third instruction defines a word (two bytes) of memory (the variable PARLIST) as data storage. The pointer to the parameter list should be stored in the variable PARLIST before executing MCALL. The fourth instruction performs a test to see if an error has occurred and branches to an error-handling routine if it finds an error condition. Finally, the subroutine ends with a return instruction (RTS, similar to the BASIC RETURN instruction).

Before executing MCALL, a program must store the correct values in the variables CNUMBR and PARLIST. If this is not done, the MLI will try to execute a call with whatever data is contained in those locations. This could be the parameters for a previous call, which would cause the MLI to repeat the previous call, or it might be data that does not meet the parameter requirements, which would cause an error.

All calls to the MLI always terminate by returning to the instruction located three bytes after the address of the JSR instruction that initiated the call. This is why we placed the BNE instruction there, so that it would be the first instruction executed after the call was completed. In this example, BOOBOO is a label (similar to a line number in BASIC) used to identify a particular location within the program. When an error condition occurs, this instruction will cause the program to execute a branch to the location specified by BOOBOO. Any value other than zero in the accumulator indicates an error.

The GET_TIME call has no parameters and might seem to be an exception to the required format for an MLI call. While the contents of the pointer to the address of the parameter list are meaningless for this call (in other words, it doesn't matter where they point to), the space the pointer occupies is meaningful. The call to the MLI always returns the program execution to three bytes after the JSR that called it. This means that you must include the call number and the pointer to the parameter list to maintain the proper spacing and make sure that the next instruction executed is the one you intended it to be. In the example above, leaving out the DW instruction would cause the program to resume by executing part of the address of BOOBOO. Since this value might be almost anything, the results of this omission would be unpredictable and almost certainly fatal to your program.

MLI ERRORS

When you issue a call to the MLI, one of two results is possible. ProDOS will either be able to process the call successfully, or the call will fail. The result is obviously important to your program. The MLI will pass data signifying the result of a call back to you by using the registers of your Apple. (The registers are special areas of memory used for recording status information and in situations where fast access to data is required.)

The following table lists the register status of your Apple after the completion of an MLI call. The columns labeled N, Z, C, D, and V represent flags composed of a single bit; they can have values of only zero or one. They are used to signal status changes. The accumulator (Acc) and the X, Y, and stack pointer (SP) registers are each eight bits wide. The PC (program counter) is composed of sixteen bits and contains the address of the next instruction to be executed. At the conclusion of an MLI call, the PC is always set to the address of the instruction that called the MLI plus three bytes. We place our instruction to test for an error at that point so that it will be executed immediately after the conclusion of the call to the MLI.

	N Z C D V	Acc	PC	X Y SP
Successful call:	0 1 0 0 x	0	JSR+3	Unchanged
Unsuccessful call:	0 0 1 0 x	Error code	JSR+3	Unchanged

The value of the N flag is determined by the value in the accumulator; it would be set to 1 only for an error code greater than

$80 (which currently does not exist). The error code itself is always returned in the accumulator in the event of an unsuccessful call. The V flag is undefined in the context of calls to the MLI (that is, the MLI does not return a result through the V flag, and it might to be set to either 0 or 1). The Z flag will be set to 1 and the C flag to 0 for successful calls, and Z will be set to 0 and C to 1 when an error occurs. The D flag will always be equal to zero.

As you can see, the Z and C flags and the accumulator are each affected by the success of an MLI call. You can test any one of these three to determine whether an error has occurred. The BNE instruction in the program segment above tests the Z flag. If the Z flag is set to zero, indicating an error, BNE branches to BOOBOO, the routine that tests the accumulator. The value in the accumulator tells you which error has occurred, represented by a code number.

The error codes you can expect the MLI to return in the accumulator are represented in Table 10.3. Any error-handling routine you write can read the accumulator to determine which error has occurred and take whatever action you choose to take. The simple course is usually best when handling errors. Since the MLI will not notify you of an error by putting a message on the screen, the minimum you should do is to have the program print a message such as

MLI CALL FAILED → ERROR #

followed by the value found in the accumulator.

The READ_BLOCK and WRITE_BLOCK calls allow you to access directly the contents of any logical block on a disk. These commands are normally used by utility programs and should be used with care. The file structure of ProDOS can be damaged if a WRITE_BLOCK command replaces necessary information with bad data.

THE MLI CALLS

MLI calls fall into three categories: housekeeping calls, filing calls, and system calls. Housekeeping calls are generally used to change

Code	Description
$00	No error
$01	Bad system call number
$04	Bad system call parameter count
$25	Interrupt table full
$27	I/O error
$28	No device connected
$2B	Disk write protected
$2E	Disk switched
$40	Invalid path name
$42	Maximum number of files open
$43	Invalid reference number
$44	Directory not found
$45	Volume not found
$46	File not found
$47	Duplicate file name
$48	Volume full
$49	Volume directory full
$4A	Incompatible file format
$4B	Unsupported storage type
$4C	End of file encountered
$4D	Position out of range
$4E	File access error or file locked
$50	File open
$51	Directory structure damaged
$52	Not a ProDOS volume
$53	Invalid system call parameter
$55	Volume Control Block table full
$56	Bad buffer address
$57	Duplicate volume
$5A	File structure damaged

Table 10.3: The MLI Error Codes

the status of a file, while filing calls are used to transfer data to and from the disk drive. System calls consist of all calls that do not fit into the first two categories. A convenient reference listing of all the MLI calls and their parameters is provided in Appendix G.

Housekeeping Calls

Under ProDOS, housekeeping calls are those file operations that either cannot be performed on or do not affect open files. This includes operations such as creating and deleting files. The Pro-DOS MLI has eight housekeeping calls:

CREATE
DESTROY
RENAME
SET_FILE_INFO
GET_FILE_INFO
ON_LINE
SET_PREFIX
GET_PREFIX

CREATE ($C0)

The CREATE call can be used to create either a standard or a directory file. It cannot be used to create a volume directory file, because volume directory files are created only when a disk is formatted. This command creates an entry in the directory specified by the path name and allocates one block of space on the disk for this file.

The CREATE call requires seven parameters. They are listed here according to the order in which they must appear, their length in bytes, and the type of parameter they are.

Contents	Length	Type
0. Parameter count	1	Value (must equal 7)
1. Pathname	2	Pointer
2. Access	1	Value
3. File Type	1	Value

4. Aux Type	2	Value
5. Storage Type	1	Value
6. Create Date	2	Value
7. Create Time	2	Value

DESTROY ($C1)

The DESTROY call deletes the specified file from the disk. The directory entry for this file is eliminated and the blocks used by the file are marked on the volume bit map as available. ProDOS places some limits on the use of this call. It cannot be used to destroy a volume directory or any file that is currently open. Nor can it be used to destroy a subdirectory file, unless that subdirectory is empty. These limitations are intended to safeguard the disk and to lessen the possibility of catastrophic mistakes, such as deleting a subdirectory file that contains other files. Locked files cannot be deleted with the DESTROY call; they must be unlocked first.

The DESTROY call requires only one parameter:

Contents	Length	Type
0. Parameter count	1	Value (must equal 1)
1. Pathname	2	Pointer

RENAME ($C2)

The RENAME command changes the name of an existing file to that specified as the new path name. The two parameters must be identical except for the last entry in each of the path names. The result of this command is a change in the file name used in the appropriate directory. This call performs exactly the same function as the Rename Files command in the Filer utility.

The RENAME call requires two parameters:

Contents	Length	Type
0. Parameter count	1	Value (must equal 2)
1. Pathname	2	Pointer
2. New Pathname	2	Pointer

SET_FILE_INFO ($C3)

The SET_FILE_INFO call is used to modify the information stored about a specific file in a directory. The effects of this call are not used by an open file until that file has been closed and opened again. The parameters used in the SET_FILE_INFO call are based on data returned by the GET_FILE_INFO call. To prevent mishaps, you should execute the latter first and modify the data before writing it back to the directory with SET_FILE_INFO.

The SET_FILE_INFO call requires seven parameters:

Contents	Length	Type
0. Parameter count	1	Value (must equal 7)
1. Pathname	2	Pointer
2. Access	1	Value
3. File Type	1	Value
4. Aux Type	2	Value
5. Null field	3	
6. Mod Date	2	Value
7. Mod Time	2	Value

While this call can be used to modify the information in a file's directory entry while that file is open, ProDOS will only recognize the changes after that file has been closed. Each open file has a file control block set up for it at the time it is opened, and that data is not changed until the file is closed and opened again. This is done to prevent changes you make while a file is open from affecting read and write operations on that file. For example, you might have opened a file as a text file with a record length of 10. While the file is still open, your program issues a SET_FILE_INFO call and changes the record length to 20. As long as the file remains open, ProDOS will continue to treat it as having a record length of 10. If you close it and then open it again, ProDOS will recognize the record length as 20.

The three-byte null field in the parameter list is intended only to maintain symmetry between the parameters of this call and the GET_FILE_INFO call. These three bytes do nothing but fill up space. This makes it easier to use the SET_FILE_INFO call with the results returned in the GET_FILE_INFO call.

GET_FILE_INFO ($C4)

The GET_FILE_INFO call returns the directory information associated with a specific file. This call can be used on open files as well as on closed files. However, if the SET_FILE_INFO command has been used to modify an open file, the access value returned by the GET_FILE_INFO command will not be valid until that file has been closed and opened again. This is because the file control block (FCB) that is set up for the file when it is opened is not affected by the SET_FILE_INFO call, as described above.

The GET_FILE_INFO call requires ten parameters:

Contents	Length	Type
0. Parameter count	1	Value (must equal $A)
1. Pathname	2	Pointer
2. Access	1	Result
3. File Type	1	Result
4. Aux Type	2	Result
5. Storage Type	1	Result
6. Blocks Used	2	Result
7. Mod Date	2	Result
8. Mod Time	2	Result
9. Create Date	2	Result
10. Create Time	2	Result

ON_LINE ($C5)

The ON_LINE call returns the names of all ProDOS volumes that are currently available for use. It can also be used to determine the name of a disk in a specified slot and drive. If an actual unit number is passed, the volume name and slot and drive numbers of the drive requested are stored in the buffer. This information requires only 16 bytes of space.

If the unit number is set to 0, however, the data buffer should be at least 256 bytes long. When 0 is passed as the unit number, the volume names, slot numbers, and drive numbers of all on-line volumes are read into the buffer. Since each one of these requires 16 bytes of storage, the buffer should be big enough for the worst case, where all eight slots each contain two drives.

The ON_LINE call requires only two parameters:

Contents	Length	Type
0. Parameter count	1	Value (must equal 2)
1. Unit Number	1	Value
2. Data Buffer	2	Pointer

SET_PREFIX ($C6)

The SET_PREFIX command sets the system prefix to the specified directory. All the rules described earlier in this book for valid path names apply. The MLI will verify that the specified directory is on line before it accepts the call. This call performs the same function as the Set ProDOS Prefix command in the Filer and the PREFIX command used from the BASIC prompt.

The SET_PREFIX call requires only one parameter:

Contents	Length	Type
0. Parameter count	1	Value (must equal 1)
1. Pathname	2	Pointer

GET_PREFIX ($C7)

The GET_PREFIX command returns the current system prefix. If there is no system prefix, a 0 is returned. Otherwise, the system prefix (bracketed by slashes) is returned to the data buffer, which must be 128 bytes long.

The GET_PREFIX call requires only one parameter:

Contents	Length	Type
0. Parameter count	1	Value (must equal 1)
1. Data Buffer	2	Pointer

Filing Calls

The ProDOS filing calls deal with the transfer of data to or from files on the disk. All files must be opened before their contents can be affected by any of the other filing calls.

There are twelve filing calls in the MLI:

> OPEN
> NEWLINE
> READ
> WRITE
> CLOSE
> FLUSH
> SET_MARK
> GET_MARK
> SET_EOF
> GET_EOF
> SET_BUF
> GET_BUF

OPEN ($C8)

The OPEN command gets a file ready to be read from or written to. It returns a reference number, which remains assigned to the file as long as the file remains open. This value must be used by all other filing calls that refer to this file. The OPEN command creates a file control block (FCB) within the IO buffer to keep track of the current characteristics of the file. The current position marker within the file is set to 0. The FCB for the file remains in existence until the file is closed.

The I/O buffer is used for all operations that require reading from or writing to the disk. It is always 1024 bytes (1K) long. Do not remove a disk from the drive while a file is still open—ProDOS does not check to see if the volume is still on line before reading or writing. If you have placed another disk in the drive, ProDOS will think the file is still exactly where it was when it was opened. With a read operation, this results in improper data being read into the file buffer. The results of a write operation are even more serious—valuable data can be written over and lost. If the area the data is written to contains a directory, the file entries on that disk become unreadable and you will be unable to access the files they represent.

To avoid this, you can do two things. First, don't remove disks from the drive while they still have open files. Second, your program can issue an ON_LINE call to check the identity of a volume before writing to it.

Remember, a maximum of eight files can be open at any one time under ProDOS. Any attempt to open more than eight files will cause the file control block table-full error.

When a file is opened, it is assigned a level number based on the value found in the LEVEL location of the system global page. The number will always be between 0 and 4. This value is important for its use with the CLOSE call.

The OPEN call requires three parameters:

Contents	Length	Type
0. Parameter count	1	Value (must equal 3)
1. Pathname	2	Pointer
2. I/O Buffer	2	Pointer
3. Reference Number	1	Result

NEWLINE ($C9)

The NEWLINE call enables or disables the newline mode for any open file. When it is disabled, a read request will end only when it encounters the end-of-file marker or when a specified number of characters has been read. When the newline mode is enabled, a read request will also terminate if the newline character is read in a file.

The value of the Enable Mask parameter determines which bits of the character read from the disk and the newline character are to be compared. When a character is read into the buffer, a logical AND operation is performed with the enable mask and the result is compared to the newline character. A match between the two causes the read request to terminate. The incoming character is not changed by the AND operation.

A value of $00 in the Enable Mask parameter has the effect of canceling the newline mode, because no bits will be compared. Any other value enables the newline mode. A value of $FF causes all bits to be compared. A value of $7F (which would set the enable mask to 01111111) would mean that bits 0–6 would be compared while bit 7 would not. When this condition exists, the ASCII character 13 ($0D) or a binary 00001101 would cause a match with either $0D (00001101 in binary) or $8D (10001101 in binary) when that character is read from the disk. This is because bit 7 is not considered in the comparison, and bits 0 through 6 are identical.

The NEWLINE call requires three parameters:

	Contents	Length	Type
0.	Parameter count	1	Value (must equal 3)
1.	Reference Number	1	Value
2.	Enable Mask	1	Value
3.	Newline Character	1	Value

READ ($CA)

The READ call transfers data from the disk to memory. The number of bytes requested and transferred will always be the same unless an end-of-file condition is encountered while reading, or the newline mode has been enabled and a newline character has been encountered. When either of these conditions occurs, the transfer count will return the number of bytes actually transferred, including the newline byte. An end-of-file error will occur only if zero bytes are transferred as a result of a READ call (in other words, the end of the file has already been reached before the call was issued).

The READ call requires four parameters:

	Contents	Length	Type
0.	Parameter count	1	Value (must equal 4)
1.	Reference Number	1	Value
2.	Data Buffer	2	Pointer

3. Request Count   2   Value
4. Transfer Count   2   Result

WRITE ($CB)

The WRITE call attempts to send a specified number of bytes from the buffer area to the specified file. This data is written to the disk starting at the current position in the file. The current position is updated to equal the current position plus the number of bytes actually transferred. Additional blocks are allocated to the file as necessary by ProDOS, and the end-of-file marker is extended when it is encountered.

The WRITE call requires four parameters:

Contents	Length	Type
0. Parameter count	1	Value (must equal 4)
1. Reference Number	1	Value
2. Data Buffer	2	Pointer
3. Request Count	2	Value
4. Transfer Count	2	Result

The value of the transfer count will always be the same as the value of the request count unless an error has occurred.

CLOSE ($CC)

The CLOSE statement must be used for all open files. This call writes any data not yet written to a file from the I/O buffer to the disk, releases the FCB and I/O buffer, and updates the directory entry for the file. It also releases the reference number assigned to a file.

If the Reference Number parameter supplied in the calls is set to 0, all open files at or above the current level are closed. You can determine the level at which files will be opened by changing the value in the LEVEL location in the system global page ($BFD8) before opening a file. This feature can be used to close files in groups with a single command. For example, your program could open two files at level 0, two files at level 1, and three files at level

2. If you then set the LEVEL value to 1 and issue a CLOSE call with a reference number of 0, all the files at level 1 and level 2 will be closed while the files at level 0 will remain open.

The CLOSE call performs exactly the same functions as the CLOSE statement that is used from BASIC.

The CLOSE call requires only one parameter:

Contents	Length	Type
0. Parameter count	1	Value (must equal 1)
1. Reference Number	1	Value

FLUSH ($CD)

The FLUSH call writes all unwritten data in an I/O buffer to a file and updates the file's entry in the directory. This command requires only the file's reference number as a parameter. If the reference number requested is 0, all open files at or above the current level are flushed.

The FLUSH call performs exactly the same function as the FLUSH statement that can be used from within BASIC.

The FLUSH call requires only one parameter:

Contents	Length	Type
0. Parameter count	1	Value (must equal 1)
1. Reference Number	1	Value

SET_MARK ($CE)

The SET_MARK call changes the current position (MARK) within a file. The new position is an absolute value relative to the beginning of the file. The new position cannot be greater than the position of the file's end-of-file marker.

The SET_MARK call requires two parameters:

Contents	Length	Type
0. Parameter count	1	Value (must equal 2)
1. Reference Number	1	Value
2. Position	3	Value

GET_MARK ($CF)

The GET_MARK call returns the value of the current position (MARK) in an open file. The MARK is always the position at which the next READ or WRITE will begin. (It can be changed by a SET_MARK command.)

The GET_MARK call requires two parameters:

Contents	Length	Type
0. Parameter count	1	Value (must equal 2)
1. Reference Number	1	Value
2. Position	3	Result

SET_EOF ($D0)

The SET_EOF call changes the size of the file to the value specified. If the EOF specified is less than the existing EOF, all blocks located after the new value are released to the system for use. The current position within the file will also be reduced to match the new EOF. If the new EOF exceeds the existing one, no blocks are allocated. New blocks are allocated only when data are written to them.

The SET_EOF call requires two parameters:

Contents	Length	Type
0. Parameter count	1	Value (must equal 2)
1. Reference Number	1	Value
2. End of file (EOF)	3	Value

GET_EOF ($D1)

The GET_EOF call returns the maximum number of bytes that can be read from a file. It gets this value from the file's directory entry. This value remains valid until the EOF is changed by the SET_EOF call or extended by using the WRITE call to add data to the file.

The GET_EOF call requires two parameters:

Contents	Length	Type
0. Parameter count	1	Value (must equal 2)
1. Reference Number	1	Value
2. End of file (EOF)	3	Result

SET_BUFF ($D2)

The SET_BUFF call allows you to change the address of the I/O buffer used by an open file. The MLI will check the system bit map to see that the new buffer is not already in use before copying the contents of the old buffer into the new buffer. The new buffer will be 1024 bytes long and must start on a page boundary in memory.

The SET_BUF call requires two parameters:

	Contents	Length	Type
0.	Parameter count	1	Value (must equal 2)
1.	Reference Number	1	Value
2.	I/O Buffer	2	Pointer (must be a multiple of $100)

GET_BUFF ($D3)

The GET_BUFF call returns the address of the buffer currently being used for I/O by the file specified in the reference number.

The GET_BUFF call requires two parameters:

	Contents	Length	Type
0.	Parameter count	1	Value (must equal 2)
1.	Reference Number	1	Value
2.	I/O Buffer	2	Result

System Calls

Any MLI call that is not a filing or housekeeping call is considered a system call. ProDOS provides five system calls in the MLI:

```
ALLOC_INTERRUPT
DEALLOC_INTERRUPT
READ_BLOCK
WRITE_BLOCK
GET_TIME
```

These routines are used to install and remove interrupt handlers, to get the time and date, and to read and write specific blocks on a disk.

ALLOC_INTERRUPT ($40)

The ALLOC_INTERRUPT call adds the address of an interrupt-receiving routine to the interrupt vector table. You should always make sure you use this call before you enable (connect and power up) an interrupt-driven device. You are responsible for making sure that your routine is placed at the location you specify.

The interrupt number that is returned by the ALLOC_INTER-RUPT function will be a value from 1 to 4. This number represents the priority given to this interrupt routine. Priorities are assigned in the order that the routines are added to the interrupt vector table.

When an interrupt is received, the ProDOS interrupt handler will call each of the routines that have been installed in the interrupt vector table in order from 1 to 4. It will stop with the first one that claims that particular interrupt. If none of the routines in the table claims the interrupt, your Apple will lock up and cease to operate until you have rebooted.

The ALLOC_INTERRUPT call requires two parameters:

Contents	Length	Type
0. Parameter count	1	Value (must equal 2)
1. Interrupt Vector Number	1	Result
2. Interrupt Handler Address	2	Pointer

DEALLOC_INTERRUPT ($41)

The DEALLOC_INTERRUPT call removes an entry from the interrupt vector table. To use it, you must provide the interrupt vector number returned as a result of the ALLOC_INTERRUPT call as a parameter. If your program will be installing and removing interrupt routines, store this value for future use. Remember that you must disable the interrupt device before executing this call. Failure to do this may cause a system failure if the device generates an interrupt after the table has been updated.

The DEALLOC_INTERRUPT call requires only one parameter:

Contents	Length	Type
0. Parameter count	1	Value (must equal 1)
1. Interrupt Vector Number	1	Value

READ_BLOCK ($80)

The READ_BLOCK call reads one logical block of data from the specified disk device. This command always reads 512 bytes from the disk, so your buffer must be at least that long.

The READ_BLOCK call requires three parameters:

Contents	Length	Type
0. Parameter count	1	Value (must equal 3)
1. Unit Number	1	Value
2. Data Buffer	2	Pointer
3. Block Number	2	Pointer

WRITE_BLOCK ($81)

The WRITE_BLOCK call writes 512 bytes (1 block) from your Apple's memory to a disk drive. Since this command always writes 512 bytes of data, you should make your buffer area at least that long. Otherwise, you will write whatever happens to be in that area of memory to the disk.

The WRITE_BLOCK call requires three parameters:

Contents	Length	Type
0. Parameter count	1	Value (must equal 3)
1. Unit Number	1	Value
2. Data Buffer	2	Pointer
3. Block Number	2	Pointer

The READ_BLOCK and WRITE_BLOCK calls allow you to access directly the contents of any logical block on a disk. These commands are normally used by utility programs and should be used with care. The file structure of ProDOS can be damaged if a WRITE_BLOCK command replaces necessary information with bad data.

You can also use these calls to read and write blocks on disks formatted under DOS 3.3. Under DOS 3.3 data is stored by track and sector number. To determine which ProDOS block number represents a given DOS 3.3 track and sector, use the formula

block = (8 × track) + sector offset

The value of the sector offset is determined by the following chart.

The half-of-block line of the chart tells you whether the sector is in the first half or the second half of the block.

Sector:	0 1 2 3 4 5 6 7 8 9 A B C D E F
Sector offset:	0 7 6 6 5 5 4 4 3 3 2 2 1 1 0 7
Half of block:	1 1 2 1 2 1 2 1 2 1 2 1 2 1 2 2

For example, if you wanted to use the READ_BLOCK call to read a block of data from a DOS 3.3 disk starting at track 5, sector 6, you would perform the following calculation to determine the correct block number. First you would multiply the track number by 8 to produce a result of 40. Then you would add the sector offset, which our chart tells us is 4, to yield a total of 44. The half-of-block line tells us that sector 6 will lie in the last 256 bytes of the block when it is read (DOS 3.3 sectors had only 256 bytes).

GET_TIME ($82)

The GET_TIME call returns the system date and time. This command has no parameters. It calls a clock/calendar routine (if one has been installed), which places the current date and time in the system date and time locations. ProDOS automatically looks for a ThunderClock in the slots of the Apple II during startup. A clock/calendar routine is automatically installed if it finds one.

The system date is stored at locations $BF91 and $BF90 in year-month-day order. The system time is stored at locations $BF93 and $BF92. Location $BF93 stores the hours, and $BF92 stores the minutes. The format for the data is the same as that used by the Create and Mod Date and Time parameters.

ProDOS and the Apple II

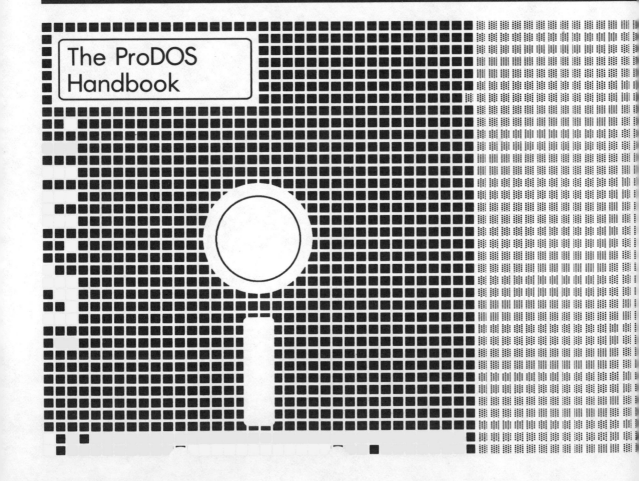

The ProDOS
Handbook

ELEVEN

This chapter consists of two distinct parts. The first is a brief description of what makes up a ProDOS system program and the resources a system program can call on. The second part of the chapter contains a description of the Monitor, a program that might be viewed as an editor for your Apple's memory. With the Monitor, you can directly manipulate the contents of any area of your Apple's memory, write machine-language programs, and still have the use of all the immediate-mode ProDOS commands.

PRODOS SYSTEM PROGRAMS

Under ProDOS a program is a system program if it makes calls to the MLI and adheres to the following three rules:

1. The program must contain the code to move itself from its load position to its execution location, if this is necessary.
2. It must update the system global page and place version numbers in the system global page at the proper locations.
3. It must have the ability to turn execution over to another system program.

These requirements will be explained more thoroughly in the next section. Beyond these requirements, all aspects of a ProDOS system program are up to you. The program can be a game program, an accounting program, or any other program.

System Program Requirements

All system programs are always loaded into memory at location $2000. When the system is booted, the first file on the startup disk with the name xxx.SYSTEM (where xxx can be any valid string of characters) and the type $FF (SYS) is loaded into memory. This program can then load any type $FF file that it wishes in its place.

After a system program is loaded into memory location $2000, it can be relocated to use any location between $0800 and $BEFF as its final execution location. This must be done by code within the system program itself.

The second requirement of all system programs is that they must update the system global page in the following manner:

1. The system bit map ($BF58 to $BF6F) should be set to protect the program by marking the appropriate areas of memory as used.
2. The number of the earliest version of the MLI with which your system program will work should be placed in location $BFFC.

3. The version number of your system program should be placed in location $BFFD.

Finally, all system programs must include a means of switching to another system program. It is important that the code which performs this operation be placed where it will not be overwritten as the new program is loaded into memory. This generally means placing it below $2000. This is the recommended method for switching ProDOS system programs:

1. Close all open files. This is a wise precaution that is heartily recommended to everyone.
2. Ask the user for the name of the desired system program. (This step might possibly be skipped in a situation where the user is not involved in the decision of which program to switch to.)
3. Open the file containing the specified system program. Determine the length of the file using the GET_EOF call from the MLI, so that you will know how many bytes to read in.
4. Deallocate the RAM used by your system program by resetting the system bit map.
5. Read the desired file into memory starting at $2000.
6. Close the file.
7. Place the desired program's path name at $0280. (Remember that first you have to place a count byte to tell ProDOS the length of the path name, and then the path name itself.) This is where ProDOS keeps the path name to the most recently loaded program.
8. Perform a JMP to $2000 to begin execution of the new program.

Steps 3 through 8 will always remain the same. If an error occurs in the MLI while the new program is being read in, your program should clear the screen and ask the user to reboot the system if the error is nonrecoverable.

System Program Resources

In an Apple II the stack is stored in page $01 of memory, starting with the high byte of the page and working down in memory. System programs have full use of this area. However, it is important to note that the low 16 bytes of the stack are used by the interrupt handler of the MLI. The interrupt handler will save these 16 bytes and restore them if the stack is more than 75 percent full. If you anticipate that a system program will be working with interrupts and the speed and efficiency of interrupt handling is one of your priorities, you should restrict your system program to using the upper three-quarters of the stack. This will eliminate the need for the interrupt handler to save and restore the lower part of the stack.

When an Apple IIe has an additional 64K bank of RAM available, the additional memory is configured as a ProDOS volume named RAM and is treated by the system as slot 0, drive 2. This extra memory area cannot be accessed directly as memory by any of the calls in the MLI or by any BASIC statement, but it can be accessed by ProDOS as a ProDOS disk volume. The extra memory in an Apple IIc is accessed in the same way. Essentially, what we are doing is fooling ProDOS into believing that the extra memory is another disk drive.

The system global page (page $BF of memory) contains the global variables used to keep track of system processing. Some of these global variables may be used by system programs, some are for information purposes only and should not be changed, and others are used for internal processing and should not be changed at all. The contents of the system global page are described further in Appendix K.

PRODOS AND THE MONITOR

The Monitor is a machine-language control program permanently located in the read-only memory (ROM) of your Apple. You can use it to examine memory locations and the contents of the registers, to dump the contents of memory, and to change the contents of memory in the registers. You can move blocks of data from one address to another, or you can compare them. In general, the monitor acts as your key to the inner workings of your Apple computer.

The Monitor is a tool for exploring and controlling your Apple. Almost all of the ProDOS commands will work from within the Monitor program (deferred-mode statements will not work). The Monitor can also be your path to direct use of the MLI. With it, you can enter machine-language programs directly into memory to call the MLI. You can also enter the data for parameters if you wish. Because the ProDOS commands will work here, you can save the results of your work with the BSAVE command.

Entering and Leaving the Monitor

If you want to enter the monitor from the BASIC prompt, you can use the command CALL − 151. The square bracket that represents the BASIC prompt disappears and is replaced with the asterisk prompt of the monitor. When you want to return to BASIC, simply press the Control-Reset keys or Control-C and Return.

Using the Monitor to Examine Memory

You can use the Monitor to examine memory in chunks of a single byte, a "word" of eight bytes, or a block of any size you specify. You examine a single byte by typing in the memory address in hexadecimal at the Monitor prompt and pressing Return. Enter the Monitor by typing CALL − 151 and enter the address of a memory location, such as FF69. The Monitor will respond with

    FF69 − A9

This is the memory location that you requested and its contents in hexadecimal. The Monitor maintains a pointer to your current location in memory and changes it every time you enter a new address.

You can display an eight-byte word of memory simply by pressing the Return key. If you have recently accessed a single location, when you press Return you will see less than eight bytes because the Monitor will only display the rest of the word you are in on the screen. When you press the Return key a second time, the Monitor will display the eight bytes subsequent to the last byte you were shown. You can easily tell the difference between these two results, because the Monitor will always show you the starting address when it shows you a complete word. It omits the starting address when it shows you only a partial word.

For example, if you type FF69 and then press Return three times, you will see the following display:

```
*FF69
FF69 - A9
*
AA 85 33 20 67 FD
*
FF70 - 20 CD FF 20 A7 FF 84 34
```

This can be an effective means of looking at consecutive blocks of memory when you are searching through memory for a particular item.

You can display a block of memory by specifying a range of addresses. You do this by typing in the starting and ending addresses separated by a period. Try typing F500.F550 at the Monitor prompt. You should get the response shown in Figure 11.1.

The first address you specify must be less than the second address, or you will see only one location displayed. If you display a range of addresses too big to be shown on the Apple screen, data will scroll off the top to make room for more data to be printed. You can use the Control-S keys to stop and start the scrolling and allow you more time to read the contents. The Control-S keys will affect only the screen display; they will not halt the dumping of contents to another device, such as the printer.

You can use another form of this command to read forward to a specified address. Because the Monitor keeps track of where you are in memory, you can specify only the ending address by preceding it with a period and pressing Return. If you have just completed the above example, type .F600 and press Return. The contents of memory locations F551 to F600 will be displayed on the screen. If you enter an ending address less than the current address, the Monitor will simply display the next byte of information.

You can also use the Monitor to examine the contents of the registers. You can do this by typing Control-E and pressing the Return key. You should see results similar to the following:

A = 96   X = 17   Y = 01   P = 00   S = 98

The actual values stored in these registers will be changing constantly, but the registers will always be the same. From left to right they are the accumulator, the index registers X and Y, the processor status register, and the stack pointer. The Monitor does not alter the contents of the registers by its operation, so these values will remain constant as long as you are in the Monitor and do not directly alter them. This feature can be extremely useful when you are debugging machine- or assembly-language programs, because it lets you see the actual contents of the registers you are working with.

```
F500- FC 85 27 60 18 A5 27 69
F508- 04 2C B9 F5 D0 F3 06 26
F510- 90 18 69 E0 18 2C 08 F5
F518- F0 12 A5 26 69 50 49 F0
F520- F0 02 49 F0 85 26 A5 E6
F528- 90 02 69 E0 66 26 90 D1
F530- 48 A9 00 85 E0 85 E1 85
F538- E2 68 48 38 E5 E0 48 8A
F540- E8 E1 85 D3 B0 0A 68 49
F548- FF 69 01 48 A9 00 E5 D3
F550- 85
```

Figure 11.1: The Monitor's Display of a Block of Memory

Using the Monitor to Change Memory

You can also change the contents of memory with the Monitor. The Monitor command to change the contents of a memory location is the colon symbol. Try using the following sequence of steps to change the contents of memory location 0310:

```
*0310
0310 - 00
*:05
*0310
0310 - 05
```

You can accomplish the same result by typing 0310:05 at the asterisk prompt. This command has the effect of placing the value after the colon at the location specified before the colon.

You can also modify more than one location at a time. This is done by typing a list of values after the colon, with each value separated from the others by a space. For example, the statement

```
0310:01 02 03 04 05 06 07 08
```

changes the contents of locations 0310 through 0317 to read consecutively 1 through 8. The memory contents affected will always be in consecutive order from the starting address. You can check whether the contents have indeed been changed by typing the command 0310.0317.

You can alter the contents of the registers by following a similar procedure. However, before you can change the contents of the registers you must examine them by typing Control-E and Return. Once you have done this, you can change the values of the registers by typing a colon and following it with the new values.

The register values must be entered in exactly the same order as they are presented to you on the screen. The accumulator is always first, followed by the X register, the Y register, the processor status register, and finally the stack pointer. If you wish to change the contents of the Y register without changing the values of any other register, you must enter the existing values for the accumulator and the X register before entering the new value for the Y register. You do not have to enter anything for the last two registers if you do not wish to affect them. This is because the changes are made consecutively, starting with the accumulator. For example, use the following steps to change the contents of the Y register:

    * (Press Control-E and Return)
    A = 96 X = 17 Y = 01 E = 00 S = 98
    *:96 17 02
    * (Press Control-E and Return)
    A = 96 X = 17 Y = 02 E = 00 S = 98

If you wish to change the contents of the stack pointer, you must enter all four of the preceding locations first. If you want to change the contents of only the accumulator, you do not have to enter a value for any other register.

Using the Monitor to Copy and Compare the Contents of Memory

The Monitor can also be used to copy the contents of memory in one location to another location. To do this, you must give the Monitor the starting address where you wish the data to be placed, the address from which you wish to start copying data, and the ending address of the area you wish to copy. The starting address of the destination always comes first and is followed by the < symbol. Immediately after this comes the starting address of the data you wish to copy, a period, and the last address you want copied. This is followed by the letter M to designate that this command is a move. For example, if you want to move the contents of locations 0310 through 0320 to the area beginning with 0350, the command

    0350<0310.0320M

will do it for you. You might do this if you wanted to copy a section of a program to create another section that was similar and needed only a few changes.

This command does not disturb or destroy the contents of the original memory location. It does, however, overwrite any contents at the destination locations. As with all range commands in the Monitor, if you specify a range where the ending location is less than the starting location, it will be treated as a single-byte instruction and only one byte of data will be transferred.

The Monitor will also compare two blocks of memory and verify that the contents are the same. The format for this command is the same as the move command, except that the letter M at the end of the line is replaced with the letter V for verify.

Suppose you want to check whether the move operation you have just completed was successful. You could list both areas of memory on the screen and then compare them by eye, or you could use the verify command. The first method is always more tedious and more prone to error. To see how the verify command works, type in the command

    0310<0350.0360V

after executing the move instruction above. If all went well, no results will be displayed and you will simply advance to the next prompt. You can prove this to yourself by listing the contents of the two areas and comparing them.

Now alter the contents of memory with a command such as 0312:12 and execute a command to verify again. You should get a result similar to

    0351 – 02 (12)

telling you that the contents of location 0351 are equal to 02, while the contents of the equivalent location (0312) have a value of 12. The contents of the destination address are always displayed last, inside parentheses. The address given is always the address of the source.

You can use this feature to compare the contents of binary files saved on disk by loading them into memory at different locations and then using the verify command from the Monitor. This can be useful when you are trying to determine the differences between two binary programs, because the ProDOS Compare Files command will tell you only that the two files don't match—it won't display the actual differences.

Other Features of the Monitor

If you want to begin executing a machine-language program, you can transfer control from the Monitor to the starting address of the program. You do this by entering the address your program starts at and following it with the letter G. For example, the command 03D0G transfers control to the instruction at location 03D0, which happens to cause your Apple to return to the BASIC prompt. If you do not specify an address, the Monitor will attempt to execute the instruction at the current address.

You can direct the output of the Monitor to your printer by entering the slot number of the card controlling the printer followed by Control-P and Return. Once you have done this, all output will be directed to the printer until you redirect the output to the screen by typing 0 (for slot 0) followed by Control-P and Return. Make sure the number you enter has a valid interface card in it, or you will have to reset the machine to regain operating control. This feature can be used to print out the contents of memory when you want a listing of a program or the data in a particular section of memory.

You can change the input device of your Apple from the keyboard to another device, such as a disk drive, by typing Control-K and Return after the slot number. The same methods and warnings apply to this command as to the command for switching output to the printer. You would use this in the same way as the IN# command in BASIC.

Entering the command I and Return causes all responses from the Monitor to be printed in inverse video. Your commands are still printed in normal video as you enter them, but you can tell you're in inverse video mode by the asterisk prompt, which is displayed in inverse video. You can type the command N and Return to reset the system to normal video mode.

You can perform binary addition and subtraction in the Monitor simply by entering the calculation at the prompt. The results are displayed on the following line and are preceded by an equal sign. The Monitor can perform only eight-bit operations and single operations with two operands. The following examples show how the

Monitor handles this function:

```
*10 – 0A
= 06
*0A + 05
= 0F
*0A – 03
= 07
*0A + 05 – 03
= 07
```

Note that the last example is clearly an error. This is because the Monitor is using only the first and last operands. The Monitor also deals only in eight-bit arithmetic, so additions that yield results above FF cause truncation. Subtractions that yield results less than 00 display the 1's complement.

The Monitor gives you the ability to define one Monitor command. You access this command by entering Control-Y and Return. This causes a jump to address $03F8. There is exactly enough room at this location to perform a jump to some other location. You can use this feature to place a machine-language program in memory, place a jump to its starting address at location $03F8, and then access it from the Monitor simply by pressing Control-Y and Return. This program could do anything at all, but the feature itself could be useful when debugging to restart the program you are testing.

ProDOS Commands and the Monitor

All the immediate-mode ProDOS commands will work from the Monitor. You can use the CAT command to see what is on a disk, the CLOSE command to close open files, or any other valid command. You can also use the BSAVE and BLOAD commands to save and load binary data to and from the disk while you are in the Monitor, where you can easily examine it. You cannot use any commands that work only in deferred mode. This means that you cannot use the OPEN, READ, WRITE, or APPEND commands.

If you try to execute a ProDOS command and an error occurs, you will drop out of the Monitor and be returned to the BASIC prompt. When this happens, you can use the same CALL −151 sequence to reenter the Monitor from BASIC. Any data or programs that you stored in memory will still be there when you come back.

The Monitor offers you the ability to directly type in machine-language programs for your Apple. This can be an important feature if you do not have an assembler. An assembler is a program that translates assembly-language instructions into machine-language instructions. To program with the Monitor, you would have to type in the machine-language instructions that correspond to the assembly-language instructions. This would require a working knowledge of assembly language and a manual containing the instruction set for 6502 assembly language. You would have to translate the instructions yourself before entering them.

The advantage that the Monitor offers to someone writing programs for ProDOS is that your machine-language programs can call the MLI directly. All you have to do is follow the assembly-language routine shown in Chapter 10. You can convert this into machine language and save it on disk with the BSAVE command. Then you can use the Monitor to enter the parameter list into memory, set up the call, and execute it using the G feature of the Monitor. If you have the patience and time to follow this approach, you can make full use of all the features of the MLI without using an assembler.

Any machine-language routine that you write using the Monitor can also be saved with the BSAVE command and reloaded with the BLOAD command. These programs can be used from BASIC by the CALL and USR statements. To do this properly you will have to place your machine-language statements in an area of memory where they will not be written over by BASIC (such as the text and low-resolution graphics page 2 area of memory), and you must supply the actual starting address of your machine-language routine with the statement.

While using the Monitor is admittedly not the easiest way to program in machine language, it is an acceptable alternative to buying and using an assembler. It takes determination and practice, but the experience of using the Monitor will reward you with more insight into how your Apple and ProDOS actually work.

Appendix: A ▓▓▓▓▓▓▓▓▓▓▓▓▓▓

PRODOS FILE TYPES

The following table represents all of the ProDOS file types. The code is a hexadecimal number that is stored in the directory file. When you use the utilities or the ProDOS CAT or CATALOG commands to display a directory file, the three-letter explanation will appear rather than the code itself. If you are using a IIc, this three-letter explanation has been expanded to an entire word.

File types are used to identify the contents of a file. Some ProDOS commands will work only with a specific type of file. For example, the LOAD, SAVE, and RUN commands will work only with BAS files.

Code	File Type
$00	Typeless file
BAD ($01)	Bad block file
TXT ($04)	ASCII text
BIN ($06)	Binary
DIR ($0F)	Directory
CMD ($F0)	ProDOS added command file
$FI–$F8	ProDOS user-defined file 0–9
$F9	ProDOS reserved for future use
INT ($FA)	Integer BASIC program
IVR ($FB)	Integer BASIC variables
BAS ($FC)	Applesoft program
VAR ($FD)	Applesoft variable
REL ($FE)	Relocatable code in machine language
SYS ($FF)	ProDOS system file
$CO–$EF	ProDOS reserved for future use

Appendix: B ▓▓▓▓▓▓▓▓▓▓▓▓▓▓

PRODOS UTILITIES ERROR MESSAGES

The following error messages are generated from the ProDOS User's Disk utilities. Each is followed by a brief description and a course of action you can follow when they occur.

CAN'T DELETE DIRECTORY FILE

This error message means that one of the DOS files you are trying to transfer to ProDOS has the same name as a ProDOS directory file. The Convert utility will not allow you to transfer this file. You must rename either the ProDOS directory file or the DOS file before trying again.

CAN'T TRANSFER DIRECTORY FILE

This occurs when you are trying to transfer a ProDOS directory file to a DOS disk. Because there is no file type under DOS that functions in the same way as a ProDOS directory, the Convert utility will not allow you to make this move.

DIRECTORY ALREADY EXISTS

This error message means either that you are trying to create a directory file using a name that you have already used for a directory or that you are trying to copy a file to a directory. You cannot do either of these things. If you are trying to create a new directory, use a different name. If you are trying to copy a file, check your path name and correct the error.

DIRECTORY EXPECTED

This error message means that you entered a file name where you should have entered a directory name. This may mean that you have the sequence of your path name wrong or that you mis-spelled a word in the path name. You can list the directories in the path name with the CAT command to check on the type and spelling of the names.

DIRECTORY NOT EMPTY

In order to keep you from accidentally wiping out a directory full of important files, ProDOS will not allow you to delete a directory that contains any other file. You can list the directory you tried to delete to see what files are there. You must delete any files in the directory before ProDOS will allow you to delete the directory itself.

DIRECTORY NOT FOUND

If for some reason ProDOS cannot find the directory you requested, you will see this message. You should check your path name to see if you have typed it in correctly. If you have, you should double-check by listing (with the CAT command) all the directories involved to make sure the subdirectories are there in the order you specified in the path name. If it still does not work, open the drive and make sure you have the correct disk in the drive.

DISK II DRIVE TOO FAST

This message will appear only when you are trying to copy or format a volume. It means that ProDOS is unable to read or write to the disk in your drive because the drive is turning too fast. In this case you must have the speed of your drives adjusted before Pro-DOS will be able to use them.

DISK II DRIVE TOO SLOW

This message will appear only when you are trying to copy or format a volume. It means that ProDOS is unable to read or write to the disk in your drive because the drive is turning too slow. You must have the speed of your drives adjusted before ProDOS will be able to use them.

DISK WRITE-PROTECTION

This means that ProDOS has tried to write something out to the disk, but the disk is write protected. This may mean that there is a write-protect tab covering the write-enable notch on the disk. You can remove the tab, but you should think twice about it. The tab was put there to prevent you from writing on the disk—are you sure you want to remove it?

DUPLICATE FILE NAME

When you see this message it means that the name you are trying to assign to a file has already been used for another file in the same directory. If this occurs while you are renaming files, try again with a different name. If it occurs while you are using the Convert utility, either cancel the transfer or proceed with it, wiping out the existing file on the destination disk.

DUPLICATE VOLUME

This error message means that you are trying to do a Compare Volume or a Copy Volume command where both volumes have identical names.

ERROR CODE = XX

This the ProDOS utilities' catch all error message. When you see this it means that ProDOS has encountered an error that the utilities cannot handle. The two-digit code following the message (represented here by XX) is a hexadecimal code for the ProDOS error messages you'll find in Appendix C.

FILES DO NOT MATCH

This means that the two volumes you are trying to compare are not identical. If you are trying to verify a backup disk, you should use the CAT command to determine which files on the two volumes have different times and dates and copy the most current one to the older one.

FILE EXPECTED

This error message occurs when you are trying to delete or alter the write-protection attribute on a file, and your path name points to a volume directory. You cannot do either of these things to a volume directory in ProDOS. The only way to delete a volume directory is to reformat the disk. The only way to write-protect a volume is to put a tab over the write-enable notch.

FILE LOCKED

This message means that you have tried to delete or rename a file that you have previously locked. If you really want to do this, you will have to use the Alter Write-Protection command to unlock it first.

FILE NOT FOUND

The file you are looking for is not where you said it is. Check to make sure you spelled the name correctly and typed the path name correctly. You can use the CAT command to make sure things are where you thought they were before trying again.

FILE TOO LARGE

This message appears when you are trying to copy a file and there is not enough room on the destination disk. You will have to either copy the file to a different disk or make room for it on this one by deleting a few files you do not need.

I/O ERROR

This is a catch-all message that may appear in many different situations. It means that for some reason ProDOS cannot read the volume you have specified. Your drive may have the door open, or it may be empty. It may be that your disk has not been formatted, or your disk drive connection has come loose. You should check all the simple things first to see if you can correct the problem; if you cannot, you may have a damaged volume and you should try another disk to see if you can read that. If none of this solves your problem, you should contact your dealer.

ILLEGAL CHARACTER

This message means that you tried to type a character that is not allowed while you were specifying a file name or a path name. Check to see if you can spot the error and correct it before trying again. If the problem persists, review the path name conventions in Chapter 4 to see if you can locate the error.

ILLEGAL WILDCARD

This message means that you tried to use more than one wild-card character in a path name. If you are trying to list a directory, you can use a wild card only in the first position and as the only character. To correct this error you will have to retype the path name in the proper format.

INSUFFICIENT MEMORY TO RUN PROGRAM

This error occurs only if your system has less than 64K of RAM memory. If this is the case, you cannot run the ProDOS operating system unless you add more memory to your system.

INVALID DATE

When you see this message you have tried to enter an impossible date into the system. ProDOS checks what you enter for validity and gives you this message if the month field does not consist of the first three letters of one of the months of the year. It will also give you this message if the year is less than 00 or greater than 99, or if the day is greater than the allowable number for that month.

INVALID DRIVE

This message means that you have typed an incorrect number when specifying the drive. You can enter only 1 or 2, because there can be only two drives connected to one slot. Simply type in the correct drive number if you want to continue.

INVALID PATHNAME

This message means that you typed an illegal character when you were entering the path name, or you had the prefix set to the wrong volume. Check the path name to see if you can spot any errors, and refer to Chapter 4 if necessary.

INVALID SLOT

This message appears when you enter a slot number outside of the range from 1 to 7. These are the only slots that ProDOS will allow you to use for your disk drive controller card. You will not get this message if you enter a slot number within this range, even if there is no disk drive controller there. (If there is no disk drive controller, you'll see the error message NO DEVICE CON-NECTED.) Simply type the correct number to continue, making sure that there is a controller card in that slot.

NAME TOO LONG

This means you typed a ProDOS file name longer than 15 characters or a DOS 3.3 file name longer than 30 characters (when using the Convert utility). Check that you have typed the name correctly.

NO DATA IN FILE

This message means that there is no data in the file you are trying to transfer. ProDOS won't let you transfer an empty file. If for some reason you need an empty file, you can use the Create command to set one up.

NO DEVICE CONNECTED

This means that there is no disk drive connected to the slot you have entered, or that it is not turned on if it is a device like a Pro-File. If you are trying to print something, it means that the printer is not connected or that the printer card is not in the slot you have specified. You should use the Display Slot Assignments option to make sure you have the right slot number for the device. If you do, check the connections to see if they have come loose.

NO DIRECTORY

This message means that at least one of the volumes connected to your system is unformatted, formatted for DOS 3.3, or formatted for Pascal. If it is formatted for Pascal, you need to use the Pascal Filer. If it is formatted for DOS 3.3, either use the DOS FID utility or convert the files to ProDOS. If it is unformatted, you can set it up for use with ProDOS by using the Format a Volume command.

NO PRINTER CONNECTED

You'll see this message when you have set your output device default to the printer and you have no printer connected to your system. Either connect the printer or reset the default to the monitor before proceeding.

NO ROOM ON VOLUME

This message means there is not enough room on the destination volume for the files you want to transfer from DOS to ProDOS or from ProDOS to DOS. You will either have to delete files from the volume to make room or use another disk.

NOT A DOS 3.3 VOLUME

This means that the disk in the slot and drive you specified for the DOS 3.3 volume in a Convert utility is not a DOS 3.3 disk. Make sure you have the right disk in the right slot and that the direction line at the top of the Convert display is correct.

NOT A PRODOS DIRECTORY

This means that the disk in the slot and drive you specified for the ProDOS volume in a Convert utility is not a ProDOS disk. Make sure you have the right disk in the right slot and that the direction line at the top of the Convert display is correct.

NOT A PRODOS INTERPRETER

ProDOS is unable to run the file you have specified in a QUIT call. This may be because the file name or the volume name is not valid for ProDOS. Assuming you have a valid ProDOS startup disk in the drive, you can get out of this situation by pressing the Control and Reset keys (the Open-Apple, Control, and Reset keys on an Apple IIe or IIc). This will cause your Apple to reboot from the disk in the default drive.

NOT A PRODOS VOLUME

This means that you are trying to use a ProDOS command with a disk that is not formatted for ProDOS. This could be a disk formatted for DOS 3.3 or Pascal, or it could be an unformatted disk. If you frequently use different operating systems on your Apple, you should devise some scheme for marking them so that you can easily identify which one you are using. Some ProDOS commands (Copy a Volume, Compare Volumes, Detect Bad Blocks, Format a Volume) can be performed on non-ProDOS disks.

NOT THE SAME DEVICE TYPE

This means that you are trying to copy or compare a floppy disk to a hard disk. ProDOS will not allow you to do this because of the potential for error. You will have to use the Copy Files command of the Filer. This message may also occur while you are setting configuration defaults to keep you from making that same mistake. This error will occur only when you are attempting volume operations with the ProDOS utilities.

NOT THE SAME DIRECTORY

You have tried to rename a file that does not exist in the directory you specified. Check the path name and prefix for errors before trying again.

PATH NOT FOUND

This means that the volume you specified exists, but the path name is incorrect. Check your spelling, and if that does not reveal the error, list the files using the CAT command to trace your path name and see if all the files in the path name exist.

PATHNAME TOO LONG

This means that you typed a path name longer than 128 characters during a transfer operation, or longer than 64 characters when you were setting the prefix. Check your spelling and trace the path name to see if you have made any errors, and correct them before continuing.

PATHNAMES INDICATE SAME FILE

This means that you are trying to copy a file onto itself. ProDOS will not allow you to do this. You will have to change the path name to give the destination file a unique name.

PREFIX NOT SET

This means that you have tried to transfer or list files from a ProDOS directory with the Convert utility, and you have not set a prefix. You will have to go back and set the prefix before you can transfer any files.

SAME FIXED DISK

This error message means that you are trying to copy or compare a fixed disk (ProFile) to itself. You cannot do this. Check the slot and drive numbers to see if you have made any errors.

VOLUME DIRECTORY FULL

There is no more room left in the directory for the file or directory you want to set up. You will have to either delete files to make room or use another directory as the destination.

VOLUME FULL

There is no room left on the disk. You will have to either delete files to make room on this disk or use another one.

VOLUME NOT FOUND

This means that ProDOS cannot find the volume name you gave it. This could mean that the disk drive door is not closed or that the wrong disk is in the drive. Check your spelling as well to make sure you did not make any typing mistakes. You can also use the List Volumes command to make sure you got the name right, that the disk is formatted for ProDOS, and that the proper disk is in the drive.

WILDCARD MUST BE IN FINAL NAME

This means that you have put a wild-card character in the wrong place in a path name. The wild card can appear only in the last name in the path name. You will have to find your error and then reenter the path name correctly.

WILDCARD NOT ALLOWED

This means that you have tried to use a wild card in a command that ProDOS does not allow you to use wild cards in. You will have to retype the full name without a wild card.

WILDCARD NOT PROCESSED

This means that when ProDOS substituted characters for the wild card the path name became too long. Check the path name for accuracy. If you have been using a lot of long names for your directories, you may have to use the Rename utility to shorten them.

WILDCARD USE INCONSISTENT

This means that you are trying to copy or rename a file with a wild card, and your destination and source path names do not match up properly. You must use the same wild card in both the source and destination path names. Correct the path names and try again.

Appendix: C ▀▀▀▀▀▀▀▀▀▀▀▀▀▀▀

PRODOS ERROR CODES

This appendix lists the error codes returned by ProDOS when it is unable to execute a command. The ProDOS Message column contains the text that is normally displayed on the screen when the error occurs, and the Most Common Cause column is intended to give you a hint to the cause of the error.

The error code is always returned in location 222 ($DE). This code will be returned by a statement such as

```
A = PEEK(222)
```

If you are using the Applesoft ONERR GOTO statement within a program, the text in the ProDOS Message column will not appear on the screen. The program will branch to the label you specify in the ONERR GOTO statement, and your code will have to peek at location 222 to determine what error occurred.

As an additional aid to you in debugging ProDOS errors in Applesoft, the line number where the error occurred is always returned in locations 218 and 219. These two values can be combined and the resulting line number calculated by the following statement:

```
EL = PEEK(218) + (PEEK(219) * 256)
```

Code	ProDOS Message	Most Common Cause
2	RANGE ERROR	The options used with a command are too big or too small. The address may be too large, or the ending address may be less than the starting address.
3	NO DEVICE CONNECTED	No device was found in the specified slot.
4	WRITE PROTECTED	There is a write-protect tab on the disk you are trying to write to.
5	END OF DATA	You have tried to read one more record from the file after the end of file has been reached.
6	PATH NOT FOUND	No file exists with the indicated path name.
7	PATH NOT FOUND	No file exists with the indicated path name.
8	I/O ERROR	The door is open on the drive, or the disk is not formatted for ProDOS.
9	DISK FULL	There are too many files on the disk you are trying to write to, or all space has been used.
10	FILE LOCKED	You have tried to write to a locked file.
11	INVALID OPTION	The option you have specified will not work with the command used.
12	NO BUFFERS AVAILABLE	Memory is full; the file you are trying to open can't be because there is no space available.

13	FILE TYPE MISMATCH	The command won't operate on the type of disk file you have specified.
14	PROGRAM TOO LARGE	There is not enough memory available to load the program you have specified.
15	NOT DIRECT COMMAND	The command you're using must be embedded in a program; it cannot be executed in immediate mode.
16	SYNTAX ERROR	You've included a bad file name, option, or comma in your statement.
17	DIRECTORY FULL	You can't create another file in the volume directory; it already has 51 files.
18	FILE NOT OPEN	You've attempted to access a closed text file; the file must be opened first.
19	DUPLICATE FILENAME	You've tried to create or rename a file, and the path name you've specified points to an existing file.
20	FILE BUSY	You've tried to open a file that's already open.
21	FILE(S) STILL OPEN	Your last program didn't close the file(s) before it ended.

Appendix: D

APPLESOFT ERROR CODES

This appendix lists the Applesoft error messages with the code returned by the Apple when an error occurs. These errors are returned in the same location (222) as the ProDOS error codes, and you will need to consult this list and the one in Appendix C to interpret the code found there.

The error message given in this list will appear on the screen unless you are running a program that is using the Applesoft ONERR GOTO or ONERR GOSUB commands. If you are, the message will not appear on the screen and your error-handling routine will take whatever action you have set it up to take. You can retrieve the error code from location 222 with a statement such as

    A = PEEK(222)

Applesoft always stores the line number where an error has occurred in locations 218 and 219. You can retrieve and calculate the line number with the following statement:

    EL = PEEK(218) + (PEEK(219) * 256)

Two error messages do not generate an error code in location 222. These are the CAN'T CONTINUE and ILLEGAL DIRECT errors. The CAN'T CONTINUE error occurs when you use the CONT command with a program that has been changed after being interrupted with Control-Reset or a STOP statement, or with a program that ended in an error. The ILLEGAL DIRECT error occurs when you use an Applesoft command in immediate mode that can only be used in deferred mode (such as INPUT).

Code	Error Message
0	NEXT WITHOUT FOR
16	SYNTAX ERROR
22	RETURN WITHOUT GOSUB
42	OUT OF DATA
53	ILLEGAL QUANTITY
69	OVERFLOW
77	OUT OF MEMORY
90	UNDEF'D STATEMENT ERROR
107	BAD SUBSCRIPT
120	REDIM'D ARRAY
133	DIVISION BY ZERO
163	TYPE MISMATCH
176	STRING TOO LONG
191	FORMULA TOO COMPLEX
224	UNDEFINED FUNCTION
254	Bad response to an INPUT statement
255	CONTROL INTERRUPT ATTEMPTED

Appendix: E ░░░░░░░░░░░░░░░

ASCII CHARACTER CODES

This appendix lists the ASCII character set used by Apple IIe and IIc computers. ASCII is the American Standard Code for Information Interchange, the most widely used scheme for encoding data for communication between computers. This table lists all the codes up to 127. There are 256 actual ASCII characters, but Applesoft BASIC uses the characters above 127 to represent the reserved words of the Applesoft language (see Appendix F). This is done to compress programs and save space when storing them.

The first column in this table gives the ASCII code for a character in decimal. The second column lists the code for the same character as a hexadecimal value. The third column gives the character on the Apple IIe and IIc keyboard relating to that character. In the cases of the ASCII characters below 32, this column does not relate to the keyboard but contains a two- or three-character name that is used to refer to that character. For example, the character ASCII 0 is referred to as NUL, and the character ASCII 7 (which will cause the speaker on your Apple to beep if you issue the statement PRINT CHR$(7)) is known as BEL.

The fourth column shows the character that appears on the screen when that ASCII character is printed. Again, the ASCII characters below 32 are control characters, and they are generated by pressing the Control key simultaneously with another key. Nothing appears on the screen when these characters are generated. For example, the ASCII character 1 is produced by the keys Control-A, and the ASCII character 4 is produced by the keys Control-D.

While it is not necessary to memorize the characters off the ASCII table to program, people who program generally end up with a working knowledge of where in the table certain characters fall. Then they can rely on looking up the answer when they need to know about a particular character. By far the most important thing is to know that the characters exist and where to look them up.

ASC	HEX	CHR	CONTROL CODE	ASC	HEX	CHR	SCREEN
0	00	NUL	Control-@	32	20	space	
1	01	SOH	Control-A	33	21	!	!
2	02	STX	Control-B	34	22	"	"
3	03	ETX	Control-C	35	23	#	#
4	04	EOT	Control-D	36	24	$	$
5	05	ENQ	Control-E	37	25	%	%
6	06	ACK	Control-F	38	26	&	&
7	07	BEL	Control-G	39	27	'	'
8	08	BS	Control-H (←)	40	28	(	(
9	09	HT	Control-I (TAB)	41	29	)	)
10	0A	LF	Control-J (↓)	42	2A	*	*
11	0B	VT	Control-K (↑)	43	2B	+	+
12	0C	NP	Control-L	44	2C	,	,
13	0D	CR	Control-M (RETURN)	45	2D	-	-
14	0E	SO	Control-N	46	2E	.	.
15	0F	SI	Control-O	47	2F	/	/
16	10	DLE	Control-P	48	30	0	0
17	11	DC1	Control-Q	49	31	1	1
18	12	DC2	Control-R	50	32	2	2
19	13	DC3	Control-S	51	33	3	3
20	14	DC4	Control-T	52	34	4	4
21	15	NAK	Control-U	53	35	5	5
22	16	SYN	Control-V	54	36	6	6
23	17	ETB	Control-W	55	37	7	7
24	18	CAN	Control-X	56	38	8	8
25	19	EM	Control-Y	57	39	9	9
26	1A	SUB	Control-Z	58	3A	:	:
27	1B	ESC	Control-[	59	3B	;	;
28	1C	FS	Control-\	60	3C	<	<
29	1D	GS	Control-]	61	3D	=	=
30	1E	RS	Control-^	62	3E	>	>
31	1F	US	Control-—	63	3F	?	?

ASC	HEX	CHR	SCREEN	ASC	HEX	CHR	SCREEN
64	40	@	@	96	60	'	'
65	41	A	A	97	61	a	a
66	42	B	B	98	62	b	b
67	43	C	C	99	63	c	c
68	44	D	D	100	64	d	d
69	45	E	E	101	65	e	e
70	46	F	F	102	66	f	f
71	47	G	G	103	67	g	g
72	48	H	H	104	68	h	h
73	49	I	I	105	69	i	i
74	4A	J	J	106	6A	j	j
75	4B	K	K	107	6B	k	k
76	4C	L	L	108	6C	l	l
77	4D	M	M	109	6D	m	m
78	4E	N	N	110	6E	n	n
79	4F	O	O	111	6F	o	o
80	50	P	P	112	70	p	p
81	51	Q	Q	113	71	q	q
82	52	R	R	114	72	r	r
83	53	S	S	115	73	s	s
84	54	T	T	116	74	t	t
85	55	U	U	117	75	u	u
86	56	V	V	118	76	v	v
87	57	W	W	119	77	w	w
88	58	X	X	120	78	x	x
89	59	Y	Y	121	79	y	y
90	5A	Z	Z	122	7A	z	z
91	5B	[	[	123	7B	{	{
92	5C	\	\	124	7C	|	|
93	5D	]	]	125	7D	}	}
94	5E	^	^	126	7E	~	~
95	5F	_	_	127	7F	DEL	

Appendix: F

APPLESOFT RESERVED WORK TOKENS

When BASIC programs are stored on a disk with the SAVE command, the Applesoft reserved words are stored as tokens, each of which occupies only a single byte of space. For example, the reserved word GOTO is represented by the ASCII character 171 and RETURN by 177. This is done to conserve space. If you examined a BAS file (say by loading it into memory with BLOAD and then using the Monitor or the PEEK command from BASIC to look at memory), you would see these codes rather than the commands they represent. All the reserved words are represented by tokens above 127 in the ASCII table. This appendix lists those codes and their corresponding reserved words.

Token	Reserved Word	Token	Reserved Word	Token	Reserved Word
128	END	164	LOMEM:	200	+
129	FOR	165	ONERR	201	−
130	NEXT	166	RESUME	202	*
131	DATA	167	RECALL	203	/
132	INPUT	168	STORE	204	^
133	DEL	169	SPEED=	205	AND
134	DIM	170	LET	206	OR
135	READ	171	GOTO	207	>
136	GR	172	RUN	208	=
137	TEXT	173	IF	209	<
138	PR#	174	RESTORE	210	SGN
139	IN#	175	&	211	INT

140	CALL	176	GOSUB	212	ABS
141	PLOT	177	RETURN	213	USR
142	HLIN	178	REM	214	FRE
143	VLIN	179	STOP	215	SCRN(
144	HGR2	180	ON	216	PDL
145	HGR	181	WAIT	217	POS
146	HCOLOR=	182	LOAD	218	SQR
147	HPLOT	183	SAVE	219	RND
148	DRAW	184	DEF	220	LOG
149	XDRAW	185	POKE	221	EXP
150	HTAB	186	PRINT	222	COS
151	HOME	187	CONT	223	SIN
152	ROT=	188	LIST	224	TAN
153	SCALE=	189	CLEAR	225	ATN
154	SHLOAD	190	GET	226	PEEK
155	TRACE	191	NEW	227	LEN
156	NOTRACE	192	TAB(	228	STR$
157	NORMAL	193	TO	229	VAL
158	INVERSE	194	FN	230	ASC
159	FLASH	195	SPC(	231	CHR$
160	COLOR=	196	THEN	232	LEFT$
161	POP	197	AT	233	RIGHT$
162	VTAB	198	NOT	234	MID$
163	HIMEM:	199	STEP		

Appendix: G ▓▓▓▓▓▓▓▓▓▓▓▓▓▓

THE MLI CALLS

This appendix constitutes a quick reference to all the calls in the MLI and their parameters. A more complete description of these calls and parameters is presented in Chapter 10.

CREATE ($C0)

Parameter count =	7
Pathname	2 bytes
Access	1 byte
File Type	1 byte
Aux Type	2 bytes
Storage Type	1 byte
Create Date	2 bytes
Create Time	2 bytes

DESTROY ($C1)

Parameter count =	1
Pathname	2 bytes

RENAME ($C2)

Parameter count =	2
Pathname	2 bytes
New Pathname	2 bytes

SET_FILE_INFO ($C3)

Parameter count =	7
Pathname	2 bytes

Access	1 byte
File Type	1 byte
Aux Type	2 bytes
Null field	3 bytes
Mod Date	2 bytes
Mod Time	2 bytes

GET_FILE_INFO ($C4)

Parameter count =	$A
Pathname	2 bytes
Access	1 byte
File Type	1 byte
Aux Type	2 bytes
Storage Type	1 byte
Blocks Used	2 bytes
Mod Date	2 bytes
Mod Time	2 bytes
Create Date	2 bytes
Create Time	2 bytes

ON_LINE ($C5)

Parameter count =	2
Unit Time	1 byte
Data Buffer	2 bytes

SET_PREFIX ($C6)

Parameter count =	1
Pathname	2 bytes

GET_PREFIX ($C7)

Parameter count =	1
Data Buffer	2 bytes

OPEN ($C8)

Parameter count =	3
Pathname	2 bytes

IO Buffer   2 bytes
Reference Number   1 byte

NEWLINE ($C9)
Parameter count =   3
Reference Number   1 byte
Enable Mask   1 byte
Newline Character   1 byte

READ ($CA)
Parameter count =   4
Reference Number   1 byte
Data Buffer   2 bytes
Request Count   2 bytes
Transfer Count   2 bytes

WRITE ($CB)
Parameter count =   4
Reference Number   1 byte
Data Buffer   2 bytes
Request Count   2 bytes
Transfer Count   2 bytes

CLOSE ($CC)
Parameter count =   1
Reference Number   1 byte

FLUSH ($CD)
Parameter count =   1
Reference Number   1 byte

SET_MARK ($CE)
Parameter count =   2
Reference Number   1 byte
Position   3 bytes

GET_MARK ($CF)
Parameter count =   2

Reference Number   1 byte
Position   3 bytes

SET_EOF ($D0)

Parameter count =   2
Reference Number   1 byte
EOF   3 bytes

GET_EOF ($D1)

Parameter count =   2
Reference Number   1 byte
EOF   3 bytes

SET_BUF ($D2)

Parameter count =   2
Reference Number   1 byte
IO Buffer   2 bytes

GET_BUF ($D3)

Parameter count =   2
Reference Number   1 byte
IO Buffer   2 bytes

GET_TIME ($82)

Parameter count =   0

ALLOC_INTERRUPT ($40)

Parameter count =   2
Interrupt Number   1 byte
Interrupt Code   2 bytes

DEALLOC_INTERRUPT ($41)

Parameter count =   1
Interrupt Number   1 byte

READ_BLOCK ($80)

Parameter count =   3

Unit Time	1 byte
Data Buffer	2 bytes
Block Number	2 bytes

WRITE_BLOCK ($81)

Parameter count =	3
Unit Time	1 byte
Data Buffer	2 bytes
Block Number	2 bytes

Appendix: H ▨▨▨▨▨▨▨▨▨▨▨▨▨

MLI ERROR CODES

This appendix contains a listing of the error codes returned by the MLI calls in the accumulator. The normal value returned is $00, which indicates the successful completion of a call. Any other value indicates an error.

Code	Description
$00	No error
$01	Bad system call number
$04	Bad system call parameter count
$25	Interrupt table full
$27	I/O error
$28	No device connected
$2B	Disk write protected
$2E	Disk switched
$40	Invalid path name
$42	Maximum number of files open
$43	Invalid reference number
$44	Directory not found
$45	Volume not found
$46	File not found
$47	Duplicate file name
$48	Volume full
$49	Volume directory full
$4A	Incompatible file format, also a ProDOS directory
$4B	Unsupported storage type
$4C	End of file encountered

$4D	Position out of range
$4E	File access error, also file locked
$50	File is open
$51	Directory structure damaged
$53	Invalid system call parameter
$55	Volume control block table full
$56	Bad buffer address
$57	Duplicate volume
$5A	File structure damaged

Appendix: I

APPLESOFT ZERO PAGE USAGE

Locations	Use
$00–$05	Jump instructions to continue in Applesoft.
$0A–$0C	Contains the USR function's jump address (see the USR function description in Chapter 6).
$0D–$17	General-purpose counters and status flags for Applesoft programs.
$20–$4F	APPLE II system monitor reserved locations. The area from $40 to $4E is used and restored by the MLI. The area from $3A through $3F is used by the ProDOS disk driver routines and is not restored.
$50–$61	General-purpose pointers for Applesoft programs.
$62–$66	Result of last multiplication or division operation performed by the program is stored here.
$67–$68	Pointer to the beginning of the program (normally set to $0801).
$69–$6A	Pointer to the start of simple variable space (where integer and real variables are stored, along with string variable pointers). This also points to the end of the program plus 1 or 2 bytes, unless this value has been changed with the LOMEM: statement.
$6B–$6C	Pointer to the beginning of the memory used for array variables.
$6D–$6E	Pointer to the end of numeric storage in use.

$6F–$70	Pointer to the start of string storage; strings are stored from this location to the end of memory.
$71–$72	General pointer used internally by Applesoft for various purposes.
$73–$74	Highest location in memory available to Applesoft plus one, unless this value has been changed with the HIMEM: statement.
$75–$76	Current line number of the program being executed.
$77–$78	This is set by a Control-C, STOP, or END statement; it contains the line number at which execution was interrupted.
$79–$7A	This points to the location in memory of the next statement to be executed.
$7B–$7C	Current line number from which data is being read. This changes when the READ statement reads past the end of the line.
$7D–$7E	Points to the absolute location in memory from which data is being read. This changes every time a READ statement is executed.
$7F–$80	Pointer to current source of input; set to $0201 during an INPUT statement; set to the data the program is reading from during a READ statement.
$81–$82	Holds the last-used variable's name. This changes every time a new variable is used.
$83–$84	Pointer to the last-used variable's value. This also changes every time a new variable is used.
$85–$9C	General use.
$9D–$A3	Main floating-point accumulator used for calculations involving real numbers.
$A4	General use in floating-point math routines.
$A5–$AB	This is the secondary floating-point accumulator used for operations on real numbers.
$AC–$AE	General-use flags and pointers.
$AF–$B0	Pointer to the end of the program (not changed by LOMEM:).
$B1–$C8	This is the CHRGET routine; Applesoft calls this

	routine every time it wants another character for input. Bytes $B8 and $B9 store a pointer to the last character obtained by this routine.
$C9–$CD	Random number; this value is placed here by the Applesoft RND function.
$D0–$D5	High-resolution graphics scratch pointers used internally by the graphics routines.
$D8–$DF	ONERR pointers also used as scratch or temporary storage.
$E0–$E2	High-resolution graphics X and Y coordinates.
$E4	High-resolution graphics color byte set by the HCOLOR statement. This determines what color the next dot drawn will be.
$E5–$E7	General use for high-resolution graphics routines.
$E8–$E9	Pointer to the beginning of a shape table.
$EA	Collision counter used by the Applesoft high-resolution graphics routines.
$F0–$F3	General-use flag.
$F4–$F8	ONERR pointers for use with the ONERR GOTO and ONERR GOSUB commands.

Appendix: J ▦▦▦▦▦▦▦▦▦▦▦

PRODOS MEMORY MAP

Decimal	Hex	
65535	$FFFF	Disk device drivers ProDOS data areas
57344	$E000	ProDOS MLI
53248	$D000	Reserved area
49152	$C000	System I/O
48896	$BF00	System global page
24576	$6000	
16384	$4000	High-resolution graphics page 2
8192	$2000	High-resolution graphics page 1
3840	$0C00	
2048	$0800	Text and low-resolution graphics page 2
1024	$0400	Text and low-resolution graphics page 1
0	$0000	Zero page, stacks, input buffer

BASIC program area

If you are using an Apple II+ that has been expanded to 64K of memory, the area from $D000 to $FFFF will be in your expansion card's memory.

Appendix: K ▦▦▦▦▦▦▦▦▦▦▦▦

THE SYSTEM GLOBAL PAGE

The system global page is an area of memory used by ProDOS for all communication with the MLI. It contains a great deal of data necessary to the proper operation of your system. If you change it, your system may lock up and refuse to operate. When this happens, you will have to reboot the system. The following table references the locations in the system global page with the information they contain.

Location	Purpose
$BF00–BF02	This is the MLI call entry point. It contains a JMP instruction to location $BFB7.
$BF03–BF05	These bytes contain a spare vector that is reserved for future use by ProDOS.
$BF06–BF08	These bytes contain a JMP instruction to the clock/calendar routine.
$BF09–BF0B	These bytes contain a JMP instruction used for reporting errors.
$BF0C–BF0E	These bytes contain a JMP instruction used when the system is unable to continue (system failure).
$BF0F	The error code is found here (when this byte contains a value of 0, there is no error).
$BF10–BF1F	This area consists of a series of two-byte pointers (vectors) used for accessing drive 1 of the disk drives. The two-byte pointers

	represent slots 0 through 7 for drive 1 on each slot ($BF10–BF11 is slot 0, drive 1; $BF12–BF13 is slot 1, drive 1, etc.).
$BF20–BF2F	This area consists of a series of two-byte pointers used for accessing drive 2 of the disk drives. These pointers represent slots 0 through 7 for drive 2 on each slot ($BF20–BF21 is slot 0, drive 2; $BF22–BF23 is slot 1, drive 2, etc.).
$BF30	This contains the slot and drive number for the last device accessed.
$BF31	This contains the number of accesses of disk devices in this session − 1.
$BF32–BF3F	These bytes contain the search list of active devices in the system.
$BF40–BF4A	These bytes are used for Apple's copyright message.
$BF50–BF57	The purpose of these bytes is unknown at the time of this writing.
$BF58–BF6F	This area contains the system bit map. It is used to record which areas of memory are in use.
$BF70–BF7F	This area consists of 8 two-byte pointers to the addresses of the ProDOS file buffers.
$BF80–BF87	This area consists of 4 two-byte pointers that contain the four interrupt vectors.
$BF88–BF8F	The values of the A, X, Y, stack, and status registers are stored here while an interrupt is being processed.
$BF90	The date is stored here.
$BF92	The time is stored here.
$BF94	The file level number used by the OPEN, FLUSH, and CLOSE statements is stored here.
$BF95	This byte is used to signal the use of the backup bit to ProDOS.
$BF96–BF97	These bytes are unused.

$BF98	This byte contains the machine identification.
$BF99	This byte tells ProDOS which slots are occupied by cards with ROM installed on them.
$BF9A	This byte is used to determine whether a prefix is in use. A value of zero in this byte means there is no prefix.
$BF9B	This byte shows whether the MLI is active. If bit seven is set to one, the MLI is active.
$BF9C–BF9D	These bytes contain the return address used by the last call to the MLI.
$BF9E	This byte is used to save the X register during an MLI call.
$BF9F	This byte is used to save the Y register during an MLI call.
$BFA0–BFFB	This area contains routines used for bank switching of memory on the language card.
$BFFC	This byte contains the earliest version number of the MLI with which the current system program will work.
$BFFD	This byte contains the version number of the current system program.
$BFFE	This byte contains the version number of the minimum compatible MLI version.
$BFFF	This byte contains the latest version number of ProDOS.

INDEX

Selections from The SYBEX Library

Introduction to Computers

OVERCOMING COMPUTER FEAR
by Jeff Berner
112 pp., illustr., Ref. 0-145
This easy-going introduction to computers helps you separate the facts from the myths.

INTRODUCTION TO WORD PROCESSING
by Hal Glatzer
205 pp., 140 illustr., Ref. 0-076
Explains in plain language what a word processor can do, how it improves productivity, how to use a word processor and how to buy one wisely.

PARENTS, KIDS, AND COMPUTERS
by Lynne Alper and Meg Holmberg
145 pp., illustr., Ref. 0-151
This book answers your questions about the educational possibilities of home computers.

PROTECTING YOUR COMPUTER
by Rodnay Zaks
214 pp., 100 illustr., Ref. 0-239
The correct way to handle and care for all elements of a computer system, including what to do when something doesn't work.

YOUR FIRST COMPUTER
by Rodnay Zaks
258 pp., 150 illustr., Ref. 0-142
The most popular introduction to small computers and their peripherals: what they do and how to buy one.

Computer Books for Kids

POWER UP! KIDS' GUIDE TO THE APPLE IIe® /IIc™
by Marty DeJonghe and Caroline Earhart
200 pp., illustr., Ref. 0-212
Colorful illustrations and a friendly robot highlight this guide to the Apple IIe/IIc for kids 8–11.

BANK STREET WRITING WITH YOUR APPLE®
by Stanley Schatt, Ph.D. and Jane Abrams Schatt, M.A.
150 pp., illustr., Ref. 0-189
These engaging exercises show children aged 10–13 how to use Bank Street Writer for fun, profit, and school work.

Special Interest

PERSONAL COMPUTERS AND SPECIAL NEEDS
by Frank G. Bowe
175 pp., illustr., Ref. 0-193
Learn how people are overcoming problems with hearing, vision, mobility, and learning, through the use of computer technology.

ESPIONAGE IN THE SILICON VALLEY
by John D. Halamka
200 pp., illustr., Ref. 0-225
Discover the behind-the-scenes stories of famous high-tech spy cases you've seen in the headlines.

Computer Specific

Apple II—Macintosh

THE EASY GUIDE TO YOUR APPLE II®
by Joseph Kascmer
147 pp., illustr., Ref. 0-122
A friendly introduction to the Apple II, II plus, and the IIe.

BASIC EXERCISES FOR THE APPLE®
by J.P. Lamoitier
250 pp., 90 illustr., Ref. 0-084
Teaches Applesoft BASIC through actual practice, using graduated exercises drawn from everyday applications.

THE APPLE II® BASIC HANDBOOK
by Douglas Hergert
250 pp., illustr., Ref. 0-115
A complete listing with descriptions and instructive examples of each of the Apple II BASIC keywords and functions. A handy reference guide, organized like a dictionary.

APPLE II® BASIC PROGRAMS IN MINUTES
by Stanley R. Trost
150 pp., illustr., Ref. 0-121
A collection of ready-to-run programs for financial calculations, investment analysis, record keeping, and many more home and office applications. These programs can be entered on your Apple II plus or IIe in minutes!

YOUR FIRST APPLE II® PROGRAM
by Rodnay Zaks
182 pp., illustr., Ref. 0-136
This fully illustrated, easy-to-use introduction to Applesoft BASIC programming will have the reader programming in a matter of hours.

THE APPLE® CONNECTION
by James W. Coffron
264 pp., 120 illustr., Ref. 0-085
Teaches elementary interfacing and BASIC programming of the Apple for connection to external devices and household appliances.

THE APPLE IIc™: A PRACTICAL GUIDE
by Thomas Blackadar
175 pp., illustr., Ref. 0-241
Learn all you need to know about the Apple IIc! This jargon-free companion gives you a guided tour of Apple's new machine.

THE BEST OF EDUCATIONAL SOFTWARE FOR APPLE II® COMPUTERS
by Gary G. Bitter, Ph.D. and Kay Gore
300 pp., Ref. 0-206
Here is a handy guide for parents and an invaluable reference for educators who must make decisions about software purchases.

YOUR SECOND APPLE II® PROGRAM
by Gary Lippman
250 pp., illustr., Ref. 0-208
The many colorful illustrations in this book make it a delight for children and fun for adults who are mastering programming on any of the Apple II line of computers, including the new IIc.

Integrated Software

MASTERING APPLEWORKS™
by Elna Tymes
250 pp., illustr., Ref. 0-240
Here is a business-oriented introduction to AppleWorks, the new integrated software package from Apple. No experience with computers is assumed.

Technical

Hardware

FROM CHIPS TO SYSTEMS: AN INTRODUCTION TO MICROPROCESSORS
by Rodnay Zaks
552 pp., 400 illustr., Ref. 0-063
A simple and comprehensive introduction to microprocessors from both a hardware and software standpoint: what they are, how they operate, how to assemble them into a complete system.

MICROPROCESSOR INTERFACING TECHNIQUES
by Rodnay Zaks and Austin Lesea
456 pp., 400 illustr., Ref. 0-029
Complete hardware and software interfacing techniques, including D to A conversion, peripherals, bus standards and troubleshooting.

THE RS-232 SOLUTION
by Joe Campbell
194 pp., illustr., Ref. 0-140
Finally, a book that will show you how to correctly interface your computer to any RS-232-C peripheral.

MASTERING SERIAL COMMUNICATIONS
by Joe Campbell
250 pp., illustr., Ref. 0-180
This sequel to *The RS-232 Solution* guides the reader to mastery of more complex interfacing techniques.

Operating Systems

SYSTEMS PROGRAMMING IN C
by David Smith
275 pp., illustr., Ref. 0-266
This intermediate text is written for the person who wants to get beyond the basics of C and capture its great efficiencies in space and time.

THE PROGRAMMER'S GUIDE TO UNIX SYSTEM V
by Chuck Hickev/Tim Levin
300 pp., illustr., Re.f 0-268
This book is a guide to all steps involved in setting up a typical programming task in a UNIX systems environment.

REAL WORLD UNIX™
by John D. Halamka
209 pp., Ref. 0-093
This book is written for the beginning and intermediate UNIX user in a practical, straightforward manner, with specific instructions given for many business applications.

INTRODUCTION TO THE UCSD p-SYSTEM™
by Charles W. Grant and Jon Butah
300 pp., 10 illustr., Ref. 0-061
A simple, clear introduction to the UCSD Pascal Operating System for beginners through experienced programmers.

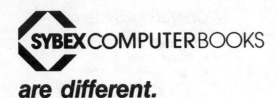

SYBEX COMPUTER BOOKS

are different.

Here is why . . .

At SYBEX, each book is designed with you in mind. Every manuscript is carefully selected and supervised by our editors, who are themselves computer experts. We publish the best authors, whose technical expertise is matched by an ability to write clearly and to communicate effectively. Programs are thoroughly tested for accuracy by our technical staff. Our computerized production department goes to great lengths to make sure that each book is well-designed.

In the pursuit of timeliness, SYBEX has achieved many publishing firsts. SYBEX was among the first to integrate personal computers used by authors and staff into the publishing process. SYBEX was the first to publish books on the CP/M operating system, microprocessor interfacing techniques, word processing, and many more topics.

Expertise in computers and dedication to the highest quality product have made SYBEX a world leader in computer book publishing. Translated into fourteen languages, SYBEX books have helped millions of people around the world to get the most from their computers. We hope we have helped you, too.

For a complete catalog of our publications please contact:

U.S.A.	FRANCE	GERMANY	UNITED KINGDOM
SYBEX, Inc.	SYBEX	SYBEX-Verlag GmbH	SYBEX, Ltd.
2344 Sixth Street	6–8 Impasse du Curé	Vogelsanger Weg 111	Unit 4–Bourne Industrial Park
Berkeley,	75018 Paris	4000 Düsseldorf 30	Bourne Road, Crayford
California 94710	France	West Germany	Kent DA1 4BZ England
Tel: (415) 848-8233	Tel: 01/203–9595	Tel: (0211) 626441	Tel: (0322) 57717
Telex: 336311	Telex: 211801	Telex: 8588163	Telex: 896939